R
60
20
0

| |

Civic Rites

The publisher gratefully acknowledges the generous support of the Classical Literature Endowment Fund of the University of California Press Foundation.

Civic Rites

DEMOCRACY AND RELIGION IN ANCIENT ATHENS

Nancy Evans

UNIVERSITY OF CALIFORNIA PRESS

BERKELEY   LOS ANGELES   LONDON

University of California Press, one of the most
distinguished university presses in the United States,
enriches lives around the world by advancing scholarship
in the humanities, social sciences, and natural sciences. Its
activities are supported by the UC Press Foundation and
by philanthropic contributions from individuals and
institutions. For more information, visit www.ucpress.edu.

University of California Press
Berkeley and Los Angeles, California

University of California Press, Ltd.
London, England

Library of Congress Cataloging-in-Publication Data

Evans, Nancy.
    Civic rights: democracy and religion in ancient Athens /
Nancy Evans.
        p.   cm.
    Includes bibliographical references and index.
    ISBN 978–0-520–26202–7 (cloth : alk. paper)
    ISBN 978–0-520–26203–4 (pbk. : alk. paper)
    1. Democracy—Greece—Athens—History—To 1500.
2. Democracy—Greece—Athens—Religious aspects—
History—To 1500.   3. Athens(Greece)—Politics and
government.   4. Greece—Politics and government—To
146 B.C.   5. Athens(Greece)—Religion.   6. Religion
and politics—Greece—Athens.   I. Title.

JC75.D36E83   2010
938'.505r—dc22   2009042190

Manufactured in the United States of America
19 18 17 16 15 14 13 12 11 10
10 9 8 7 6 5 4 3 2 1

This book is printed on Cascades Enviro 100, a 100% post
consumer waste, recycled, de-inked fiber. FSC recycled
certified and processed chlorine free. It is acid free,
Ecologo certified, and manufactured by BioGas energy.

For Jesse and Jalia

Great are the plunges and throes and triumphs and falls
      of democracy,
Great the reformers with their lapses and screams,
Great the daring and venture of sailors on new
      explorations.

Great are yourself and myself,
We are just as good and bad as the oldest and youngest
      or any,
What the best and worst did we could do,
What they felt . . . do not we feel it in ourselves?
What they wished . . . do we not wish the same?

WALT WHITMAN
Leaves of Grass (1855)

CONTENTS

ILLUSTRATIONS

FIGURES

MAPS

PREFACE

THE WORLD IS CHANGING FAST these days. During the time that I worked on the manuscript for this book, America faced two ongoing wars, crises in major financial and industrial institutions, and growing awareness of changes in the earth's global climate. We also saw the election of the first African American president. In the meantime, rapid developments in what is called information technology modified how we communicate with each other on a daily basis, while providing a degree of access to images, videos, music, and publications of all kinds that was unimaginable only fifteen years ago. Americans revere progress—new and improved!—and they approach times of volatility as rare openings for growth. What might be experienced as a period of anxiety is framed instead as a desirable opportunity. This capacity to reimagine ourselves and our common future is one of our better qualities as a people.

A society that idolizes progress can also marginalize the study of the past—especially stories from the ancient past of a society on the other side of the globe. Saying "That's ancient history" is simply a way of dismissing an event and indicating a determination to move forward. "Ancient history" for many people is history that has lost all relevance and no longer has any practical connection to the present. But as a teacher, scholar, and feminist committed to justice and education, I firmly believe that more of us can benefit from a better understanding of the Mediterranean societies of antiquity. The ancient world itself may be long gone, but our understanding of it is constantly changing. Archaeologists uncover new evidence; sophisticated new technologies help scholars retrieve additional information from fragmentary physical remains; new critical approaches developed by researchers in the social sciences and humanities encourage scholars of antiquity to reevaluate the ancient evidence. Like everything else in the modern world, ancient history does not stand still.

It was the people of ancient Athens who fashioned the first democracy, and even coined the word from their Greek words meaning "people" and "power," but the Athenians do not provide us today with a model of the exemplary democratic state. Some decisions made by the Athenians were far from admirable. Athenian society was highly stratified by class, and the economy would not have functioned without slave labor. The lives of women were severely restricted, and they had no role in the political process. The political process itself was flawed, and ambitious men sometimes led the voting public astray. But at the same time Athenian philosophers, poets, architects, and artists created works of lasting beauty, proportion, and grace. Their ideas infuse the modern world we inhabit, and their symbols steal into our dreams. The intellectual leaders in ancient Athenian society were members of a rich and sometimes quirky community, and they all lived and worked during a time of great change.

In fifteen years of teaching and leading discussions in college classrooms, I have been repeatedly reminded that the ancient world is good to think with. Historians often say that we cannot know where we are going without an awareness of where we have been. I agree, and I would add to this that a deep and *deeply practical* understanding of the past enables us to better analyze the present, better evaluate possible options for change, and better plan for a viable *and* desirable future. The ancient Mediterranean was a complex place inhabited by diverse peoples and nations who tackled problems similar to the ones we face today. Power, ambition, and greed. Maintaining access to the material resources necessary for growing economies. Questions about the nature of justice, and appropriate ethical behavior. The changing place of religion in society. Conflicts with foreign peoples too frequently regarded as aggressive barbarians. Internal tensions and heated debates about whether a democratic state could, or even should, create and sustain an empire.

Though ancient and modern democratic governance are topics that deserve our reflection, the subject of religion also warrants careful reexamination. Religion has always been a powerful factor in American society. But the differences between ancient and modern religious practices are great, and we could easily disregard ancient religion, believing the gap between it and our belief systems to be so great that we can get little practical benefit from bridging it. Even so, it is a mistake to conclude that the peoples of antiquity were generally superstitious peasants who clung to childish myths, while an elite group of educated men rejected all traditional practices as irrational and primitive, thanks to their vigorous intellectual curiosity.

The outlines of Athenian history are well-known to many, from the Persian invasions and the decades dominated by Pericles to the Peloponnesian War and Sparta's defeat of Athens, but the significant impact of religious culture on Athenian public and political life during this time is familiar mostly to specialists and scholars. In large part this ignorance is due to the completely alien nature of Athenian religion. I have written this book for a more general audience to show how the ancestral rituals of Athens were thoroughly intertwined with its emerging democratic institutions. Here I rely on the openness and intellectual curiosity of my readers to follow me into a descriptive analysis of some traditional Greek religious rites. The festival calendar of the Athenians honored many deities at scores of festivals during the year, which they reckoned from summer to summer, starting with the first new moon after the summer solstice in our month of June. In this book I have chosen to analyze only three major divinities, namely Athena, Demeter, and Dionysus, plus a handful of their civic festivals. I have had to exclude some important material. But I hope that I have included enough description and analysis to make the customs of animal sacrifice and public festival a bit more understandable to twenty-first-century readers.

Students, friends, and colleagues have helped me think through this book since I started seriously working on it in 2003. The idea to organize the book as I have, interweaving historical chapters with chapters on cultural and religious context, came from classes that I taught during the '90s and '00s at Wheaton College and Smith College, and I learned a great deal from students at those institutions. I wrote the book in part with sabbatical travel support from the Alden and Beverly Fiertz Award at Wheaton College, which funded study at the Fondation Hardt in Geneva and a trip to Athens. Once I started actually writing I benefited from conversations and correspondence with many whom I would now like to thank. Roy Evans, Geoff Bakewell, Clara Hardy, Ra'anan Boustan, Susan Dearing, and Flora Keshgegian read drafts and offered guidance in the project's early phases. Colleagues at Wheaton read early drafts of chapters and gave good advice throughout the process: Lisa Lebduska, Connie Campana, Paula Krebs,

Claire Buck, John Partridge, Joel Relihan, Gen Liang, Fran Fernandez de Alba, James Mulholland, and Rolf Nelson. Many thanks to Lauren Provost and especially Chris Hyde for help with images. Joe Cambray's curiosity and insights often helped me make connections I had missed before. Alan Boegehold generously offered his time, and I have always learned a great deal from talking with him about Athens. Elita Pastra-Landis also shared with me her love of Greece, and I look forward to more trips with her to Brauron. Laura Cerruti at the University of California Press supported this project early on and I am most grateful to her, and to Eric Schmidt, for seeing the project through at the end. Stephanie Fay and the anonymous readers at the Press were helpful too. Jay Samons, Becky Sinos, and Alice Falk offered invaluable corrections and advice on the final drafts of the entire manuscript, and this project would be much poorer without their keen insight. All were ideal readers. I am grateful for John Golebiewski's attention to detail with the final proofs. Finally, thoughts of my own teachers and mentors were never far from my mind as I worked on this project, foremost among them Thalia Pandiri, Walter Burkert, and Martha Nussbaum. Each of them has deeply influenced my writing, my teaching, and my approach to the ancient world. All errors and oversights that remain are entirely my own.

Heather, Ron, Mary, Jesse, Jalia, and my mother have given me unfailing support over the years, and taught me the most important lessons about living a good life. This book is lovingly dedicated to them, and to the memory of my father.

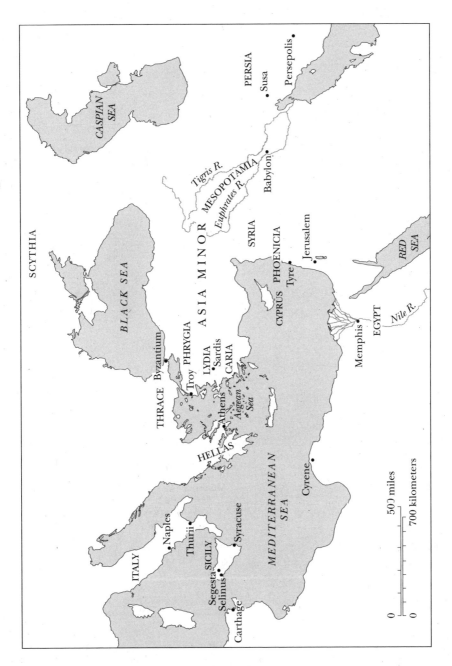

Map 1. The ancient Mediterranean and western Asia

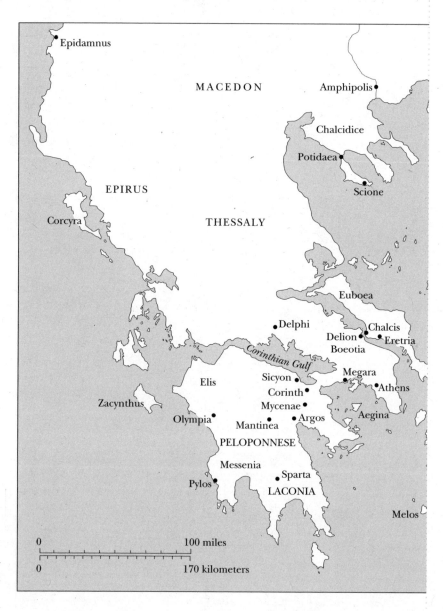

Map 2. Greece, Asia Minor, and the Aegean

THRACE

Byzantium · Chrysopolis

Propontis

Bithynia

Thasos

Samothrace

Aegospotami

Hellespont

PHRYGIA

Lesbos

Mytilene

Arginusae

LYDIA

Scyros

· Sardis

Chios

AEGEAN
SEA

I O N I A

Notium · Ephesus

Samos

Miletus

CARIA

Delos

Paros

Naxos

Hallicarnassus

Rhodes

Map 3. Attica and central Greece

Introduction

The City of Pericles and Socrates

IMAGINE THE GREEK MEDITERRANEAN, just over 2,400 years ago. A surprisingly strong spring sun warms the limestone buildings in the Athenian Agora, the commercial and communal center of the city. High above on the Acropolis marble monuments and a great bronze statue of the armed goddess Athena glint in the sunlight. In the city streets brightly colored red and yellow wild flowers spring up amid the grass growing along the edges of the paving stones, and they barely stir in a faint morning breeze. In a large, walled courtyard in the Agora on this morning, a group of well over 500 men have gathered. They are a sampling of the citizens of democratic Athens, men of all ages chosen by lot to serve on a jury. They stand clustered in groups as they listen intently to an elderly man who begins speaking before them in a strong and unfaltering voice. He clearly is no stranger to teaching and persuasive argument. He is a confident and engaging speaker, even if some of his claims do provoke surprise and murmuring in the courtroom.

A small committee of civil magistrates seated on a dais presides over this trial, and next to them the steady trickle of a *klepsydra,* or water clock, measures time as a thread of water slowly runs from one large terra-cotta vessel into another placed on a shelf just below. Each speaker is allotted a fixed amount of time in this courtroom, but the old man shows no signs of anxiety, no urge to rush his words under the pressure of the running clock. He takes his time as he defends himself. In other ways, too, this man is an oddity to those serving on the jury. While his voice resonates with unusual strength and clarity, his appearance raises a few eyebrows. He is shortish, and barefoot, and his old, worn cloak hangs awkwardly askew over a noticeable paunch. This attire, combined with his bald pate and a curious snub nose, inspires smiles of derision in some of the more elegantly dressed jury members. Along the back edges of the courtyard behind the jurors stand a dozen other men and a handful of heavily veiled women, the old man's family, friends, and supporters. The expressions on their faces betray their worst fears, as well as their fierce devotion, their resolute pride, and their love.

This somewhat unkempt elderly man has been accused of religious impiety, and he is being tried by a jury of his peers in a state court. Some today might wonder about these facts: Did Athens, the city that first gave the Western world the democratic form of government, really permit its citizens to be tried for religious crimes? Did the leaders of this democracy actually allow religious behavior—and alleged misbehavior—to be considered a legitimate concern of the state? Although our modern notions of democracy endorse the separation of church and state, the historical facts about ancient Greece point in the opposite direction: Democratic Athens did concern itself with the religious lives of its citizens. Impiety was a deadly serious charge for the members of this democratic community. Citizens could be exiled or even executed if found guilty of violating the sacred laws governing the proper worship of the state's many gods and goddesses. Death at the hands of the state was in fact the fate of this 70-year-old man who stood trial for impiety in 399 BCE. As luck would have it, we even know the name of the man who defended himself on this day. He was the philosopher Socrates.

Athens was Socrates' home, and the great philosopher came of age during the decades when the visionary leader Pericles was making Athens the commercial and cultural center of the northeastern Mediterranean basin. Under Pericles Athens experienced unprecedented growth, prosperity, and influence. Athenians were proud of the radical new form of government they called *dēmokratia,* democracy. In their innovative system all male citizens had a voice, and not just those from the wealthy, established families as in many neighboring cities. Although he came from an aristocratic family Pericles enthusiastically supported the democracy, and he gave new political privileges to the laborers and working men of Athens whose ability to participate in government had long been restricted. Pericles also guided

Athens into a position of international prestige, advocating the development of an Athenian naval empire that for decades ruled the Aegean Sea, the eastern Mediterranean, and the shipping lanes into the Black Sea. Some cities allied with Athens experimented with implementing more democratic forms of rule, and other cities suffered the imposition of democracy forced upon them by the Athenians.

Athens was a city that Socrates deeply loved, and he lived within the city's walls nearly every day of his life. The only time he was away was during those few months as a mature man when he took part in military campaigns in the mountainous country north of Athens. Even during those times when he was not living in his beloved Athens, he was still fighting as an infantryman alongside his fellow Athenian citizens. As much as Socrates loved his home city, he had even more regard for the men who made Athens the extraordinary place it was during the second half of the fifth century before the common era. During this period dominated by Pericles' leadership, Athenians completed the great building projects on the Acropolis, and they celebrated the careers of renowned playwrights such as Sophocles, Euripides, and Aristophanes. Innovative natural scientists and clever philosophers from throughout the known world came to teach Athenians, who could not get enough of the new ideas. Socrates earned his living as a stonemason and may well have worked on Pericles' building projects; he no doubt attended the theater and conversed with the visiting scientists and philosophers. Socrates thrived in the heart of Pericles' Athens. He was the sort of man who spoke the truth as he saw it, and his criticisms of the Athenians could at times be withering.

But the so-called golden age of Athens ended almost as suddenly as it began. At the time of Socrates' trial in 399, Athens was just emerging from the greatest period of political and social tumult that it had ever experienced. The Athenians had only recently finished fighting a war that had dragged on for nearly three full decades. Sparta, Athens' chief rival, was victorious in the end. Barely five years before the trial of Socrates, the Spartan army had occupied Athens and torn down the defensive fortifications that surrounded the city. Meanwhile, the Spartan navy reduced the Athenian fleet and made the Athenians promise that they would never again rebuild their navy. After fifty years of commercial, financial, and military leadership in Greece, the mighty Athenian naval empire was finally at an end.

While the Spartans achieved victory, the citizens of Athens were experiencing further troubles. Tensions between wealthy aristocrats and the common people, the skilled craftsmen and modest farmers of Attica, had rarely been greater. The decade between 413 and 403 had seen repeated coups d'état as the government careened wildly between an unsteady democratic rule of the people and an oppressive oligarchy headed by old, wealthy families. A moderate oligarchy of 5,000 ruled for a short while. A noble general and popular leader of the people arose in this time of crisis and won over the people, only to betray the Athenians to their enemies not once but twice: first to the Spartans, and later to the Persians. Twice democracy itself was abolished in Athens, and one of these times it was the Athenians themselves who voted to change the government. Each time that the short-lived, repressive regimes seized power, hit men assassinated prominent, as well as not-so-prominent, democratic leaders. But each time, by some miracle—including the remarkable intervention of Sparta in 403—the Athenian people bounced back and regained control of the government.

It was a wonder that anyone survived those years of chaos and terror. Hard feelings lingered even after the democracy was restored a second time in 404/3, and a general amnesty was declared in the wake of trials for the most hated and violent leaders of the oligarchic coups. In light of these events, it is not wholly surprising to see Socrates on trial in Athens just five years after the final restoration of democracy. Socrates was a recognizable, if eccentric, public figure in his own right, known for frequenting the public square in the city, where he questioned fellow citizens on their opinions and assumptions concerning justice and the proper, ethical behavior of citizens. It was common knowledge that Socrates had ties to some of the oligarchs who led the repeated and briefly successful attempts to undermine the democratic government. Some believed that Socrates had anti-democratic, aristocratic sympathies, even though he was himself only a poor stonemason who could barely support his own family. And Socrates was widely known to be an intimate friend of that man who had twice betrayed the Athenians to their foreign enemies during wartime.

The suggestion that Socrates' trial and execution were almost entirely politically motivated is an attractive one. This idea has been put forward and pursued in recent years, most notably by I. F. Stone in his popular 1988 book *The Trial of Socrates*. But while there may be some truth to this thesis, it is at best only partially true. Looking to purely political motivations for the death of Socrates overlooks an essential fact about Athenian society: religious observance played a central role in the world's first democracy. While some, including Stone, have come to view the "religious" nature of the impiety charges against Socrates as a mask for the more political motives of his accusers and their cronies, other scholars have continued to explore the full range of life in ancient Athens, including the diversity of religious behaviors and expressions. These scholars have pointed out that today we have a duty to take the Athenians' religious customs quite seriously. Doing so requires that we try to reimagine and reconstruct the varieties of human experience from an ancient Greek perspective and not from our own modern one. We need to reexamine our own categories of thought, and not heedlessly apply our categories to their world—especially if our categories do not comfortably fit in that world.

Religion is one of those concepts that cannot be easily transferred from modern to ancient societies. When we fail to acknowledge the full impact of religion on the civic institutions of ancient Athens, we blind ourselves to the full complexity of the world that Athenians themselves inhabited. The Greek political world was one that was governed by civic rites. The democratic government in Athens, like the regimes in every other Greek city at that time, relied on countless religious practices in every aspect of its daily functioning. Citizens stood not only in political and social relationship to each other but also in religious and cultic relationship to each other, to their children and ancestors, and to the city's gods. It was the duty of Athenian citizens to take part in the common civic and religious life of the city and to express disagreement and dissent when they saw or heard things that did not conform to accepted practice. This book will explore some of the religious aspects of democratic institutions in ancient Athens, and examine how the exercise of traditional practices had a substantial impact on Athenian political and social history in the fifth century.

The deepest roots of Athenian democracy that scholars can identify today lie in a distant past that was common to all Greeks. Athens was just one of many city-states that flourished in antiquity in the northeastern corner of the Mediterranean Sea. As is still true today, Greece was known then among its inhabitants as "Hellas," and Greek culture in general was called "Hellenic." Panhellenic shrines and customs were those that were shared by all the independent Greek city-states: the festival of Zeus called the Olympic Games was panhellenic, as was the sanctuary at Delphi, an oracular shrine sacred to the god Apollo. Another significant component of panhellenic culture in Greek antiquity was the epic poetry of Homer, and the shared mythological traditions surrounding the city of Troy and the warriors who fought there in a distant and heroic past. Though Homer's *Iliad* and *Odyssey* celebrate the sometimes conflicting heroic values of physical strength and mental cunning, the preeminence of honor, or *timē,* and manly virtue, or *aretē,* is common to both poems. Both poems also embody the heroic pursuit of undying fame: *kleos.*

The ancient panhellenic warrior values of fame, *timē,* and *aretē* featured in Homer's epics remained influential many generations later in the democratic Athens of Pericles and Socrates. Socrates and Pericles both knew the myths and oral traditions of Homer and the epic past, but they had only a dim idea of why that warrior society faded. Scholars today know that the destruction of the Bronze Age citadel at Troy in the thirteenth century BCE marked the end of a flourishing civilization in the eastern Mediterranean. The Trojan prince Hector and the Greek lords Agamemnon, Odysseus, and Achilles may never have existed as genuine historical personalities, but similar warriors lived during what archaeologists now call the Mycenaean period. The fall of the Mycenaean palace cultures was accompanied by waves of immigration throughout the Mediterranean and an economic lull that lasted for several generations. During this time there was decreased trade in the Aegean Sea, no significant Greek cities to speak of, and relative poverty throughout Hellas. But the region recovered, and the Geometric (ninth–seventh centuries) and Archaic (sixth and early fifth centuries) periods brought political stability to Hellas, along with increased trade and cultural contacts with other more developed cultures in the eastern portion of the Mediterranean basin, such as Egypt and Phoenicia.

The political stability and economic growth during the Geometric and Archaic periods also fostered the rise of the independent Greek city-state, or *polis.* There were hundreds of these city-states (*poleis*) throughout the Greek-speaking world, and each one maintained its own legal, political, and religious customs. The vibrant Archaic period drew to a close with the invasions of Persian armies in 481 and 480. Some Greek *poleis* formed an alliance, and their victory over Persian forces in 479 marks the start of what scholars call the Classical period. In Athens that victory contained the seeds of a new empire that would last several generations. Later empires—the Hellenistic empires of Alexander the Great and his successors and the Roman Empire following them—severely restricted the institution of the *polis.* But these subsequent empires would never forget what was accomplished in the Athens of Pericles and Socrates.

We still live with and nurture public institutions that started in Greece, thanks in large part to the Romans, who preserved what they valued in Greek culture by wedding it to their own particular strengths in government, law, and engineering. After a long hiatus the Renaissance and Enlightenment brought back democracy, theater, athletic competition, and a certain classical sensibility recognizable in the art and architecture of Europe and the Americas. So much of ancient Greece has survived and been woven back into Western culture over the centuries that today we may feel we already know these ancient people and the world they inhabited. But we need to be cautious. What appears so familiar may actually be more foreign than we first realize.

Anyone who learns a foreign language can tell you that words in one's native tongue are not necessarily congruent with the words in another. Words within each language have subtle gradations of meaning, and concepts in one language awkwardly overlap with "equivalent" notions in the other. At the same time, linguistic connections and associations in one culture are often wholly absent from the other. The same holds true for religious concepts. Like spoken languages, cultures also comprise lived frameworks of their own, and they can be analyzed as symbolic systems with their own order and organization that work to create meaning within their own context. These lived symbolic and religious systems are in some ways related to spoken languages; and as we do with foreign languages, we can make an effort to learn the symbolic language of religion and ritual in other cultures—even those in the distant past.

Yet the religious systems of antiquity, including polytheism, may be more challenging to understand than a foreign language. It is a strange and difficult thing to comprehend or even discuss polytheistic religion in a modern, post-Enlightenment world. Christianity has been the dominant tradition in Europe and the West for many centuries, and Christianity defines religious thought and behavior with an emphasis on the centrality of belief. Ancient Greek religion had little to do with belief, and a great deal to do with practice and observance of common ancestral customs. Jewish, Christian, and Islamic notions of religiosity and belief are also rooted in large part in holy books and sacred narratives. Observant Jews and Christians believe the accounts recorded in their scriptures, to greater or lesser extents; some believe the scriptures themselves to have been divinely created, or at least divinely inspired. An association that ties religion to belief in traditional narratives still persists in the work of some modern secular historians of Greece and Rome. This book does not share the assumption that Greeks viewed religion through the lens of belief in the ways that Jews, Christians, and Muslims do today. Such an assumption about the central place of sacred narratives continues to support a common misconception that Greek and Roman religiosity were both based on explicit belief in the manifold myths of the gods.

This book will mention famous myths only incidentally, and will rather be concerned with what modern students of religion and anthropology term cult practices. The meaning of "cult" here is closely linked to the Latin *cultus,* from the verb *colo* meaning "tend, cultivate; take care of; nourish." Cult practices in this sense do not describe the secret rituals of disreputable religious communities that brainwash well-intentioned but weak and suggestible devotees. Rather, cult practices were traditional customs that enabled the Greeks (and Romans) to tend to the gods—or better, to nourish social and political relationships in the present by maintaining long-standing relationships with ancestors and ancestral gods. The place of cult practices in antiquity was quite unlike the role of religion in the modern world. Indeed, the governments of all Greek *poleis* were responsible for maintaining certain religious customs; current scholarship calls this mode of public worship "civic religion" or "civic cult." Democratic Athens was famous even among other neighboring ancient Greek *poleis* for the expense of its civic cult. The bloody ritual killing of animal victims at the city's altars, called *thysia* (described in detail in chapter 2), occupied a central position in Athenian civic religion.

The chapters that follow look to the beginning of Western democracy, and they explore the thoroughly intertwined relationship of politics and religion in ancient Athens. The structure of the book mirrors this intertwining; odd-numbered chapters provide historical narrative and analysis, while even-numbered chapters pause the flow of time to examine certain religious festivals and customs that shed light on significant historical events. Chapters 1 and 2 reveal the religious roots of Athenian democracy and the cultic aspects of its political institutions. After providing a historical narrative for the origins of democracy, including the military and cultural conflicts surrounding the Persian Wars, chapters 3 and 5 describe the push toward imperialism that resulted in a long and destructive war that very nearly put an end to all earlier democratic impulses. Since the growing pains of Athenian democracy were not evident just in the political and military history of the fifth century, chapters 4 and 6 explore Athenian religious institutions that were rooted in the surrounding landscape and that encouraged criticism of ruling structures and powerful individuals. Athenians participated in their city's customs of theater and in the "mysteries"; both of these religious traditions allowed for political dissent and gave a voice to those who had no recognized political role in the citizen body. Finally, chapter 7 turns to three impiety trials that were held in 399, and examines how the democratic system appeared to be working in the period following the Peloponnesian War and yet ultimately failed its citizens. An epilogue briefly looks forward to Athenian religion and politics in the era of the Macedonian kings Philip and Alexander, who conquered Athens and forever changed Athenian civic traditions.

In this book I have made no assumptions about the reader's level of familiarity with ancient Greece, and therefore have written each chapter from the ground up, so to speak. Each chapter narrates material centered on a historical personality or a deity. Students and general readers can uncover the city of Athens, its history and culture, and by the end they will have before them a portrait of an ancient city that was complex, powerful, at times self-contradictory, and beguiling. More advanced students and scholars can skim the material they know well, and trace the larger argument that ties together two distinct subfields in classical studies that have normally been kept apart—namely, political history and religion. For these readers chapters 2, 4, 6, and 7 may be the most engaging. I have supplied references to the most important primary sources in the text and appendix, and readers looking for extensive quotations and close analysis of the ancient texts may consult the suggested readings.

Studying ancient Greece is at best an exercise in creative reconstruction and the articulation of persuasive argument, tempered with strict attention to the details of available evidence. The remaining extant sources are never as plentiful as scholars wish they were, and often they are simply fragmentary and incomplete. Sources for fifth- and fourth-century Athens are more plentiful than for any other city from this period. Thankfully, some Greek literary sources have survived to modern times in a reasonably whole state. We can study these works much as they existed in the Athens of Socrates and Pericles, a city where the traditional epic poetry of Homer was heard alongside the dramatic works of Aeschylus, Sophocles, Euripides, and Aristophanes. The histories of Herodotus and Thucydides emerged from the same Athenian community that produced the philosophic dialogues of Plato. Taken as a whole, the literary output of fifth- and early fourth-century Athens is second to none. In addition, later authors such as Plutarch and Pausanias writing during the Roman period in the second century CE had strong antiquarian interests, and they preserved many details of Greek history and culture that otherwise would have been lost.

Those scholars who study the societies and cultures of the ancient Mediterranean world can supplement literary evidence with physical remains: all the major artwork and archaeological materials from areas that have been excavated. Graves, inscriptions, coins, and small finds can fill out the larger picture created by the vases, sculptures, buildings, and monuments that have survived. Even the layout of a city can reveal something of its inhabitants who lived many centuries ago. Physical evidence can be frustratingly broken and fragmentary at times, but when it is read alongside the literary evidence scholars can reconstruct a reasonably accurate picture of ancient Athenian society. Modern academic disciplines can also help an ancient historian interpret the remaining evidence. Various forms of literary and critical theory can open up ancient texts to deeper understanding, and insights from the social sciences (political science, sociology, anthropology, religious studies, and women's studies) can play a part in illuminating the social dynamics at work in an ancient city.

Spelling and transliteration of Athenian proper names and Greek terms can be confusing, because some names bear the marks of having been Latinized before entering into English (e.g., the Latinized Pericles vs. the direct transliteration Perikles). Wherever possible I have used the spellings of proper names and Greek terms found in the third edition of the *Oxford Classical Dictionary*, the standard English reference book for all things having to do with ancient Greece and Rome. All dates given in this book are BCE, before the common era. Since the Athenian year started at midsummer, some dates provided have slashes: for example, the year 480/79 denotes that year that began in the summer of 480 BCE and ended twelve months later in 479. A glossary of transliterated Greek terms and technical English words that appear throughout the text with some frequency is provided in an appendix.

Specialized and rather esoteric debates among classical scholars and ancient historians are still simmering about nearly every topic covered in this study. I have therefore included a bibliographic appendix that lists the most important ancient sources, along with discussions keyed to each chapter that provide current bibliography on both sides of debates. I encourage readers to turn to the interpretations of other scholars, and whenever possible to the ancient texts. There is no substitute for getting back to the sources themselves, in the original languages whenever possible, and becoming thoroughly engaged with the issues they raise.

Let the conversations and discussions continue. The Greeks loved—and still love—a good debate, and their past lives on through us. The outbreak of the Peloponnesian War, the debacle of the Sicilian expedition, the execution of Socrates—these events may appear to be remote and distant, and yet when seen in a certain light they do remain with us today, whether we are making choices that concern our personal and private lives or debating courses of action that will determine the common future of our larger communities. We may be conscious or unconscious of our relationship to what we casually refer to as "antiquity," but there is nothing ancient or outdated about how personal and societal attitudes toward religious practice have influenced—and continue to influence—public life in any democratic community.

ONE

Cleisthenes

The Family Curse behind Athenian Democracy

THE ATHENIANS WHO TRIED SOCRATES for impiety in 399 BCE and found him guilty were heirs to a set of democratic practices that had been in existence for a little over a century. The breakthrough to what we would recognize today as a democratic form of government had come around the year 507, when an Athenian aristocrat named Cleisthenes suddenly emerged as a leader and guided the Athenians through a series of reforms. But Cleisthenes was not the first democratic reformer; he was building upon foundations laid by generations of Greeks before him.

As is the case with most figures in Greek history, especially Greek history before the wars with Persia in the first half of the fifth century, we can know very little about Cleisthenes as an individual, just as we know little about how he persuaded the Athenians to implement the changes he proposed. The limited knowledge we do have about Cleisthenes stems from what is probably best considered an oral tradition of Athenian history that encompasses both fact and fiction. It was fifth-century Greek historians such as Hecataeus and Herodotus who first recorded the oral traditions about the more distant Athenian past; the historical genre was further developed by Thucydides, who mainly reported contemporary events but sometimes paused to digress about well-known stories from the past that illuminated the present. The main story connected to Cleisthenes preserved in Thucydides and Herodotus concerns his lineage, an aristocratic family that had long been accursed. Cleisthenes and his family—the Alcmaeonidae—lived under a shadow of suspicion because of an act of impiety committed by a distant ancestor. The tradition related how, at a pivotal moment in the history of Athens, two opposing political groups came face to face at a shrine sacred to the city's gods. In the ensuing clash, members of one faction killed some men who had taken refuge at a public altar. The egregious act of impiety had serious political repercussions, and it resulted in what came to be known as the "curse of the Alcmaeonidae" (Herodotus 5.70–72; Thucydides 1.126).

The details of this episode as reported by Herodotus and Thucydides may not be entirely trustworthy, and we will never know for certain what exactly happened in the middle of the seventh century, the traditional date for when the curse was initially called down. But the larger story behind this curse and the way the curse reportedly came about does reveal a good deal about the world the Greeks inhabited, and their assumptions about this world. An analysis of these assumptions can then uncover the very human hopes and fears of the Athenians who over time fashioned what later generations would come to know as democracy. This chapter provides a first glimpse into that ancient world.

THE LAY OF THE LAND

The Athens that we are familiar with today is the sprawling, sunny Mediterranean metropolis near the Aegean. It spreads itself out below the remains of temples perched high atop the Acropolis. The city recently remade itself into a cosmopolitan international destination as it prepared for the twenty-eighth modern Olympic games in 2004. But this modern urban center has a continuous history of human settlement that stretches back without break for at least 3,500 years, as construction projects for the new underground subway revealed. The period that brought democracy to the world occurred more than 2,500 years ago, in the fifth century. The emergence of democracy in Athens was not an inevitable outcome but rather the result of countless decisions made over many generations—the responses of real people to real and pressing situations. The all-too-human impulses of fear and sometimes greed motivated them to make the decisions they did, as did the wish to enjoy life in the present while ensuring that their families and descendants would thrive in generations yet to come.

But in the changeable environment of the ancient Mediterranean it was not easy to establish a stable government. A traveler to Athens and its neighbors in the fifth century would have seen a landscape dominated by mountains, islands, and the sea, looking much as it does today. Isolated harbors and valleys sheltered small villages and encouraged the development of localized dialects and customs. Mountains made regular travel over land difficult, or at least inefficient and time-consuming, while the jagged coastline of islands, gulfs, and harbors offered safe anchorage for ships that regularly sailed the surrounding waters. The Athenians, like many other Greek-speaking peoples, relied on the sea for their livelihood. As much as the political and social circumstances changed during the course of the fifth century, the connection to the sea remained essential for Athenians.

Patterns of settlement and land use on the mainland and the islands of Greece were dictated by the landscape and its relationship to climate. Mainland Greece and the islands received little rainfall, and Attica, the name for the countryside surrounding the city of Athens, was among the driest areas, with as little annual rain as falls in some of the drier regions of the U.S. desert Southwest. The prevailing Mediterranean wind came in from the west, and Attica, being on the east side of a mountain range, received even less rainfall than some of its immediate neighbors. The arable land in the plains of Attica stretched between the mountains and the sea, and it was highly valued for the cultivation of grains—primarily barley, but wheat and rye were also grown. Wheat was the preferred cereal because it was a finer grain when milled, but barley was the preferred crop because it was more drought tolerant. When the rains did arrive, they came in November or December and fell until early March. During these wet winter months farmers planted and cultivated the grain crops, and sailors stayed off the stormy seas. During the long, windy, and dry summers the sailors, traders, and itinerant craftsmen turned to their ships, while farmers tended their principal warm weather crops: figs, olives, and grapes.

Because the availability of good, arable land was so limited, the plains were not used for pasture. Consequently, there were precious few herds of cattle, an important fact with implications for both diet and religious life that will be discussed in more detail in chapter 2. Only the richest aristocrats kept and bred horses. Sheep and goats were much more common, and these herds were pastured above the plains in the uplands, and even further up in the mountains during the warm summer months. Herd animals were bred and maintained primarily for the goods they produced year-round—wool and milk—and only secondarily for their meat. The demands of animal sacrifice were stipulated in the traditional civic calendar of religious festivals, and they were based on the implicit recognition that resources were scarce.

The deities in the polytheistic system of the ancient Greeks ranged from the most powerful and widely recognized gods to lesser known, local spirits. The gods and goddesses of ancient Greece mirrored both the natural environment that the people relied on to make their living and the social world that governed the daily lives of real men and women. Some were gods whose power over the natural world lay in those agricultural resources that the Greek diet so heavily depended on—for example, Demeter, the goddess of cereal crops; Athena, who oversaw the cultivation of the olive; and Dionysus, the god of the vine and the production of wine. There were also lesser deities like Pan, who oversaw the work of shepherds, and the innumerable nymphs who imbued the springs that streamed from the hills and snowy mountaintops.

While the gods that the Greeks worshipped can reveal to us the resources that they valued, at the same time we can today discern a good deal about human social relations in ancient Greece by analyzing the interactions among these gods. A whole panoply of deities was arranged into an elaborate and interconnected family headed by the supreme patriarch Zeus, "father of gods and men" as he was called by the traditional poets Homer and Hesiod. Zeus the divine patriarch had authority over all the immortals (with the notable exception of three ancient goddesses called the Fates) and over all the earthly mortals. Zeus ruled the other deities not because he was the oldest, or the wisest, and not because he had a special connection to the land and the natural environment of Greece. Zeus ruled because he had successfully wrenched power from his father, Cronus. Cronus had once done the very same thing when he became ruler over his father, Uranus. This mythic pattern of an intergenerational power struggle between male deities and their fathers occurs in neighboring eastern Mediterranean cultures; contemporary scholars call it the Succession Myth. As heir to the Succession Myth, which required the son to dethrone his father (often with the duplicitous assistance of his mother), Zeus modeled a pattern of behavior that was unconsciously and consciously imitated by generations of Greek men. Certainly mortals did not kill their fathers (or even wish to), but in the natural order of things the son grows up and takes the father's place in the world and thus symbolically defeats him.

This mythic social order that Zeus modeled placed power in the hands of a few who needed the obedience and labor of many others to maintain the status quo and keep the world from returning to a primeval state of chaos. Viewed within the economies of archaic and classical Athens, the pattern manifested itself in the small fraction of men—those of a hereditary, aristocratic class—who governed everybody else. The category "everybody else" embraced many different subcategories, including less well-to-do ordinary citizens, some of whom were small landholders and independent farmers, while others worked as sharecroppers in a semifeudal system, cultivating land belonging to a wealthier class. The most unfortunate became debt bondsmen, who lost their liberty and citizen privileges until they could repay their debt. "Everybody else" also meant noncitizen but free resident aliens called metics, many of whom were specialized and professional craftsmen who worked in Athens or its port. Finally, all the slaves, regardless of where they labored, all the women, and all children counted as "everybody else," too. There were far more people in this category of "everybody else" than there were actual citizens. At best only 25 percent of the total population of classical Athens were citizens with full political privileges.

Because running farms was labor-intensive, many people lived in the countryside villages of Attica; but by the end of the sixth century, Athens was a small urban center that existed in a mutually dependent and beneficial relationship with the outlying rural districts, called demes. Athens was the recognized name for the larger autonomous civic entity called the *polis* (city-state), and it was a large town that contained the seat of centralized government for that *polis*. The surrounding countryside of Attica encompassed hills and mountains as well as the broad plains with their scattered districts, villages, and towns extending from the Aegean Sea in the south and east to the mountains in the north and west. When scholars speak of Athenian democracy, Athenian citizens, or the Athenian empire, they are referring both to the urban center of Athens and to the rural districts of Attica. Neither could exist without the other.

Athens as a city looked like many other cities in archaic and classical Greece. It lay in a broad plain between two ranges of hills. The plain was no more than 10 miles wide, and in the middle of the plain stood a small cluster of hills. An outcropping of bedrock, the Acropolis, towered above the hills and the plain (figure 1). An acropolis, literally the "peak of the city," had the obvious advantage of being an easily defensible height and a natural fortress; acropolises were sites of palace complexes as far back as Mycenaean times, before the thirteenth century. Other major urban centers in Greece had this same topographical feature—cities such as Corinth to the south of Athens, and Thebes to the north. Athens and the Acrop-

Figure 1. Athens: the Acropolis with the Parthenon viewed from the south. Photo by author.

olis had the further natural advantage of being situated only 4 miles due north of the harbor of Phaleron, and only 5 miles from a complex of three natural harbors to the southwest, collectively called the Piraeus. In the fifth century, Athens and its harbors were physically linked by the construction of defensive walls. These walls would play an important role in the course of the Peloponnesian War later in the fifth century.

The overall picture, then, might well resemble a walled city in medieval Europe. Classical Athens was a well-fortified but small (by our standards) urban center with temples, markets, and the seat of the democratic institutions alongside urban neighborhoods with their homes, businesses, and workshops. Further suburban neighborhoods and businesses developed outside the fortifications. Cemeteries and other sacred precincts were also traditionally found outside the city walls. Farms and villages in the outlying districts of Attica were all interconnected, but these villages maintained direct contact primarily with Athens, since the city housed the central markets, the assemblies, and the law courts that formed the backbone of Athenian democracy. The most important public shrines of the gods were also located in the center of Athens. This relationship between one city and the surrounding countryside created a type of centripetal energy that moved toward Athens. Such an arrangement was unusual among Greek cities, which more often organized themselves along an axis with two or more public centers—one center for cultic activity and another for commercial and political activity.

RESOURCES, COLONIES, AND CULTURAL CONTACTS

For all the natural advantages enjoyed by Athens, life in the archaic and classical city still entailed hard work. More often than not the majority of residents were familiar with poverty, privation, and the ever-present threat of hunger. Starting with Hesiod's seventh-century poem *Works and Days,* Greek literature explored the themes of man's never-ceasing labor and the suffering that accompanies human existence. Alongside the toil Hesiod also presented traditional tales of the Olympian gods and goddesses, and the very different sort of existence that they led. Hesiod remained a favorite poet of the Athenians throughout the fifth century; along with Homer, Hesiod was often quoted by Socrates.

But the Greeks were well aware that human life need not always be so tough. While the farmers throughout Attica maintained their rough, traditional way of life for many generations, by the late sixth century the commercial center of Athens had developed a thriving import and export economy, and a merchant class became acquainted with new prosperity. Athens' chief export products were wine, the finest olive oil, and exquisitely rendered ceramic ware, the famous black-figure and red-figure vases that were so prized during antiquity throughout the Mediterranean basin. Athens was also fully exploiting natural resources from its silver mines at Laurium, in the southern hills in the direction of Cape Sounion. With this silver the *polis* minted hard currency (a relatively recent innovation) and used that money in foreign trade.

Even with all the wealth generated by these various resources, famine remained a continual threat. Although the plains of Attica were fertile enough when the rains fell, some years brought drought, and there simply was not enough consistently arable acreage to feed a burgeoning population. The Athenians were faced with constant pressure to import grain, and to export residents to colonies around the Mediterranean basin. The need to colonize and expand had been a factor in the larger Greek world since at least the tenth century. At that time Greeks began to settle other lands around the Mediterranean, founding cities such as Corcyra (modern Corfu), Cyrene on the North Africa coast (today's Libya), Syracuse in Sicily, and Naples in Italy. Even a city as far west as Marseilles on the coast of France started out as a Greek colony. To the east, Greek settlements spanned the entire coast of Asia Minor (now Turkey) around to Byzantium (Istanbul), famously situated along the trade route to the Black Sea. Athens was not prominent among the colonizers of the Archaic period; Corinth and the Euboean cities of Chalcis and Eretria took that honor. But colonization of a new sort would become an Athenian focus later in the fifth century.

When centuries of colonization did not fully alleviate the pressure of the growing population of Attica, the Athenians started importing considerable amounts of grain. The importation of this staple had unforeseen economic and social repercussions. The continual need to import grain kept pressure on the silver mines at Laurium, which made possible the hard currency that could be used to purchase foreign cereals. Mining at Laurium in turn maintained the demand for expendable slave labor—the mines at Laurium were notorious for their cruel conditions. The institution of slavery itself depended on vigorous foreign trade, and slave dealers exploited foreigners from overseas markets. But the need to import so much grain had important implications for Athenian foreign policy as well. Some grain came from Greek colonies in Sicily and southern Italy, which were considerably less arid than mainland Greece and far more fertile. But most imported grain came from what the Greeks considered the breadbasket of their world: the expansive and fertile plains north of the Black Sea in the area that today constitutes Ukraine. Grain was shipped from Black Sea ports, through the straits of the Bosporus and the Hellespont, and then across the Aegean Sea. The constant need to import grain encouraged the growth of an energetic maritime industry, and it also meant that Athens felt a compelling interest to preserve open trade routes.

Wherever the Greeks went as colonists and traders, they carried with them their institutions and their distinct culture. This meant first of all the Greek language and the oral traditions that stretched back generations into the heroic past of the Homeric warriors who had fought at Troy. Hand in hand with this mythology went the ancestral customs of religion and cult practice, the regular and obligatory rituals through which Greeks maintained contact with their ancestral gods. Finally, tightly interwoven with religious customs were the political and legal structures. In fact, the same word, *nomos,* designates religious custom as well as civil law. Although these two concepts are considered quite different in today's Western democracies, throughout ancient Greece the customs, or *nomoi,* of civic governance and ritual observance reinforced each other. This complete interdependence of religious and political institutions is perhaps for us today the most strange and unexpected feature of democratic Athens. Accustomed as we are to a post-Enlightenment form of democracy with its separation of church and state, we take for granted that the daily functions of government stand well apart from the priestly functions of ritual and prayer. Yet for any Greek *polis,* from the most traditional monarchy to the most radical democracy, such a separation was simply inconceivable. This interdependence was as strong in the later centuries of Mediterranean antiquity as in the earliest, and many famous episodes in Greek history bear witness to it.

Polis is a Greek word most often translated as "city-state." *Polis* is the ancestor of such English words as "politics," "political," and "politician." A *polis* was, quite simply, an independent and autonomous body of citizens, or *politeis.* Some *poleis* (plural) were ruled by hereditary kings or tyrants, some were oligarchies ruled by an ancestral aristocracy, and by the early fifth century a very few were self-ruling democracies. In the fifth century there were literally hundreds of *poleis* in the Greek world. Most were small municipalities, indeed more like large market towns than nation-states. Athens was exceptional for its large size: 930 square miles, nearly the size of the state of Rhode Island (1,045 square miles). Athens' principal rival, Sparta, was likewise an unusually large *polis* in terms of land area, though nowhere near as large as Athens in its combined citizen/resident population.

The political boundaries of Athens developed in slow stages from the eighth to the sixth centuries. Like much of Hellas after the fall of the Mycenaean palace culture in the twelfth century, Attica before the eighth century was a collection of insignificant and impoverished villages that were beginning to come together and establish a distinct identity. The continual scarcity of resources over the generations created a polarized society that was composed of a small class of elite nobles and a much larger class of less well-to-do citizens who competed with the aristocracy for political power. The aristocracy drew its strength from lands in the outlying rural districts in Attica while ruling from the chief urban center of Athens. Border disputes with neighboring *poleis* were common.

Establishing and maintaining conspicuous religious sites throughout Attica became a way for Athenians to mark the frontiers of the *polis.* Rural villages often contained sanctuaries—land, altars, temples, and sometimes entire building complexes set aside for the traditional worship of the gods. Long before Athenian power in the Mediterranean reached its peak in the fifth century, Athens took control of sanctuaries near other *poleis* in the rural countryside of Attica. Examples of significant border sanctuaries in Attica include the sanctuary of Artemis at Brauron on the eastern coast, the sanctuaries of Athena and Poseidon at Cape Sounion on the southern tip of the Attica peninsula, the sanctuary of Demeter at Eleusis on the western border with Megara, and the much-contested sanctuary of Amphiaraus on the northern border between Attica and Boeotia. Chapter 4 will examine one of these sites, the sanctuary of Demeter at Eleusis, in fuller detail, and chapter 6 will describe the complex interaction of religion and politics surrounding a religious tradition that was associated with a "foreign" god, Dionysus, who reportedly entered Athens from the borderlands to the north and east.

In earlier times these sites on the frontiers of Attica had housed local cults that were politically independent of Athens; but as Athenian territory grew and its borders became better defined, both political and religious power became centralized in Athens. While rites continued to be celebrated at border sanctuaries as they had always been, the official homes of these cults were transferred to new civic sanctuaries constructed in the civic center of Athens. One conspicuous example is the city's Eleusinion, an urban sanctuary sacred to the goddess Demeter, whose main cult site was located on the western border of Attica in the town of Eleusis. The reorganization of these border sanctuaries during the Archaic period enabled political and religious authority to radiate out from the center to the margins of the *polis*. The *polis*'s political boundaries were sharpened and defined by Athens' official religious and political connections to ancient rural cults.

THE REFORMS OF SOLON AND THEIR
POLITICAL AFTERMATH

Although the political boundaries of Athens probably had stabilized by around 700, Athenian democracy did not emerge whole and fully formed; Athenian democracy was not the inevitable outcome of what scholars call the synoecism of Attica, or the union of its separate communities to form a single, larger sovereign community. The classical *polis* of fifth-century Athens, with all its political and religious institutions for which we now have so much physical and literary evidence, was the result of centuries of slow change punctuated by a few moments of major innovation. In some ways the stress of these slow changes left indelible marks that even the most radical expressions of democracy could not erase. The most visible of these marks points to the gap between the various economic classes of Athenians. The distinctions between the elite aristocrats and the common people were preserved in the rituals, offices, and hierarchies of the *polis.*

For the generations leading up to the Classical period, the main distinctions recognized among the male inhabitants of Attica highlighted the links between civic, military, and economic status. A typical citizen in the *polis* of archaic Athens was an adult freeborn male who owned land in Attica and was not a debt bondsman working on someone else's land. Some of these citizens were quite successful, while others might live more precariously, subject to changeable weather and the unpredictable success of crops, but they at least maintained enough wealth to own the weapons and armor of a warrior. Their limited resources enabled them to serve as hoplites, or armed infantrymen. A small number of poor citizens owned no land at all and could not afford even the most basic armor; these men, called *thētes,* worked purely as hired laborers and their civic roles in the *polis* were the most restricted. There were also citizens with considerably more wealth. A small number of elite families owned enough land to raise horses, and these nobles served in the citizen army as "horsemen," *hippeis,* or knights. This three-tiered citizen body made up the foundation of most *poleis* in archaic Greece, not just Athens.

Where Athens began to diverge from the other Greek *poleis* in the Archaic period was in its slow development of governing procedures that gradually gave political power, *kratos,* to the common citizens, called the *dēmos,* in English "the people." Combining these two words produces *dēmokratia,* hence our word "democracy"—the "power of the people." The first round of significant pre-democratic changes came during the rule of Solon early in the sixth century. Solon was a traditional aristocrat, but during his year of elected rule as archon or chief executive magistrate (traditionally dated to 594/3) he initiated the passage of a series of laws that had a profound and lasting impact on Athenian society. While many details of the changes remain lost to us today, we know their broad outlines: the Solonian laws encompassed fundamental changes to the life of all inhabitants of Attica, changes that affected areas ranging from religious rites to homicide laws to a new definition of citizen status. Recognizing the corrosive effects that debt had wrought on the common citizens—particularly since debt was so easily incurred by farmers trying to cultivate crops in the unpredictable climate of Attica—Solon banned debt slavery and freed any existing debt slaves. Solon then banned all agricultural exports, with the notable exception of olive oil, thereby encouraging better use of the available arable land.

Religious reforms were central to the Solonian reform program. Solon pushed through sumptuary legislation that limited the extravagance of funerals, which had become elaborate public events designed to display power and were potentially disruptive, especially when a member of the aristocracy was buried and the streets were full of grieving crowds and wailing women. Solon then revised and published a new, standardized civic calendar of religious festivals for the residents of Attica, and he redefined the distribution of ritual privileges among the economic classes. Again, the inclusion of this sort of religious reform runs counter to our notion of the role of government in public life, and we are reminded that *nomos* in Athens encompassed both of the modern categories "church" and "state." Public life in the Greek *polis* demanded citizen participation in ritual, and eligibility for religious offices was the first step to power and political authority in the *polis*. Solon brought about great social and political change when he reformed laws relating to worship of the gods.

By far, the most influential changes Solon instituted involved the creation of four citizen property classes that defined four distinct, graduated degrees of political and ritual rights. The wealthiest aristocrats still had the sole access to the most powerful civic offices, but now the mass of non-aristocratic people, newly freed from the threat of slavery and debt bondage, had a limited voice in the Assembly, the *ekklēsia*. Balanced against this Assembly was the *boulē*, the Council of 400 citizens (perhaps from the upper classes) who deliberated the laws. He may have given limited citizen privileges to craftsmen and hired laborers, some of whom were foreign born. Though these craftsmen owned no land at all, they worked in growing numbers in the urban center of Athens. This evidence suggests that Solon's reforms tied political privileges to economic class rather than to birth. While the richer citizens continued to have more political opportunities, the lower classes for the first time had some voice in how the city was to be governed.

Solon was also responsible for innovations in the judicial system: he instituted a new appeal process, and he invented what in Athenian parlance was called a "public" action to supplement the more customary "private" forms of legal recourse. This reform allowed any citizen, not just the injured party or his family, to prosecute certain kinds of injury. Moreover,

Solon reviewed the oldest written Athenian laws, the law code of Draco, which had been published just a few decades before his own archonship (perhaps in 621). Solon abolished much of the harsh Draconian code with its reliance on capital punishment, and retained only those laws that addressed homicide. But one aspect of Draco's tradition that Solon did keep was the commitment to making the *nomoi* visible to all. Solon had his new laws, including the laws regulating cult practices and the worship of the gods, inscribed on big wooden tablets and publicly mounted in the Agora, where citizens of all property classes could refer to them. The beginning of public accountability is evident in the publication of the Solonian reforms. Even if basic literacy was not yet widespread among all classes of Athenians, this action marked the beginnings of the notion that the law remained the same regardless of who was in power and implied that the educated nobles were now being held accountable by those who could not necessarily read the laws as published.

Athenian tradition relates that Solon went into a self-imposed ten-year exile once he had completed his full program of reforms—but only after making the Athenians promise that they would not tinker with the reforms during his absence. Solon declined any offers to stay in power; he insisted that the Athenians live with the reforms and give them a chance to work. Solon's reforms broke the monopoly on political power long held by the noblest and wealthiest families, but at the same time his laws failed to please any single group completely. His new political compromise between the privileged aristocrats and the more humble working poor did not bridge the structural gap that Athenian society was based upon, and no type of political reform could change the arid climate of Attica and the unpredictable environment that helped maintain the economic gaps. But Solon's reforms did give a boost to those who had less wealth than the landed aristocracy.

Political tensions between the classes remained and even increased in the years after Solon stepped down, eventually resulting in a period of aristocratic "tyranny" when the noble-born Pisistratus first seized power around 560. Pisistratus's initial bid to become sole ruler, or *tyrannos,* in Athens did not go smoothly. Despite alliances with political factions and other noble families, Pisistratus was forced out of Attica twice before he actually succeeded in establishing a stable tyranny in 546. "Tyranny" in today's sense of a harsh and oppressive despotic rule overstates the situation as it existed in archaic Greece. Tyranny at that time was a common form of extra-constitutional monarchical rule, based perhaps on political models found to the east in Lydia, located in modern-day Turkey. Indeed, the Greek word *tyrannos* is not native to the Greek language but is a loan word from Asia Minor. In the ancient model of tyranny an aristocrat became tyrant when he seized power in a coup, or inherited power that had been so seized. In sixth-century Greek usage, *tyrannos* came to mean something close to our word "king"—Oedipus was *tyrannos* in the city of Thebes in Sophocles' famous tragedy *Oedipus the King,* whose Greek title is *Oedipous Tyrannos.*

In sixth-century Athens, Pisistratus the *tyrannos* ruled mildly. He enjoyed the support of certain aristocratic families and gained popular approval through his sponsorship of major civic and religious festivals. During his reign Athens became an important Greek city with grand public sanctuaries and civic festivals for the goddesses Athena and Demeter. Pisistratus constructed new buildings and commissioned artwork for sanctuaries on the Acropolis, and he built an altar to the twelve gods in the Agora. Dramatic festivals for the god Dionysus probably became popular during the rule of Pisistratus and his sons. Pisistratus used traditional cult practices to consolidate his power and advance a sense of cohesion and civic identity among the Athenians. An anecdote in Herodotus illustrates how Pisistratus's sense of political theater eased his first return from exile: he found an unusually tall and beautiful woman, and dressed and armed her like Athena. This image of the goddess rode into Athens on a chariot announcing that she was bringing Pisistratus back to rule. When a rumor of Athena's appearance reached the rural villages of Attica, townspeople rushed to Athens to see the performance and welcome Pisistratus back (Herodotus 1.60). The earliest theater produced in Athens in the sixth century likewise relied on a dramatic conceit in which costumed actors impersonated the gods; Pisistratus simply played off this traditional cultural pattern, and let the *dēmos* participate alongside him in the civic drama.

Pisistratus apparently intended to establish a hereditary aristocratic dynasty, and rule passed to his son Hippias at his death in 527. The case of Pisistratus and his sons shows us how democratic impulses in Athens developed slowly and unevenly. The innovative reforms of Solon gave way to the renewed energies of the elites, led by the Pisistratid family for more than fifty years. After the death of Pisistratus, public sanctuaries and civic festivals continued to play a crucial role in the history of Athens. When an uprising against the Pisistratid tyranny did finally occur, it unfolded during a *polis*-wide annual festival honoring Athena. The celebration called the Panathenaea was famous for its elaborate and lengthy religious procession through the Agora and up the Acropolis; priests, civic magistrates, and armed warriors accompanied the sacrificial animals to the altar of Athena. Hippias, like his father, used such civic festivals as a public stage to display his civic power. Visibly leading the worship of Athena, the divine guardian of Athens, provided Hippias with a good opportunity to connect with the *dēmos,* display his largesse, and demonstrate his piety.

Behind the scenes, elite resentment was growing against Hippias and his younger brother Hipparchus, and a small conspiracy was hatched among some aristocratic families. A group of Athenian men attending the Panathenaea armed themselves as though they were part of the procession, but in fact their target was Hippias. The attempted coup was unsuccessful. In the confusion before the procession started, Hippias dodged the assassin's knife, but the weapon found its mark in his brother Hipparchus (Herodotus 5.55; Thucydides 6.54–59; cf. Thucydides 1.20). The public murder of Hipparchus in 514 provided Hippias with the impetus to live up to the modern meaning of the title tyrant and he instituted a far more repressive regime. This new regime would be short-lived. Two conspirators, Harmodius and Aristogeiton, lost their lives at the Panathenaea that day, but the two "tyrant slayers," as they later came to be known, would be honored by coming generations as the liberators of Athens. Statues of the two were set up in the Agora, where the *dēmos* went about its daily business of honoring the gods and governing the *polis.*

THE CAREER AND DEMOCRATIC REFORMS OF CLEISTHENES

Like the tyrants Hippias and Pisistratus, the democratic reformer Cleisthenes came from an aristocratic family, indeed one of the most famous families in archaic Greece. His father's family had a long tradition of political service to Athens, and had funded public building projects in Delphi. His maternal grandfather, also named Cleisthenes, had been *tyrannos* in the nearby *polis* of Sicyon in the Peloponnese, and members of his family had married into the ruling family of Pisistratus. In Athens it seems that the aristocratic Cleisthenes distinguished himself as leader in a different way. He gave real political power to the ordinary citizens, the *dēmos,* while creating a political advantage for his own family. Cleisthenes went about preparing for political reforms in a particularly militaristic fashion. As an aristocrat with close family and political ties to *poleis* beyond Athens, Cleisthenes used his influence to enlist the aid of Cleomenes, king of Sparta. The Spartans were known to resist tyrants in their own *polis* and to dislike them in neighboring *poleis*. Cleomenes marched to Athens with a small contingent of Spartan infantry and overthrew the tyranny of Hippias. Following the coup, Cleisthenes struggled with another Athenian leader for power, and he came out on top.

While Solon had paved the way for a fairer distribution of wealth several generations earlier, it is Cleisthenes who is perhaps best credited with instituting the reforms that mark the beginning of a true, recognizable Athenian democracy. Like Solon before him, Cleisthenes realized that democratic power was closely tied to the rural villages of Attica, even if the democratic institutions—the assembly places, council houses, and law courts—were housed in the urban center of Athens. Keeping in mind the Athenians' ties to the traditional rural way of life, Cleisthenes gave power to the ordinary citizens in Attica by distributing power throughout the villages or demes of the *polis*. More importantly, he redefined the very notion of what constituted a deme. Originally "deme" simply was the word for any of the towns, villages, and rural districts in the countryside of Attica. But after Cleisthenes a deme became the smallest political unit in the *polis*. The deme became the building block for clustering citizens into manageable units that could function easily in a preindustrial society that lacked the Internet, telephones, or newspapers. Demes were grouped to form two larger political units—namely, the thirty sections (*trittyes*) and the ten new tribes (*phylai*) into which the *trittyes* were then folded.

Traditionally, every male citizen born and living in Attica was a member of a *phratria,* an ancient word that designated social groups that followed lines of male descent and had control over who was and was not recognized as a legitimate member of the Athenian citizen body. "Phratry" is cognate to the English word "brother" (compare the words "phratry" and "brother" to the Latin *frater* and German *Bruder*), and as hereditary brotherhoods the phratries had worked for generations to maintain blood ties and political power among the aristocrats. Phratry members worshipped the gods together at state-sponsored festivals, and they dined together on certain civic and religious holidays. Active phratry membership was essential for enjoying political privileges in the archaic *polis*.

Cleisthenes' reforms kept the institution of the phratries, and then cleverly supplemented them by transforming the deme into the smallest constitutional unit that shared with them some of the same political, social, and religious functions. Rather than designating a mere rural or suburban village as it had always done, the deme became the foundation supporting the whole democratic apparatus. Cleisthenes' reforms officially recognized

139 demes, and deme membership became a component necessary for Athenian citizenship, in addition to traditional phratry membership. Membership in one of the demes, like that in a phratry, was inherited through the paternal line. But the new Cleisthenic deme no longer simply designated a physical place. The deme name was not necessarily an indication of the village where a citizen resided; it suggested which village his ancestors came from. After Cleisthenes, the deme was a political unit, and Athenian male citizens came to be identified by their deme name in addition to their father's name—for example, Socrates' full Athenian name was "Socrates, son of Sophroniscus, from the deme of Alopece."

One strength in Cleisthenes' plan was that demes and phratries reinforced each other. They remained separate social groups, but they shared important social, ritual, and political functions. Since official written record keeping did not yet exist, citizens relied on each other and on their communal groups to determine citizenship in the *polis*. The *polis* sponsored life-cycle rituals that celebrated the birth, political maturation, and marriage of phratry and deme members. Deme and phratry members worshipped the gods together on a regular and predictable schedule of civic festivals. Membership in a phratry and deme thus meant that peers in a citizen's communities witnessed him taking part in civic festivals and public feasts. In this way demes and phratries shared a common purpose: both were social and political groups that defined membership through active participation in civic rituals that also fulfilled a religious function.

As a consequence of the new civic and religious roles of the deme envisioned by Cleisthenes, every citizen had multiple and overlapping peer groups that both established and continually validated his civic status. The complex and interdependent bonds of civic identity in Athens were revealed even more starkly in the combinations of demes to form the larger social networks of citizens, namely the thirty sections and the ten tribes. Cleisthenes grouped each village (deme) with neighboring villages to constitute a section, or a *trittys;* he defined thirty sections in all, roughly equal in population. Three sections were then grouped to constitute one of the ten tribes (the word for section, *trittys,* literally means "a third"). The ten tribes were in part a holdover from more ancient times, but Cleisthenes also reworked the archaic notion of "tribe." Before him there had been four tribes, the so-called Ionian tribes that had performed certain ritual functions, and he left them intact for some cultic purposes; he handed over other religious rites and nearly all the political functions to ten newly created tribes, each named after a different semi-mythical hero, such as Cecrops or Aegeus.

The great innovation in Cleisthenes' plan was in the composition of each of the ten tribes. The politics of Attica had been growing increasingly complicated because of local tensions that were arising between three geographically identifiable interest groups: the people of the coastal region, the inland agrarian residents, and the growing number of urban dwellers in and around Athens. To combat the potentially crippling effects of fractures along geographical lines, each of the ten tribes was composed of three sections, drawn equally from each of the three regions of Attica. In this way the ten Cleisthenic tribes had a geographically scattered membership, and regional special interests could not rule the day.

If the demes are viewed as the building blocks for the foundation of Athenian democracy, then these ten new tribes are what provided a working structure for the Cleisthenic system. Public offices of every imaginable sort were filled either by direct election or, more commonly, by a lottery system within each tribe. A combined process of election and lottery was used to select the important officers known as archons (*archontes*, "leaders"). The archonship was an ancient office that predated the Solonian and Cleisthenic reforms. After Cleisthenes' reforms, nine archons and a secretary were selected annually, one official from each tribe, for one-year terms as magistrates with religious and judicial duties. The process of selecting the archons in the new system involved first direct election of a pool of candidates, and then a lottery. This procedure apparently layered the older aristocratic method beneath the newer Cleisthenic idea. Upon leaving office all ex-archons were eligible to serve on an ancient advisory board called the Council of the Areopagus, which retained judicial powers for certain legal proceedings including homicide and some religious cases. This council was one of the oldest institutions in Athens—it existed long before the reforms of Solon and Cleisthenes—and though its duties were gradually reduced over time, its core responsibilities illustrate a deep-seated assumption that the religious and political aspects of the state overlapped.

After the reforms of Cleisthenes, decision making and legislative powers were located in two democratic bodies. The body called the *ekklēsia*, or Assembly, was open to all citizens, and it met about every ten days on a hillside in Athens called the Pnyx (figure 2). Athens probably had tens of thousands of citizens, but judging from the size of the Pnyx a maximum of 6,000 to 8,000 attended the meetings. In some instances the Assembly also functioned as a large jury. The smaller Council of 500 called the *boulē* replaced the earlier Council of 400 established by Solon, and it met more

Figure 2. Athens: the Acropolis viewed from the hill of the Pnyx. Photo by author.

often than the *ekklēsia* to take care of legislative and judicial business. Each of the ten tribes supplied an annual quota of fifty citizens for the *boulē*, chosen by lot from all but the lowest property classes. It was assumed that every citizen would sit on the *boulē* at least once during his lifetime, and service on the *boulē* was limited to two years total for each citizen. Each tribe's committee of fifty was given the responsibility of presiding over the *boulē* and *ekklēsia* for a portion of each year called a prytany. During that time the citizens were known as the fifty *prytaneis*, or presidents, and for one-tenth of the year (a little longer than a lunar month) they performed the executive functions and daily governance of the *polis*. The fifty presidents were required to live in the city, and they dined at public expense in a public building called the Tholos. The office of the fifty *prytaneis* rotated by lot through the ten tribes established by Cleisthenes, and even the daily chairmanship of the fifty presidents, the office of the *epistatēs*, was selected by lottery each day.

The ten Cleisthenic tribes fulfilled other duties for the *polis*. Quotas of hoplites for the infantry were determined on an equal basis for each of the ten tribes. Each tribe annually elected one of the ten generals, the *stratēgoi*, who made the military decisions for that year. The office of general was one of the few in democratic Athens that was elected directly and not selected by lottery. Boards of magistrates were also selected equally from the ten tribes. Each tribe even sent competing teams of athletes, singers, and dancers to represent it at *polis*-sponsored festivals.

The direct democracy of Cleisthenic Athens described here is more radical than the modified forms of representational democracy in place today. Athenian democratic institutions as they existed after Cleisthenes and into the age of Pericles in the fifth century ensured that every citizen could regularly participate in communal decision making. The only impediments to participation were practical: a combination of time, distance from the city, and money. If a citizen could afford to take a day off from work, then he could go to Athens and exercise his political privileges by serving on a jury, attending the Assembly, or participating in a civic religious rite.

According to one tradition Cleisthenes also implemented the institution of ostracism (another theory dates it a few decades later). Every year the *dēmos* as a body was given the opportunity to send away one citizen deemed to be potentially too powerful or dangerous for the good of the *polis*. First the Athenians determined whether they wished to hold an ostracism vote; if an ostracism was held, citizens met in the Agora two months later and voted by scratching the name of a candidate onto an *ostrakon,* or broken piece of pottery—the ancient equivalent of a piece of scrap paper. Whoever received a plurality of the votes was banished from the *polis* for a period of ten years. In this way the democracy placed a check on the political influence of powerful leaders. Before the institution of ostracism, Athenians had relied on the wisdom of their leaders to limit their own political power by voluntarily going into exile, as Solon had done at the end of his period of rule. Even after ostracism became official, few men actually received enough votes to be ostracized, but it did occasionally happen. Because Cleisthenes abruptly falls out of the historical record following the year of his reforms, some scholars have proposed that Cleisthenes himself was immediately ostracized upon leaving office; others suggest that he left Athens on his own, in the tradition of Solon.

The democratic reforms of Cleisthenes instituted in the last decade of the sixth century were put into place against a backdrop of broader changes that were occurring all throughout the Greek-speaking *poleis* of the eastern Mediterranean. Greek cities continued to experience economic growth as trade expanded, and this growth led to the increasing importance of port cities that took full advantage of their excellent natural harbors. Athens is only one of the cities that followed this pattern; others included Corinth, which lay at the strategic isthmus between mainland Greece and the Peloponnese, and Miletus in Asia Minor. The mounting influence of port cities also renewed tensions between residents of urban centers and rural areas—between those men whose wealth depended on the aristocratic connections to land and those who could build wealth despite being landless. Often these tensions were played out in the development of religious practices within cities. While the response to these changes took a democratic form in Athens, democracy was not the only possible outcome. Indeed, Athens was considered unusual by its peers, and the governments of most other *poleis* either continued with the traditional forms of kingship and aristocratic rule or experienced tyranny, the extra-constitutional form of monarchy.

The *polis* that Cleisthenes left to the Athenians was far different from the other Greek city-states in the year 500. In Athens even men of modest means were free to speak out and disagree with the wealthy and powerful. The *dēmos* took an active role in helping to make decisions that would be in the interest of everyone, not just of the wealthy aristocrats. Common citizens ruled their peers, and in turn were ruled by them. Ancestral tribal forms of community and worship continued as always and were even augmented and elaborated on. The brilliance of Cleisthenes was that he used the traditional political and cultic communities and religious customs to reinforce new institutions that gave more power to the *dēmos*. His reforms created an ever greater degree of accountability among all citizens. Politics and civic religious practices both played an important role in the systems of accountability.

Cleisthenes himself had perhaps a curious familiarity with a brand of civic accountability that looked to both the man and to the community from which the man came. He was a member of an old and well-established noble clan called the Alcmaeonidae, or the heirs of Alcmaeon. According to Athenian oral tradition, the Alcmaeonidae family had long been tainted by a curse. In the days of Cleisthenes' great-grandfather Megacles in the mid-seventh century, an Athenian aristocrat named Cylon, flush with a recent victory at the Olympian games, gathered a group of friends and allies and attempted a coup d'état. According to the historian Herodotus, Cylon had married into the powerful ruling family in the neighboring *polis* of Megara, where the aristocrat Theagenes was then *tyrannos*. This was well before the rises of Pisistratus, and Cylon had his eye on establishing the first tyranny in Athens. With his supporters Cylon seized the Acropolis. At this time Megacles was probably serving as archon, and under his leadership the Athenians swiftly put an end to Cylon's coup. When a group of Cylon's allies took refuge at an altar on top of the Acropolis, Megacles and his supporters promised to let them go if they would hand over their weapons. Cylon's men did so—but Megacles and his followers did not live up to their part of the agreement, and in their outrage and fury they murdered some followers of Cylon. Cylon, the man who wanted to be the first tyrant in Athens, managed to escape the carnage.

Violating the sanctity of an altar of the gods was deadly serious business. Murder was a capital crime, but spilling human blood on ground holy to the deathless gods was doubly intolerable and could taint a family and a whole city for generations to come. For this crime Megacles and his entire family were found guilty of impiety and expelled from Attica. But it was not only Megacles and his sons who were forced into exile. The Athenians were so offended by Megacles' impious actions against the *polis* and its religious traditions that at a later time they expelled even the bones of Megacles' ancestors, and cursed all of Megacles' descendants. When Megacles' son Alcmaeon and his sons (the Alcmaeonidae) later returned to Attica and to public life, they too were haunted by the curse and the loss of their ancestral ties to the land, symbolized in the exiled bones of the ancestors (Herodotus 5.71–73; Thucydides 1.126; Aristotle *Athenian Constitution* 1).

Alcmaeon's son Megacles felt the effects of the curse when trying to marry off one of his daughters. The tyrant Pisistratus agreed to marry her, but because of the curse on the family he reportedly would not run the risk of having children by her, and they apparently never had intercourse. When Megacles learned of this he became enraged. It was left to his son Cleisthenes to finally escape the taint of the "curse of the Alcmaeonidae." As a grandson of Alcmaeon and one of the family of the Alcmaeonidae, Cleisthenes also lacked the ancestral ties to Attica common among Athenian citizens. Cleisthenes' early career shows him serving as one of the archons under the tyrant Hippias, perhaps in an effort to fit in and cooperate with Athenian aristocrats who supported the tyranny, but later he went into exile and encouraged the Spartans to overthrow the tyranny of Hippias. When the Spartan general Cleomenes forced Hippias from power, he feared the rise of another *tyrannos,* namely Cleisthenes. So the Spartans again reminded the Athenians of the curse that dogged the Alcmaeonidae.

But here Cleisthenes outsmarted the Spartans: he counteracted the curse on his family's ancestors by symbolically aligning himself with the Athenian *dēmos,* and against tyrants and aristocratic governments that would use any means available to restrict the opportunities and power of the common citizens. As a result, the Alcmaeonidae in generations to come were known in Athens as the "tyrant haters." According to Athenian oral and later written tradition, democracy emerged in Athens when the heir of an accursed aristocrat who had lost the security of his ties to his homeland established new ties to the *polis* by empowering the *dēmos* and reenergizing the political and religious life of the communities of Attica.

TWO

Athena

Religion and the Democratic Polis

ON WARM SUMMER WEEKEND EVENINGS across suburban America, the smell of grilled meat wafts across neatly clipped lawns. While children snack on hot dogs and hamburgers and romp in the backyard, adults sit on the patio sipping drinks. Wisps of smoke rise in the evening dusk. Perhaps the grown-ups are chatting about a recent movie, or party politics, or perhaps they trade neighborhood gossip before they consume their charbroiled beef. Throughout the evening, the host stands at the grill and oversees the social ritual of the great American barbeque. Barbeque grilling can be seen as a custom that unites America from coast to coast; it encapsulates the democratic American values of community and family cohesion, and it also embodies every person's individual right to the pursuit of happiness.

If some citizens from ancient Athens could travel in a time machine and visit this scene of the American family enjoying a backyard summer barbeque, they would find it strange. Where are the priests, they would ask; where are all the other civic officials? Why are these families each eating alone or in such small groups; why are they not all mixing together in the public town square, feasting on beef at public expense? What is so "democratic" about a society that does not occasionally fund a civic festival for the gods, or a public banquet for its citizens?

Twenty-five hundred years ago, the citizens of Periclean Athens called their custom of civic sacrifice and feasting *thysia*. In the practice of *thysia*,

35

Figure 3. Sacrificing a pig at an altar. Attic red-figure cup by
the Epidromos Painter, ca. 500 BCE. Paris, Louvre G112.

domesticated animals—mostly pigs and smaller herd animals such as sheep
and goats, but on special occasions larger cows and bulls—were ceremoni-
ally slain at the altars of the gods, as the two men prepare to sacrifice a pig
in figure 3. The body of each animal was butchered on the spot. The thighbones and tailbones were wrapped in fat, and the bundles were burned for
the gods on a stone altar. Seers with specialized training examined the entrails and lobes of the livers for divine signs. Priests and civic officials immediately roasted and ate the *splanchna,* or innards, of the victims—the
heart, kidneys, entrails, and other organ meat. Once the gods had received
their smoky portion and the civic officials had eaten their tasty bits, the remainder of the flesh was butchered, cooked, and distributed to those present. On such a festival day the people of Athens honored their gods, feasted,
and celebrated—all at public expense.

These customs of public animal sacrifice formed the core of what scholars have come to call the civic religion of ancient Athens. The smoke that
wafted to the sky linked the social and political world of humans with the

powerful realm of the immortals. The most basic customs of *thysia* existed throughout all Greece long before the reforms of Cleisthenes, and over the years customs were modified in Athens as Athenians worked to improve access to the decision-making positions in government for all classes of citizens, the wealthy and the poor alike. This complete integration of what we today might call sacred and secular is evident in the way that the Athenian *dēmos* and its leaders funded public worship. The same institutions that made and enforced laws also demanded that citizens actively participate in festivals that honored the city's gods. Religious customs permeated the fabric of Athenian society and politics. This fundamental difference between Athenian democracy and democracy in modern states, especially in the West, cannot be underestimated. For Athenians there was no separation between what we today consider church and state.

CULT AND DEMOCRACY FROM A POLYTHEISTIC PERSPECTIVE

The *polis* of Athens emerged from the sixth century with a new form of government: *dēmokratia*. During the fifth century, Athens also found itself in other new roles. Athens formed an alliance with some neighboring Greek *poleis* and overcame a foreign invasion. Later in the fifth century, Athens would even for a time pursue the dream of empire. But regardless of the policies that the Athenian government pursued during these decades of rapid change, democratic governance in Athens would never be separated from the institutions and officials that maintained traditional cult practices and worship of the gods. In this regard, the democratic reforms of Cleisthenes did not produce a regime that differed from other *poleis*. In Athens a common assumption was passed down through the generations: the bedrock of the Athenians' shared experience was the mutual reinforcement of religion and politics, which expressed a common goal. A prosperous city demonstrated its prosperity in the celebration of public rituals, and this city ensured its future prosperity by keeping to the old ways of the fathers: *ta patria*.

Scholars who study ancient Greece have described fifth-century Athens as a direct democracy. Policies were determined by direct vote of the citizens, and almost every state office was filled with citizens who were directly selected by lot. Athenians developed elaborate lottery systems to select the citizens who would serve their turn in a particular office for a fixed period. The most significant reforms to the governance of the *polis* were made under the leadership of Solon and Cleisthenes, who redefined property classes, established the demes, and made the decision-making bodies more egalitarian by opening up additional public offices to citizens of modest means. Most public offices were held a relatively short time, often for one month or even one day, and rarely ever for more than one year. After Cleisthenes, the only major offices not filled by lottery at some level were the ten generals or *stratēgoi,* directly elected from each tribe, who led the army and navy and determined military strategy during times of war. During the period of the Athenian empire, the officials in charge of the treasury were likely also chosen by direct election. These Athenian practices stand in contrast to familiar, modern forms of democratic bureaucracy. Many of the higher offices in the United States are held by elected officials who rely on professional civil servants and private consulting firms to carry out the mundane tasks of governing the nation and implementing policy. Even the U.S. military has been made up entirely of professionals since the elimination of the draft at the end of the Vietnam War, and today much of the work that supports the U.S. armed forces is performed by private contractors. But there was no professional class of civil servants in ancient Athens.

Athens also became a cultic democracy after the reforms of Cleisthenes, in the sense that all public offices in the *polis* were committed to upholding the ancestral practices of polytheistic worship. Altars of the gods were located in or near the places where citizens met to debate and discuss affairs of state, and formal relations between *poleis* likewise included the worship of the gods. These ancestral polytheistic practices, called *ta patria* and *ta nomizomena,* themselves were a visible expression of the social and political values in which Athenians in the fifth century took great pride.

It is well-known today that the Greeks were polytheistic. Even children who watch Disney's animated cartoon of Hercules can say that the ancient Greeks believed in many gods and told stories about these gods and heroes. The ancient world of multiple deities differs starkly from that of the single, monotheistic God who stands behind the contemporary Western traditions of Judaism, Christianity, and Islam. But ancient polytheism cannot be reduced to a Technicolor cartoon world of exaggerated gods and colorful heroes. Polytheism is not an intermediate stop on the road from primitive pantheistic chaos to rational and unitary monotheism, as was once argued by historians of religion who worked within the same nineteenth-century intellectual frameworks that produced Darwin's theory of evolution. For these earlier scholars, ancient polytheism was labeled "paganism," and today some—especially those whose main point of reference is largely Christian or monotheistic—still call it that.

The eighteenth and nineteenth centuries also produced secular humanists who set aside the personal God of traditional Christianity and valued virtuous knowledge and an impersonal deity above all else. Enlightenment figures in the seventeenth and eighteenth centuries looked to the Greeks and Romans for sources of secular, humanistic wisdom. Philosophers and literary scholars read such Greek authors as Homer, Plato, and Sophocles; they culled passages and quotations from the ancient texts that reinforced their own beliefs in a rational and comprehensible cosmos. While the efforts of secular humanists did yield some valuable insights, their method largely ignored the details of Greek religious behaviors, and in the end their understanding of ancient cultures was limiting. Secular humanists tended to skip over the gory details of cult practice, perhaps because it seemed too "primitive" for their taste. But twentieth-century sociologists and anthropologists learned how to read the grammar of ritual and make sense of it. The ancient civic custom of polytheistic worship required all citizens to regularly participate in traditional rites. A religious system like that of the Greeks and Athenians valued human actions and demanded interaction with the recognized divine powers. Modern scholarship has suggested that questions of individual belief and personal faith were of little consequence in an ancient polytheistic worldview.

What we recognize as Mediterranean polytheism emerged relatively recently in the span of human history—probably during the past ten thousand years, when nomadic societies were learning to domesticate herd animals and cultivate cereal crops. Polytheism, a coherent system for organizing a divine world, was articulated in response to networks of human social and economic relationships. As men and women began to live in more permanent settlements, their early urban societies developed social hierarchies that had the task of controlling and distributing food surpluses. The people living in organized towns worshipped deities who controlled the natural environment and determined the fertility of crops and herds. Greeks, like their neighbors around the eastern Mediterranean basin, reckoned that there were as many powerful deities as there were skills necessary to maintain human communal life. Polytheism, then, in part delineates an ancient landscape of practices and stories that projected the human physical and social world onto a parallel cosmos of divine personalities.

The gods that the Greeks worshipped and told stories about were both familiar to them and at the same time undeniably foreign. Like humans, the gods had a recognizable human form and individual personal traits—each god possessed distinct strengths and weaknesses. Taken collectively, the gods and goddesses formed a social network of complex familial relationships not unlike human family groups. But the gods were also fundamentally different from mortal humans, because their divine lives were not dictated by want and loss. The gods' well-being and very existence did not depend on the rhythm of the seasons or the physical labor involved in food production. The gods did not carefully watch the weather, cultivate the land, tend the flocks, or plan for future shortages by setting aside current surpluses.

Nor could the gods be touched by the finality of death, *thanatos*. The Greeks recognized blood as the warm stuff of life that courses through the veins of humans and animals alike, and that causes almost certain death when it flows too freely from the body. But blood was absent from the divine circulatory system. Instead, the gods' veins were imagined to be filled with a special liquid called *ichōr* that did not share the same mortal properties as blood. "The deathless ones" was one name for the gods in the Greek language, the *athanatoi* (the prefix *a-* negates *thanatos*). Their divine food, *ambrosia*, likewise means "immortal stuff." The opposite of immortal is *brotos*, mortal, and a *brotos* is a mortal man who toils upon the earth for his livelihood.

These links between work, food, blood, and death are deeply embedded in the language, myths, and rituals of the Greeks and other peoples who lived around the eastern end of the Mediterranean. The archaic Greek poet Hesiod tells of how mortal men once lived and dined in ease among the gods. Mortals lived in this work-free and pain-free utopia until they were punished for a mistake involving the preparation and distribution of food at a feast. As a consequence, mortals were forever separated from the immortals, and mortal men were required to live with women and toil ever afterward (Hesiod *Theogony* 507–616 and *Works and Days* 53–105). We know this story as the Greek myth of the god Prometheus, who gave the gift of fire to mortal men and was responsible for the creation of the first mortal woman, Pandora. The themes and narrative pattern of this myth resonate with another familiar story in the Western tradition—the story of the garden of Eden in Genesis. Here again an immortal god banishes the mortal from paradise, and sentences him and his wife to a harsh life of toiling upon the earth until they succumb to old age and inevitable death.

In both the Greek and Israelite stories, mortal women are singled out for special punishments that draw attention to their sexual and reproductive status in society. Other similarities between West Asian myth and the myths of the Greeks made popular by Homer and Hesiod in the seventh century have led some scholars to reconstruct likely avenues of influence and cultural exchange in the eastern Mediterranean. In fact, some of what we think of as Greek mythology may have originated further east and south in Asia and Africa, and then traveled by word of mouth along trade routes to the Greek-speaking peoples of modern-day Turkey. In time the eastern motifs and patterns were adapted and assimilated into preexisting stories, many of which had entered Greece in the second millennium BCE with the invasions of nomadic tribes from the north. The cultural interchanges that took place from the ninth through the sixth centuries are a complex phenomenon that scholars continue to explore and document.

After some generations of influence from technologically more advanced cultures to the east and south, Greek myth took on a recognizable form in the art and poetry of the Geometric and Archaic periods in the eighth through the sixth centuries. The gods of Homer remain familiar today: Zeus, Aphrodite, Athena, and Apollo. Yet our common supposition that there existed a fixed pantheon of Greek divinities may well be too neat. The canonical number is twelve—those deities depicted on the east pediment of the Parthenon in Athens, over the main entrance to the great temple built at the height of imperial Athenian power. But the nature of polytheism in antiquity is far too fluid for precise categories. Gods and heroes were constantly being added to the great family of deities, including foreign gods that the Greeks encountered in such far-flung places as Egypt, Syria, and Persia. The cosmopolitan world of classical and Hellenistic Greece welcomed all gods into the city. The word "polytheism" itself was not even needed in Periclean Athens; the concept was unimaginable until the Greeks encountered monotheism in the Roman world of the first century CE. At that time Philo, a Platonic philosopher and native Greek-speaking Jew living in Roman-ruled Egypt, coined the word "monotheism" when he wrote Greek philosophical commentaries on the traditional Hebrew scriptures. Like the modern world, antiquity was a time of intense intermingling of cultures and peoples of diverse ethnic backgrounds.

As is the case with the word "polytheism," there is no separate, unique word in the Greek language that scholars can translate as "religion." Instead, Greeks spoke of acts and behaviors when they talked about what we think of as religion. In place of "religion" and "polytheism" they used common words denoting pious and impious actions. *Eusebeia* (commonly translated as "piety") and its opposite *asebeia* (impiety) meant the proper and improper observance of ancestral customs of worshipping (*seb-*) the appropriate gods at the proper times in the proper ways. Worshipping the gods properly required being aware of the natural rhythms of the seasons and of the agricultural year, and celebrating the social institutions that characterize human community. *Eusebeia* in ancient Athens encompassed all three realms: the natural environment, the human social world, and the divine cosmos of the gods. The sequence of festivals observed by Athenians demonstrates how the natural, the human, and the divine are constantly overlapping and working in response to one another. Since life in the Greek cities depended on the successful cycles of cultivation and agricultural labor, there were major public festivals scattered throughout the year dedicated to the gods who oversaw the fertility of the land. Both the production and storage of cereal crops and the manufacture and storage of wine were essential for life in Attica, and festivals of Demeter and Dionysus became major public events; these deities and their festivals will be discussed in more detail in chapters 4 and 6 below. For Athenians the ancestral customs that honored the city's patroness Athena also defined them politically, and these civic rites came to express feelings of Athenian pride and, sometimes, superiority over neighboring *poleis.*

Beyond meeting the physical demands of the environment, daily life in Attica and the mechanisms of Athenian democracy were organized around smaller social groups of citizens, namely deme and tribe. Regularly scheduled civic rites brought these smaller communities together and enabled citizens to honor the gods at the same time that they marked membership in their human society. For example, civic festivals in each of the 139 demes marked the official coming-of-age for youths, called ephebes, and civic festivals incorporated new wives and new babies into the ten tribes established by Cleisthenes. At the same time, Athenians marked the unity of the larger *polis* by celebrating Athena and Theseus, the mythical hero who long ago took the members of the ten tribes and combined them into a single political unity. Today many know Theseus as the hero who traveled to Crete to slay the Minotaur, but the Athenians knew him as their founding hero who was credited with uniting the scattered villages of Attica. During the fifth century Theseus gained in popularity as a figure in art and in the Athenian political imagination. Some contemporary scholars have linked his increasing presence in Athenian art and myth to the late sixth-century political reforms of Cleisthenes. It was only after Cleisthenes' reforms that the common *polis*-wide festival in honor of Theseus came to celebrate the political unification of the state, just as the festival called the Synoikia celebrated Athena and the unification of Attica.

In the generations after the unification of Attica, Athenians fixed an official calendar for their state-sponsored civic feasts. The complex civic and polytheistic systems of the ancient Mediterranean resulted in the complete absence of a commonly accepted Greek calendar, a situation that seems strange and awkward today. It was not uncommon to refer to historical events by the season of year, the phase of the moon, or even some other unusual celestial event such as a lunar or solar eclipse. Athens itself functioned with several overlapping calendars; the archon's calendar was lunar, but the *boulē's* was solar. In Athens inscriptions could refer to the eponymous archon (i.e., the archon for whom the year was named) or the secretary of the *boulē* to date events, but this method had little meaning for people outside of Athens. The four-year cycle of the panhellenic Olympiad was common to all Greeks, and numbering the Olympiads also became a shared reference point. But beyond this there was no standard Greek way of reckoning time.

While a handful of panhellenic festivals were celebrated by all Greeks (e.g., festivals at Olympia and Delphi), few holidays were shared by every city-state. A particular festival in Attica was probably not celebrated in neighboring Corinth or Sparta at the same time. Two recognized ethnic/linguistic groups among Greek *poleis,* the Dorians and Ionians, did observe many of the same festivals, but differences remained in the details of each calendar. The different civic calendars of the Greek *poleis* did not even recognize the same New Year's celebration. In Athens the new year began in summer, but in other cities like Delphi the new year began in the spring. Regardless of when the year started, the Greeks commonly did divide the solar year to into twelve lunar months, and each month began with the new moon. But there was no seven-day week in the Greek world, and no weekend or day of rest. These innovations came with the Roman Empire almost a thousand years later, and were based on the rites of a Persian god named Mithras and on the Jewish calendar as inherited by early Christians.

Without any weekly structure to make up the month, each month had its own unique rhythm of work days and festival days. The name of each month was drawn from a major festival particular to that month, and since each *polis* designated its own festivals, even the names for the months varied from *polis* to *polis*. For instance, Thucydides reports that when the peace of 421 took effect, it was "the fourth day from the end of the month of Artemision" for the Spartans, but for the Athenians it was "the sixth day from the end of the month of Elaphebolion" (Thucydides 5.19). In

Attica the Athenian Assembly legislated the official calendar of monthly civic festivals celebrated by all. Then each deme was responsible for organizing its own community festivals that supplemented those at the larger *polis*-wide level. In fifth-century Athens this meant that each of the nearly 140 demes followed its own separate deme calendar, in addition to following the civic calendar common to all Athenians. Three good examples of these deme calendars have been preserved. Like many Athenian laws, the festival calendars were inscribed on stone and placed in public where citizens could refer to them.

The Athenian calendar also preserved festivals that existed before Cleisthenes' reforms and the institution of the demes. The Apatouria, a three-day Ionian festival in the fall, was set aside to celebrate the phratries and their new members, including any new wives who married into the tribe. The Apatouria celebration appears to be a very ancient one that predates the period of Ionian colonization; it was celebrated in Athens and in related Ionian cities of Asia Minor (cities such as Ephesos and Miletus). The Cleisthenic system allowed for overlapping political and cultic communities, and the demes played a similar role in welcoming and enrolling new members. Males were enrolled in their deme at the age of 18 in a ritual not entirely unlike the Apatouria. Each of the ten Cleisthenic tribes also organized an annual festival honoring the hero who gave his name to that tribe.

Two particular deities were prominent in the Athenian civic calendar. The extended family headed by a patriarch was the cornerstone of Greek society, and this pattern of human social interaction was mirrored in the festivals sacred to Zeus, the patriarch of the Olympian family of deities. Zeus, the acknowledged father of gods and men, was honored at countless altars in the city and throughout the countryside. Pisistratus began work on a massive temple for Zeus during his reign in the mid-sixth century. Construction of the Olympeium, situated to the southeast below the Acropolis, came to a halt at the death of Pisistratus, and the temple was not fully completed until the reign of the Roman emperor Hadrian more than 600 years later. In the meantime Athenians worshipped Zeus at his other altars, as when they honored Zeus Polieus, the god in his role as protector of the *polis,* at a festival called the Dipolieia held in the sanctuary of Zeus on the Acropolis in early summer.

Even more important to the Athenians as a civic group was the goddess Athena. Because Athens had been since prehistoric times a city sacred to the virginal daughter of Zeus, festivals for Athena were prominent, especially during the summer months when farmers enjoyed a bit of leisure time before the harvests. The goddess was worshipped in her different manifestations experienced by mortals: for example, Athena Parthenos (the unmarried daughter of father Zeus), Athena Nike (the goddess of victory in battle), and Athena Polias (the goddess of the civic *polis* complementary to Zeus Polieus). First among the festivals of Athena was the Panathenaea, an annual civic celebration of Athena Polias that every four years became a grand international event called the Great Panathenaea. The Panathenaea featured processions that wound through the city and ascended the Acropolis, where the sanctuary of the goddess crowned the highest point in the city. It was at this festival that the tyrant Hipparchus was assassinated in 514 shortly before the Cleisthenic democratic reforms.

Zeus and Athena may have been worshipped at the city's most prominent altars and sanctuaries, but throughout the urban center of Athens the *polis* built and maintained many other major temples and shrines, places that were sacred to other gods and heroes who helped the city function properly. Those honored in the city included figures such as the god Dionysus and the hero Theseus. Many more shrines lay scattered throughout the countryside of Attica, where Athenians could pay homage both to major deities such as Poseidon, Artemis, and Demeter and to the minor divinities of the rivers, woods, and pastures that helped nourish the *polis*.

Worship of ancestral deities was not visible in the public realm alone, however. Every household possessed small shrines and altars. The hearth of each household was sacred to the goddess Hestia, and the symbolic civic hearth of the city that guarded an eternal flame was located in a building called the Tholos, which also functioned as a public dining room for the citizens who served their terms as *prytaneis*. Private observances among families in individual households mirrored what happened in the shared social world of the city. A citizen man raised up prayers both at home among his family and in the *polis* amid his fellow citizens. Figure 4 depicts an intimate domestic moment as a warrior heads off to war, the husband pouring a libation while his wife and perhaps his father (on the far left) look on. Private individuals dedicated thank offerings to the same gods that public magistrates and state ambassadors honored on behalf of the city.

The full range of personal and household traditions even included "magical" practices: curses and incantations were aimed at rivals in business, love, and sports. Ancient Greek society was highly competitive, and resorting to these traditional practices was not uncommon. Although the practices of so-called magic may seem today more like primitive superstition than solemn worship of great heavenly powers, evidence suggests that

Figure 4. Pouring a libation at home before a warrior
heads off for battle. Red-figure stamnos by the Kleophon
Painter. Munich, Antikensammlungen 2415.

these customs were widespread. An example of a clay doll, complete with
pins and attached curses stuck into it, has been excavated from a well
abandoned in fourth-century Athens. Curses inscribed on pliable sheets of
lead foil have been found buried near the finish line at athletic stadiums,
and curses aimed at rivals in love and business were also buried in cemeteries or thrown down abandoned wells, most likely under cover of night.
Such curses invoked the attention of the powerful underworld gods Hecate,
Persephone, and Hades.

While the chthonic underworld deities all had authority over curses,
their powers did not undercut the rule of the divine patriarch Zeus. Persephone and Hades had recognizable authority precisely because of the inti-
macy of their relationships to Zeus—Persephone was his daughter, and
Hades his brother. Hecate's powers were even more ancient than the patriarch's, but still inferior, since Zeus had earlier defeated her generation of
gods in battle. The worship of these three gods actually worked to rein-

force the hierarchical divine family of polytheistic Athens, where each deity had a known position and function. Zeus remained the recognized patriarch who called the gods to assembly, measured out impartial justice, and oversaw the legitimacy of human oaths. He could not be easily connected to curses and sinister incantations; such activity was not appropriate to him. But some of Zeus's closest relatives were given dominion over these darker powers. The divine division of labor in this family network reveals another specialized skill that was considered necessary for the *polis* to function as it should—the skill of malevolent cursing that was better practiced far from the light of day.

The responsibility of managing the complex patterns of traditional worship in the *polis* fell to the people themselves, the collective *dēmos*. As the Athenian constitution changed during the sixth and fifth centuries and the *polis* became more democratic, so did the religious and social customs. The ten magistrates called archons exercised religious authority along with other civic duties for one-year terms; after reforms in the early fifth century, archons were chosen by lot from a list of candidates approved by the *dēmos*. Young men were socialized into the customs of Athens. Upon reaching the age of 18 boys became ephebes, and most probably left home at this time to undergo a period of intense training. Much of the instruction was aimed at honing physical and military skills, but there is evidence that the ephebes fulfilled ritual duties for the *polis* at sacrifices, processions, and certain festivals, including the Eleusinian Mysteries, the Dionysia, and the Plynteria.

Additional civic priests and officials present at festivals and sacrifices were male citizens who were also selected by lot. But the offices of priesthood revealed vestiges of the pre-democratic past, and they were not always distributed so openly. Although guidelines were changed so that some priesthoods could be filled by citizens other than the wealthy aristocrats, other priestly offices—far more ancient than the new democratic institutions—continued to be held for life. These hereditary priesthoods were handed down through the paternal line and stayed within ancient tribal lineages. Yet other priesthoods were direct appointments held for a fixed time. Some priestly offices were even put up for sale, a practice that made them available only to the aristocracy, and the *polis* used the monies to help finance the festivals and purchase the necessary sacrificial animals.

Regardless of the particular type of priestly office, being a priest was not normally an activity that required specialized knowledge or training beyond that with which any male citizen would be familiar. While the ancestral customs of the *polis* did require religious specialists who read entrails, divined omens, and butchered carcasses, every adult male citizen was considered qualified to perform the ancestral customs of *ta patria* and could therefore officiate as one of the priests at a sacrifice. This ability to function as a priest was one of the privileges of being a male citizen in Athenian society. Foreigners and noncitizens could not be priests, and female priestesses generally required a male butcher and civil magistrate to complete a sacrificial slaying. Any individual male citizen could serve as priest in his deme or in his own household at a family feast, and he could butcher the meat (if he knew how) and distribute it to the invited guests. What all the priestly functions have in common, though, is that they enabled ordinary men to exercise a powerful type of authority within the human social sphere. Citizens could assume the authority of communicating directly with the gods on behalf of the political community.

'THYSIA': CIVIC SACRIFICE AND THE 'POLIS'

A public festival in ancient Athens filled what today we consider separate civic, religious, social, and nutritional human needs. Politics and religion in the ancient world had social functions and meanings that fully intertwined; the modern categories "church" and "state" had no place in any Greek *polis.* Concern for the proper worship of the gods was deeply embedded in all levels of society, and the giving of gifts was laden with symbolic importance. Ancestral customs demanded specific offerings for certain gods at certain festivals. Acceptable offerings varied. Personal items such as clothing, locks of hair, toys, or household items could be given as votive gifts. Terra-cotta votive plaques and miniature vases were manufactured expressly to be given as offerings at sanctuaries. Even the consumption of food was invested with religious meaning, and perhaps the most common gifts to the gods were foodstuffs: wine, milk, or honey could be poured directly into the earth, while grains, cakes, vegetable offerings, and animal offerings could be deposited or burned at an altar.

As alien as it may seem for citizens in modern Western democracies, perhaps the most important Greek political custom was the complex of rituals that surrounded the custom of *thysia,* or animal sacrifice. This practice of *thysia* stood at the very heart of *ta patria,* the ancestral customs. Greek custom and myth both maintained that *thysia* was meant to please the gods—although not every sacrifice always went according to plan. When something did go awry during the ritual, the sacrifice was considered not pleasing and it was rejected. At the same time, the practice of *thysia* offered the inhabitants of the ancient city one of their only opportunities for the consumption of red meat. Meat was a precious commodity in the ancient economy, especially as cities expanded and urban populations grew. The land of Attica could not support herds large enough to feed all the city's inhabitants with a regular diet of daily—or even weekly—meat protein. Red meat was not commonly for sale in large quantities in the markets where seafood and agricultural products were sold. Commercial refrigeration did not exist, of course, and there were no ways available to preserve meat and keep it fit for human consumption. In place of red meat as a source of protein, Athenians relied more on fowl and fish. Seafood was a central part of the Athenian diet, particularly fish, which could be readily salted and preserved. But according to ancestral custom, the gods did not require humans to sacrifice fish blood and make it holy at an altar. While those who lived in the countryside may have enjoyed red meat more often than their city-dwelling peers (only after sacrificing at an altar in a village, or at a household shrine), it is clear that ancient technological and economic conditions did not allow for meat eating in the manner familiar to us today.

The customs of *thysia* combined civic and religious meanings with the biological necessity for protein in the healthy human diet. Because Greek *poleis* organized the distribution of meat only after political officials dedicated part of the animal to the gods, meat eating became explicitly linked in this society to political identity. Elected civil magistrates stood side by side with the citizen priests at the altar, and saw to it that the sacrifice was done in accordance with law and custom. The priest exercised the authority to lead the complex proceedings and carry them out as always had been done; this was the very essence of *ta patria* and *ta nomizomena*. After prophets and seers with specialized training examined the lobes of the liver and looked for signs from the gods, the *mageiros,* another civic official present, worked as butcher, cook, and religious specialist all rolled into one. The entire inner circle of citizens who actually performed the various components of the *thysia* ceremony were considered the closest to the gods. These men made sure that the gods received their portion first, and then they were honored by consuming what were considered the choicest bits of the animal's flesh: the *splanchna,* which consisted largely of organ meat. Once these morsels were roasted and eaten by the priests and civic officials, the *mageiros* supervised the butchering and cooking of the animal's carcass, and the equal distribution of the meat to the other citizens who were in attendance. In classical Athens, democratic political forms imitated religious *nomos.*

The customs of *thysia* were ancient even to the Greeks, and they were beyond question. The gods' festivals and rites were woven into the annual civic calendar, as one god was honored at one particular festival, and another god at a different time. This was the essence of *eusebeia*, piety. Each rite demanded its own customary species of animal. Female goddesses such as Athena and Artemis tended to get female victims (sometimes even a pregnant one), but not always. Sheep and goats were common offerings. Zeus liked bulls, and the pig was especially beloved by the earth goddess Demeter. Some rites even excluded the blood of animal sacrifice and instead demanded food offerings of fruit, vegetables, or grains. The price for making the wrong sort of offering could be very high: one fourth-century priest, charged with dedicating a bloody animal offering to Demeter when a vegetable one was required, appeared before his peers in court to defend himself on charges of impiety, *asebeia*. His fellow Athenians voted to put him to death. Violations of the traditional sacred laws were taken very seriously by Athenian citizens—not because they were superstitious about future outcomes, but because they were committed to their civic duty of upholding the customs of their ancestors.

THE PANATHENAEA

Perhaps the best way to get inside the Athenian experience of civic religion and cultic democracy is to look closely at one festival that was particularly sacred to Athenians. The Panathenaea was an Athenian festival that honored Athena Polias, the patron goddess of the city. The role of *thysia* at the Panathenaea was essentially similar to its role at other civic festivals in Attica. Analyzing the rituals and their urban and social settings can bring us closer to the Athenians, whose worldview embraced ancestral gods and customs related to these gods, and who worked hard to maintain connections between what was considered the overlapping worlds of gods and mortals.

Athena had long been the patron goddess of Athens. Physical evidence for her worship stretches further back than the literary record. The principal site for observing her cult was the summit of the Acropolis, which shows traces of having been a fortified palace complex in the Mycenaean period. The archaeological remains do not at present precisely indicate when Athena's shrines and altars were first built, but her most ancient shrine may well have been on the site of the fifth-century building called the Erechtheum, and by the mid-sixth century Athenians were building monumental stone temples for their goddess. The origins of the Panathenaea festival itself likewise appear to date from the Archaic period; Pisistratus may have had a hand in popularizing the festival. Athena was an unmarried daughter of Zeus and a perpetual virgin who fiercely defended her chastity. With her warrior skills and uncommon wisdom she was in many ways more like her father than were some of his well-known sons, gods such as Hermes and Dionysus. As a virginal *parthenos* who remained unmarried, Athena was never required to join the household of another man. Athena resided forever within the household of Zeus, under the influence and authority of her father, the greatest patriarch of all. The Athenians respected such loyalty in their patron goddess, and both Athena and Zeus were worshipped on the Acropolis, though first honors seem to have gone to Athena.

The main feature of the early Panathenaea festival may have involved presenting the goddess with a gift. For the Athenians the most appropriate gift for this goddess was a dress, *peplos,* that celebrated her victories in past battles. Famous scenes from the exploits of the virginal warrior goddess were perhaps woven into the *peplos,* especially a scene that featured Athena's role alongside Zeus in the gods' victory over the monstrous Giants. This scene would later be depicted in the artwork that adorned her temple complex on the fifth-century Acropolis. When she was not battling monsters and beasts, the unmarried Athena was also well-known for her skill at the loom. In a similar way Athenian *korai,* the unmarried daughters of citizen families, were raised to become skilled textile workers who prepared wool and wove at looms set up in homes alongside the hearth. For the festival of the Panathenaea, girls of varying ages from the best aristocratic families were chosen to practice and perfect their wool-working skills in service to the goddess of the loom. For nearly a year these girls worked together to weave the goddess's intricately decorated new *peplos.* At some point (we do not know exactly when) the festival was imagined as the birthday of Athena, and the *peplos* was the gift that the *polis* gave their protectress. Athena's birthday was celebrated in the midsummer month of Hekatombaion, the first month of the Attic calendar; by starting their civic year with their goddess's birthday the Athenians showed honor to their powerful patron.

The sixth century was a time of significant changes in the fortunes of Attica: Athens became a major economic center and a thriving city that attracted artisans from all over the Aegean region. In perhaps the middle of the sixth century, Athens took the important step of reorganizing the birthday celebration of their goddess, opening it up to other Greeks and making it a panhellenic event. Tradition has it that the tyrant Pisistratus was ruling over Athens when these changes took place; scholars are unsure whether he personally pushed for these changes to the civic rites or the desire for change arose elsewhere within the *polis* and he just facilitated the reorganization.

The Athenians chose the panhellenic athletic festival as their model when they refashioned the Panathenaea. For two centuries already, Greeks from different autonomous *poleis* had been gathering to honor the gods with athletic games celebrated at a sanctuary in Olympia—a small, centrally located village in the rural Peloponnesian peninsula. Homer sang of similar athletic games in the *Iliad:* these are the funeral games that showed respect for the gods while honoring the fallen warriors who died on the plains surrounding Troy. The games for Patroclus in *Iliad* 23 highlighted the *aretē*, or manly virtue, of the best warriors. The games the men played and the skills they honed were the skills needed on the Homeric battlefields: footracing, boxing, javelin throwing, chariot racing. These were precisely the same games and contests held at the panhellenic athletic festival. But another essential aspect of the funeral games and the athletic festival was the celebration of *thysia*. The gods were honored with animal sacrifice, while the athletes celebrated human community with the shared sacrificial meal.

The Olympian games celebrated in the rural sanctuary sacred to Zeus were actually the oldest of four sets of panhellenic games celebrated among the Greeks. The Olympian games were probably established in the eighth century, and by 150 years later three other athletic festivals had been added to the panhellenic calendar: the Nemean games (also sacred to Zeus), the Isthmian (sacred to Poseidon), and the Delphic (sacred to Apollo). Each festival was held in a different region of Greece, and the games were celebrated in either a two- or a four-year cycle. Because each festival was celebrated in a different year of the cycle, at least one athletic festival was celebrated each year. Sacred truces were in place for the duration of the festivals, putting any military hostilities on hold for as long as the Greeks were united in honoring the gods and celebrating human community and manly *aretē*. Using these panhellenic festivals as their model, the Athenians reorganized the Panathenaea in the sixth century: they celebrated Athena with an athletic festival every four years at the Great Panathenaea. For each of the other three years they honored the goddess's birthday with the more modest, traditional *polis* celebration.

The festival of the Great Panathenaea lasted at least four days. The first days were devoted to the panhellenic competitions. Male athletes from three age classes (boys, ephebes, and men) competed in the traditional athletic and equestrian events. First- and second-place winners were awarded jars of fine olive oil—the olive being a fruit associated with Athena and widely cultivated throughout Attica. The olive oil was presented in costly and beautifully painted vases known as Panathenaic amphorae. These unique vases depicted the warrior Athena on one side and the particular athletic event on the other.

Alongside the better-known athletic competitions of the pentathlon, the footrace, and the four-horse chariot race, participants from all over Greece competed in other traditional events that did not remain a part of the modern Olympics when the games were revived in the late nineteenth century. Oral recitations of poetry, as well as musical and dance competitions, attracted men with more artistic talents. Solo musicians who played the harp and flute competed against each other, and performers of lyric poetry tried to win over the judges. Rhapsodes, the itinerant professional singers who memorized and recited epic verse, also performed. Some scholars believe that it was the poetic competitions at the Great Panathenaic celebrations under the Pisistratid tyrants in the sixth century that helped rhapsodes fix the canonical forms of Homer's epics, the *Iliad* and *Odyssey*. Another opportunity for song and dance came on the night after the last of the athletic competitions. This special evening, called the *pannychis,* featured choirs of Athenian youths and maidens who sang sacred songs in honor of Athena. The event lasted late into the night and ushered in the day of the great procession up the Acropolis.

Team sports of various kinds were also played at the Great Panathenaea, though these events were not panhellenic. Rather, these group events were reserved for the citizens of Attica. Each of the ten Cleisthenic tribes were required to supply teams for the events, and the ten tribes would then compete against each other. There were sailing contests and ship regattas, and competitions of an old-fashioned war dance performed in full body armor—the pyrrhic dance. Torch races were also run by competing teams from the ten tribes. Prizes for these Athenian-only events were not vases of olive oil but oxen and money. The clear purpose of such prizes was to allow the winning tribal team another opportunity to sacrifice and feast together.

Special festivals called for special offerings, and the highlight of the Great Panathenaea was the procession on the final day. It was then that the Athenians presented the goddess with her animal sacrifices and her birthday gift. The Panathenaea celebrated in the month of Hekatombaion featured major civic sacrifices of scores of cows: Hekatombaion refers to a hecatomb, literally "one hundred cows." The first month of the Attic calendar was thus named for this day of public worship and civic feasting consecrated to the patron goddess Athena. Visitors today to the British Museum in London can see among the Elgin Marbles the sculpted frieze that ran about the interior portico of the fifth-century Athenian Parthenon. This frieze is thought by some to depict the Panathenaic procession itself, and the preparations for the great ritual of *thysia*. Men, youths, maidens, horses, sheep, and cows all make their way to the summit of the Acropolis, carrying the items necessary for the ceremonial slaughter of the sacrificial animals and the feast afterward.

The grand *pompē* or procession of the Panathenaea started near the city gates in the Kerameikos quarter, where participants gathered along with the animals. In the early fourth century, Athenians would build a monumental civic building for this very purpose, the Pompeion. The *pompē* first followed the Panathenaic Way through the residential and commercial quarter of the Kerameikos, and from there into the city center and the Agora before finally ascending the slopes of the Acropolis to the altars and the temple that housed the image of the goddess. A few women and girls marched alongside the men in the procession, and the *peplos* of Athena, the handiwork of Athenian maidens and women, was displayed on a cart for all to see. When the Acropolis was rebuilt after the devastations of the Persian Wars and Athenians again processed through the city to honor their goddess, the *peplos* was displayed as a sail on the mast of a wheeled cart styled like a ship. Such a dress was a fitting gift for the patron goddess of a naval empire.

At the foot of the steep Acropolis the procession halted. The *peplos* was removed for the final ascent, and the decorated cart was left at the base of the hill. Since cows do not climb steps with ease, Athenians constructed a paved ramp parallel to the monumental stairs that ascended the Acropolis— a sort of ceremonial track for the animals to climb. When the *pompē* reached the sanctuary at the top of the Acropolis, sacrifices were performed at a monumental altar near the main entrance to Athena's temple. The interior of any Greek temple was not a meeting place or a house of prayer; rather, it housed an image of the deity and contained storerooms for treasure and votive offerings, and for the tools and implements needed during the sacrificial rituals.

The proper sacrifice of whole herds of cows required organization, expertise, and precision. The Parthenon frieze and images on vases depict the many people who were involved in the process, each with his or her own

Figure 5. Sacrificial scene from an Athenian red-figure vase, ca. 510 BCE. Attic red-figure lekythos, the Gales Painter. Boston, Museum of Fine Arts 13.195, Francis Bartlett Donation.

role. Older citizens who were priests and magistrates oversaw the rites and prayers. Youths helped lead the animal victims up the steep paths and helped control and lift the beasts once they reached the altar. A young maiden was a part of every sacrifice in the role of *kanēphoros*, or basket carrier. Figure 5 shows two young men leading the cows to the temple, represented by the solitary column on the right, while the maiden carries the basket. Since the Greeks believed that the animals were, in a sense, being tricked into offering their lives, *ta patria* required that the sacrificial knife be hidden amid barley grains in the basket carried by the *kanēphoros*. No one was to witness the tool that would bring death to so many unaware and blameless animals.

The officials most closely involved in the rites of *thysia* had to be ritually pure to perform the ceremony, so a ritual hand washing was done when the first victim reached the altar, as shown in figure 6, and prayers to the gods were offered with outstretched hands. Libations of wine were poured into the ground. Grains of barley taken from the basket were sprinkled onto the forehead of the bull. When the bull threw his head around in response to the stimulus of grains showering his face, the priests took the movement as a sign that the bull was giving his assent. The animal victim was now willingly offering its life for the good of the *polis* community.

Now is the moment of death, and the beginning of the slaughter. An official wielding a sacrificial axe stuns the animal by hitting it in the head

Figure 6. A priest washes his hands before sacrificing a
sheep. On the right a youth holds the basket containing the
grains and the knife. Attic red bell-krater, ca. 450–425 BCE.
The Hague Gemeentemuseum, OC (ant) 5–71.

with the blunt end of the heavy tool. Then the ephebes step up. The bull
is still alive, but is dead weight. It takes several athletic young men to lift
the head and forequarters of the bull so that the correct—and fatal—
incision can be made. The cut is made at a main artery in the neck, and
the neck is supported so that the blood can be drained and collected in a
special bowl. The blood that preserves life can also take life away when it
flows too freely from the body: for this reason the animal's blood is considered powerful, and very sacred—provided that it is contained and used
in the proper way set forth by ancestral custom. Blood spilled with no
thought to the proper observance of traditional rules and guidelines of *ta
patria* constitutes *miasma,* or ritual pollution.

The animal dies as its blood fills the bowl. A civic priest splashes the
contents of the bowl on the base of the altar, making the first offering to
the immortals. At this point things begin to happen quickly: ephebes help
roll over the bull's carcass so that the *mageiros* can begin his tasks, first
making a long incision from the neck down the length of the abdomen.

Figure 7. Roasting the innards and reading the liver. Attic red bell-krater, ca. 425–400 BCE. Paris, Louvre G 496.

The *splanchna* are extracted and roasted by the proper civic officials, and the liver is removed so that seers can interpret the lobes for signs from the gods. In figure 7 a youth roasts the innards on a long spit and another youth pours a libation while a priest examines a liver in his right hand; at far right the god Apollo, holding a branch of laurel, oversees the sacrifice. The gods require their portion, too; with the accumulated experience of generations before him, the *mageiros* works quickly to disjoint the legs from the body and reserve two particular bones for the gods. The tailbone and the thighbones are wrapped in fat and set to burn upon the altar. The smoke that ascends into the skies reaches the gods, who were said to be pleased with the burning savor of the sacrificial offerings. Through this custom of *thysia* the immortals received their proper respect and honor from mortals. Indeed, it was thought that the gods' immortal existence would be diminished if the honors of *thysia* ever ceased.

The thighbones sanctified on the altar were not the only gifts Athena received that day. Athenians also presented Athena with her new *peplos,* which had been woven by the young women of Athens. A vestige of aristocratic privilege is apparent in this ritual: the actual presentation of the gift, an act that was itself a great honor, was reserved for women who belonged to one particular old Athenian family. The statue of the goddess was not dressed in its new robe at the Panathenaea; that ritual act was apparently reserved for a festival called the Plynteria ten months later, when women from that same aristocratic family removed the adornments from the statue and washed it—probably in the sea. There were many images of Athena on the Acropolis, especially after the artistic program put into place by Pericles, and scholars are not sure which image was presented with the new *peplos*. Several new statues were executed in the mid-fifth century, and there was an old wooden statue of the armed Pallas Athena, but equally important to the Athenians was an ancient wooden image said to be a crude and a nearly featureless plank of wood, which was nonetheless venerated.

Athena had many altars on the Acropolis in addition to the great altar. Judging from inscriptional sources, each celebration of the Panathenaea devoted a great deal of time to sacrifices at the altars. Offerings were made to all aspects of the patron goddess present in the shrines on the Acropolis: Athena Polias, Athena Nike, Athena Parthenos, and Athena Hygieia (Athena of the City, Athena of Victory, Athena the Maiden, and Athena Who Preserves Health). The distribution of the sacrificial meats varied: portions from the offerings for Athena Hygieia were distributed mainly to important civic officials. Portions from the animals sacrificed to Athena Polias and Athena Nike were set aside for all the Athenians; meat was distributed from designated places in the Agora and Kerameikos according to deme. The civic rites of Athena unified the city and nourished the citizens, who displayed their public piety by feasting on the meat purchased at state expense.

THE CENTRALITY OF CIVIC FEASTING
AND SACRIFICE IN ATHENS

As a practice that was central to the well-being of the community, *thysia* was the subject of many laws and ordinances passed by the Assembly. The Athenians were proud of their customs. The frequency of their purchase and distribution of meat set them apart from Greeks in other *poleis;* while the practice of *thysia* was common to all Greeks, the Athenians were said to finance more festivals and public banquets than any other *polis.* Some scholars have reckoned that as many as one-third of the days in the Athenian calendar included some sort of civic animal sacrifice, though surely every Athenian did not observe every festival. But as one aristocratic commentator noted in the late fifth century, Athens had an unusually large number of festival days when the official business of the *polis* conducted in the *ekklēsia* and the law courts could not be held. In the fourth century before the rise of Alexander, when Athenian democracy was still functioning as it largely had during the fifth, corrupt demagogues occasionally came to power and misused the funds set aside for sacrifice, celebrating public holidays and feasts with an extravagance that some aristocrats viewed as excessive.

Of course the common citizens may have enjoyed the public banquets with more relish than aristocrats who still recalled old-fashioned ways. At an earlier time banquets for citizens had meant dining at a symposium in the intimate company of a few of one's social equals. The symposium was an elite institution from an earlier, pre-democratic age; it was a custom that had transmitted traditional warrior values at a time when the aristocracy had little obligation to share power. The civic festivals of Periclean Athens distributed meat more equally among the masses of citizens, regardless of birth, class, and social status. The *polis* even built public dining rooms in common areas. A building called the South Stoa was completed in the Agora during the last quarter of the fifth century. This long porticoed structure, which contained fifteen dining rooms with couches for as many as 105 men, was built by the state to serve Athenian citizens who were spending the day in the Agora. The Pompeion in the Kerameikos, constructed a few decades later, also contained dining rooms with spaces for at least sixty-six men. On festival days men could use these spaces to dine together on sacrificial meat, and on business days they could use the rooms for meetings.

Not every festival with sacrifices was a major holiday and a day off from public business; some festivals were certainly minor affairs, attended by only a small fraction of the citizen body. Some demes held sacrificial banquets on days that were workdays for other demes. But even on business days when the courts and the assembly met, *thysia* was still a visible part of the public proceedings. Stone altars where *thysia* was performed were a necessary component in the design and construction of any public space, from the council building (Bouleuterion) and the law courts to theaters and athletic stadiums. Every *polis* meeting opened with offerings and prayers to the gods, with libations of wine and the sacrifice of an animal at an altar. Priests performed the bloody sacrifice of an animal on the battlefield before battle in a rite known as *sphagia,* and seers carefully inspected the entrails. Negotiations and treaties with foreign states were sealed with cult practices that connected the human realm of foreign affairs to the divine powers recognized by all men; the word for "treaty" or "negotiated truce" is the same word as "libations for the gods," *spondai*. Here words of prayer accompanied a stream of wine that spilled to the ground as the parties involved called upon the gods to witness their intentions. Athenian laws published on wood and stone *stēlai* and placed in the Agora or elsewhere opened with formulaic phrases stating that the gods sanctioned the deliberations of the assembly and the ordinances passed. Hundreds of these Athenian laws inscribed on *stēlai* are extant, and a surprisingly large number of them record the minutiae of how the Athenians publicly financed the banquets and festival that constituted the civic calendar.

Public dining rooms were a standard feature in the landscape of fifth-century Athens, but civic festivals and the public banquets that followed were not the only occasion for publicly financed meals. One civic building deserves particular notice: the Tholos, located near the Agora. Regular dining at public expense in the Tholos had a political function in Athens at least since the reforms of Cleisthenes. During its tribe's turn at *polis* administration, each group of fifty citizen *prytaneis* was fed at public expense for a month in the Tholos. We do not know the precise menu that was served in the public dining rooms, but meat from the civic sacrifices performed daily could well have turned up there when it was available. Other public officials and guests of the *polis* also ate either in the Tholos or another public dining hall called the Prytaneion; these diners included the handful of citizens who were honored by the *polis* with the privilege of permanent maintenance at public expense, or *sitēsis*. One of the reasons Socrates so angered the jury of fellow Athenians at his trial in 399 is that he apparently asked not only to be found innocent of the charges filed against him but even to be granted this unusual honor of public maintenance in the Prytaneion for the remainder of his life.

Participating in *thysia* and in the public banqueting that took place afterward was one of the central ways in which male citizens formed and validated their identity as citizens. A citizen in this democracy was someone with whom other citizens sacrificed and dined. Although public record keeping was a regular part of Athenian civic life by the mid-fifth century, no central bureau yet existed where citizens could go to register themselves when they came of age. There is some evidence that lists of citizens to serve in the military were drawn up, but we know of no written records for birth or marriage, no voter lists, and no death certificates beyond the epitaphs in the Kerameikos cemetery. Instead of centralized written records Athenians relied on their memories of who attended *polis* festivals and public banquets—who worshipped the gods of the city alongside other citizens. *Eusebeia* was tied to active participation in civic groups. Anyone who did not participate was an *idiōtēs*, a completely isolated private individual (hence our word "idiot").

Citizens in Athenian cultic democracy came of age and were socialized into their demes and phratries, where each man was known by family members and peers. Not only were fellow demesmen well acquainted with each other and often related through blood and marriage, but they also knew the networks of families and could name each other's grandparents and grandsons. When a citizen needed to prove his identity in court, should his citizen status come into question, he called witnesses from his deme and phratry to vouch for his presence at civic sacrifices and banquets. When a defendant wanted to establish in a court of law who his blood kin were, he called witnesses from his family who swore that over the years the defendant had sacrificed to the gods in the presence of other family members at both major and minor civic festivals. An Athenian jury considered such testimony adequate proof of identity and citizen status. Even Plato and Aristotle, in their theorizing about how to form and manage the ideal state, included *thysia* and the subsequent public banqueting as the backbone of their societies. Both philosophers claimed that the customs surrounding *thysia* provided occasions for fellowship, and for courtship leading to marriage. These ancestral customs surrounding festivals and public banquets, *ta patria,* provided the foundation for important bonds and networks of families. *Thysia* and the communal meals were not simply beneficial to the *polis,* nor were they excuses for merriment. They were, in fact, completely necessary for Athens to function.

And yet the custom of *thysia* was not fully egalitarian in this democratic society, because significant portions of the population were excluded. The male citizen body constituted perhaps one-quarter of the residential population of Attica. Respectable wives reclined on couches only at their wedding, and they never dined in the public dining rooms. Women had no place in the governing democratic institutions, and although citizen women of all ages did perform significant cultic functions in the *polis* it is unclear whether they took part in the civic banquets alongside men. There is some evidence that women, even women of the upper classes, suffered from malnutrition. Slaves were not citizens at all, even after they gained their freedom, and in fifth-century Athens there was an additional group of noncitizens who were excluded from the civic functions of cultic democracy. Resident aliens called metics, many of whom were citizens of nearby *poleis,* settled in Athens in large numbers. Although some metics were wealthy businessmen who could enjoy the culture and pleasures of Athens and take advantage of its economic opportunities, they were little better than women or slaves when it came to participating in the official political structures, though they did often dine on couches alongside citizens and could be compelled to serve in the military.

Some people in Greek antiquity actually declined to eat meat for reasons of principle. Philosophers such as Xenophanes and Heraclitus criticized traditional customs common to all Greeks that recognized the power of blood pollution and the necessity of sacrifice to please the gods. Tradition has it that Pythagoras's theory of the transmigration of souls kept him and others from eating meat. But true vegetarianism was rare, because rejecting meat necessarily meant rejecting the *polis* and the cult of animal sacrifice that bound citizens together. *Thysia* was the bedrock of every political community in ancient Hellas, and vegetarians found themselves outside the political structures wherever they went. Since they did not dine with their peers and exhibit recognizably pious civic behaviors, they were considered politically and socially suspect.

Eusebeia, or public piety, in the cities of ancient Greece was not a matter of belief or superstition. A pious citizen in Athens was not a meek and humble man who submitted to the will of the gods; nor was he a cautious and superstitious one who observed every festival and every ritual down to the last detail. Ritual practice was so thoroughly integrated into political and social life that a pious citizen was a man who took his civic responsibilities seriously. He participated in public life and civic rites alongside his citizen peers. When he consumed the sacrificial meat slaughtered at the altar of Athena, the pious citizen's observance of civic rites and ancestral customs, *ta patria,* signaled his willing inclusion in the Athenian body politic.

THREE

Pericles

Empire and War in the City of Athena

CLEISTHENES BRIEFLY ASSUMED A LEADING role in Athens in the late sixth century when he led the *polis* following the expulsion of the Pysistratid tyrants. The reforms he advanced drew on an inherited understanding among the Athenians that their government was charged with funding and maintaining the civic rites of its citizens: at festivals and civic sacrifices the citizen body worshipped the ancestral gods while it feasted on meat purchased by the state. Cleisthenes' political opponents raised the memory of the curse of the Alcmaeonid family, but Cleisthenes nevertheless won over the respect of the Athenian *dēmos,* who benefited from the significant reforms he instituted in the governance of Athens. But while Cleisthenes quickly disappeared from the Athenian historical record, the aristocratic family of the Alcmaeonidae did not fade into obscurity. In fact two of the most important political figures in fifth-century Athens—Pericles and Alcibiades—were directly related to Cleisthenes. Both prominent political leaders were outstanding military commanders as well; Pericles was repeatedly elected general and Alcibiades had his share of significant military accomplishments. Pericles and Alcibiades left indelible marks on the political history of Athens, as well as on the cultural and religious life of the city. Like Cleisthenes before them, both men had to address the legacy of the curse on their Alcmaeonid ancestors. But unlike Cleisthenes, both Pericles and Alcibiades at certain points in their public lives found themselves connected to civic trials for impiety.

Pericles is perhaps best known for leading Athens during the period that is sometimes called its Golden Age. Indeed, those decades between the Persian and Peloponnesian wars are often named after him: the Age of Pericles, or Periclean Athens. The fifty years following the withdrawal of Persia also witnessed the creation of a naval empire in Athens, a complex process that started well before Pericles came to power. Pericles' name has come to be closely connected with the Athenian empire, although some have perhaps unduly credited him with its rise. During the years of Pericles' leadership, Athens experienced significant changes in civil governance and the observance of traditional religious festivals. Many of these changes reflected the impact of empire on the *polis*, its religious customs, and its citizens. The civic rites of Athens in time came to convey what it meant for a democracy to maintain an empire. While Pericles was only one of many who advanced the empire, he was the acknowledged leader of those Athenians who voted to support the changes in the city's communal and religious life.

WEST MEETS EAST IN A FIERY TEMPLE

The roots of the Athenian empire stretch back into the Archaic period, well before Pericles and Cleisthenes. This first empire in classical Hellas unfolded in response both to internal pressures within the *polis* of Athens and to the changing political circumstances of those *poleis* that Athens felt special cultural and political connections to. Since at least the eighth century, the Greeks living alongside the sea had been on the move, leaving the mainland of Greece and sailing east and south across the Aegean Sea. As they explored they established trading posts and settlements in the Aegean islands and along the east coast of the Mediterranean. Greek cities could be found as far south as the modern-day border between Turkey and Syria. Greeks also sailed west and expanded into Sicily and southern Italy.

One of the waves of settlers were the Ionians, an extended group who spoke a common dialect, organized their communities around the four recognized ancient tribes, and celebrated a common set of annual religious festivals. The Athenians were traditionally understood to be the common ancestor of the Ionians; this supposition is probably not entirely accurate, but over the years a shared religious and cultural heritage reinforced the conviction. Oral traditions recounted how Ionians had set out from Attica shortly after the Trojan War and sailed across the Aegean to Asia Minor, and in time the west coast of modern-day Turkey became known in Greek as Ionia. Ionians were not the only ones settling across the Aegean: Dorian Greeks from the southern parts of Hellas also settled in the islands and along the eastern edge of the Mediterranean coast. Dorians spoke a different dialect of the Greek language, and celebrated a calendar of festivals distinct from the Ionians'. Newly founded Dorian and Ionian communities brought Greek customs and language to non-Greek lands, and they maintained close political and religious ties with their relatives across the sea in Hellas.

Cultural transmission is a two-way street, and throughout Ionia and the eastern Mediterranean Greek settlers and traders mixed with many different ethnic peoples who shared their own knowledge and customs. These non-Greek peoples became known as "barbarians," or *barbaroi,* a Greek word coined to describe all those who did not speak Greek but uttered some combination of indecipherable sounds that struck the Greek ear as nonsense—"bar . . . bar . . . bar." The most consequential of these barbarians lay to the east and south of Hellas: the Lydians and Carians, both Indo-European peoples who inhabited coastal Asia Minor; the Phoenicians and other Semitic-speaking peoples along the Mediterranean coast to the south of Caria in present-day Lebanon, Syria, and Israel; and the Egyptians along the Nile River and its delta in North Africa. One ancient text from this region relates how Ionian Greeks were known to a certain Semitic people who dwelled in the inland regions east of the coastal Phoenicians. The ancient Israelites in the book of Genesis called the Greeks the Javan, or Iawan—the Hebraicized spelling of "Ionian."

One of the benefits of trade in the Mediterranean basin was the robust exchange of cultures. Ancient Greece and the subsequent Western tradition could not have developed as they did without the influence of the eastern peoples called barbarians. Indeed, the Greeks in the eighth and seventh centuries borrowed the alphabet of the Phoenicians, the coastal cousins of the more nomadic and pastoral Israelites. Early Semitic scripts contained around twenty-two symbols representing the sounds of consonants. This system contained no vowels, which were filled in by the reader as he went along. When Greeks adapted the Phoenicians' alphabet for their own tongue, they introduced written vowels into the script by assigning vowel sounds to the Semitic consonantal symbols that the Greek language did not need. At the same time the Greeks also borrowed other things from the neighboring Phoenician and Semitic cultures—musical instruments, modes of dress, stories, and myths. Even some religious practices common in Athenian civic cult were probably passed along to Greeks from this part of the world during the eighth century, above all some forms of divination practiced during sacrifice. Hepatoscopy, or interpreting the lobes of a sheep's liver, was one of the most common prophetic customs practiced by seers in the east, and it played a role as well in the civic rituals of *thysia* in archaic and classical Athens.

Much further inland and east of the Egyptians, Phoenicians, and Lydians lived the Persians, who inhabited what to the ancient Greeks constituted Asia proper. The heart of the region known then as ancient Persia is today called Iran. While Athens was experiencing shifts between aristocratic regimes, tyrannies, and emerging democracy, the Persians were amassing one of the largest empires the world had yet seen, one that straddled three continents and stretched from the Indus River through Mesopotamia and all the way to the eastern shores of the Mediterranean Sea. As Persia loomed in the east, Greek *poleis* were constantly struggling to maintain stability both at home and abroad. Border wars and struggles for influence within Hellas brought about shifting alliances that often came into conflict with each other. The result for fifth-century Greece was two periods of protracted warfare: the Persian Wars and the Peloponnesian War. During these two conflicts Greeks became sensitive to perceived differences in ethnic background as manifest in dialect and religious custom, especially those identified by the ethnic labels "Ionian" and "Dorian." In Athens traditional Ionian festivals that honored Apollo and Athena took on new social and political meanings, and civic rites themselves changed over time.

These political conflicts and cultic changes had their roots in earlier generations, when the mainland Greeks kept close contact with their cousins in the Aegean and along the Ionian coast. The political fortunes of Ionian Greeks depended on developments in the kingdoms immediately surrounding them. As a result, some Ionian Greek *poleis* in the sixth century came to be governed by foreign kings. Not all these kings were oppressive—indeed, some brought about positive changes for their subjects. The Lydian king Croesus is the first ruler known to have adopted a monetary system that minted coins for use in trade. The institution of coinage in the early sixth century helped bring great wealth to Lydia and Ionia, and it facilitated the development of an international trade economy in the eastern Mediterranean. The Athenian tyrant Pisistratus is credited with introducing the first metal coinage in Athens around 550 (not long after the Lydians' innovation among the Ionians).

In the mid-sixth century the Lydian kingdom of Croesus was overpowered by the growing Persian Empire, and Ionian Greeks became subjects of the Persian king Cyrus the Great. The Persian mode of imperial administration relied on regional governors called satraps who oversaw the management of local cities and kingdoms, which were themselves governed by client-kings and tyrants. In this way most of the Greek *poleis* in Ionia came to be governed by native tyrants who answered to satraps and the Great King of Persia. In time Greeks began to chafe under foreign rule. Ionian Greek resistance increased as the ambitions of the Persian Empire expanded; stiffer taxes were levied against the Ionian cities and greater numbers of ethnic Greeks were conscripted into the Persian army. The Aegean island of Naxos resisted Persia from the start, and Miletus, the most prosperous of the Ionian cities along the Asia Minor coast, found Persian rule especially oppressive. In 499 some Ionian cities followed the lead of Miletus and revolted against the Persian Empire. When they did rise up against the barbarian Great King, the Ionians of Miletus asked their relations on the Greek mainland for assistance. The Athenians willingly provided twenty ships and a moderate-sized force. It was not yet ten years since the reforms of Cleisthenes.

This revolt in Ionia marks the first official meeting of Athens and Persia, and it was a memorable one that brought together religion and international politics. In 498 an Athenian contingent of soldiers fought alongside Ionians at Sardis, the capital of the Persian province of Lydia. In the midst of battle the Athenians sacked and burned the city. A temple of the native goddess Cybele went up in flames in the conflagration, a temple that was sacred to the resident Lydians and protected by the ruling Persians. Destroying the enemy's sanctuaries was an accepted tactic to demonstrate military and cultural superiority, and Athenians did not shrink from it. The Persian king Darius was so enraged at the act of impiety that he reportedly assigned a slave the task of reminding him of the sacrilege. Three times a day—whenever the Great King sat down to eat a meal—the slave repeated, "Master, remember the Athenians." The victory in Sardis led to further campaigns in Asia Minor, but in the end the Persians put down the revolt once and for all with the destruction of Miletus in 494.

This anecdote about Darius and his slave was recorded by the historian Herodotus (5.105), himself a Greek from Halicarnassus, a Greek city located in Caria on the southern coast of Asia Minor. Herodotus's history of the Persian Wars stands as the oldest surviving example of Greek narrative history. Considered the father of history, Herodotus is the first author known to use the word *historia*, which means in Greek something close to "researches," or "reports of eyewitness accounts." His nine-book account of the

Persian Wars was published in the last quarter of the fifth century, and it reaches back to the sixth-century background of the conflict between Persia and Greece. It also includes countless interesting ethnographic details from his inquiries and travels throughout the then-known world. Herodotus's history maintains throughout a strong moral perspective that warns his audience of the dangers of unchecked pride, or *hubris:* in his worldview, divine retribution, or *nemesis,* is inevitable if man reaches beyond the limits that the immortal gods have set. Some of this moralizing is conveyed in anecdotes about Persian rulers from the more distant past, but the message about *nemesis* was perhaps also addressed to the Greeks of the late fifth century— especially Athenians—who were similarly faced with the issues that accompany building and maintaining an empire.

Herodotus directed his research toward the origins of empire in the past, and he related how the Persian Empire began in the sixth century in the generations leading up to Darius I. This empire was centered in the capital cities of Persepolis and Susa, and as it grew it reached as far as the Indus valley of Pakistan and India, while to the west and south it encompassed modern-day Iraq, Turkey, Syria, Lebanon, Israel, and Egypt. To the north the Persian Empire stretched up and around the Black Sea—though here nomadic Scythians stubbornly eluded its grasp. The far western frontier from the Persians' perspective comprised Ionia, the islands of the Aegean Sea, and mainland Greece. These Greeks in the sixth century were not particularly wealthy or powerful. The Persians may well have considered them less-developed, poor inhabitants of a remote backwater of the Mediterranean basin. After quelling the Ionian revolt with the destruction of Miletus in 494, Persia may have assumed that Hellas would be easily absorbed into its empire. And yet that initial encounter between the Persians and the Athenians—the Athenian destruction of a temple at Sardis that proved so memorable for the Great King—resulted in the greatest of surprises for the Persians. Darius "remembered the Athenians" in 490 and sent across the Aegean forces who invaded Greece, but his men were defeated at the plain of Marathon on the coast of Attica a little more than 25 miles northeast of Athens—hence the modern distance of the runner's marathon.

At the time of the battle of Marathon the Athenian democratic reforms put into place by Cleisthenes were still recent, and there remained the possibility that the new institutions would not be stable enough to survive the combination of foreign invasions and internal political pressures. The latter soon became pressing with the reappearance of the former Athenian tyrant Hippias. When Hippias had been driven out of Athens by the Spartan

Cleomenes in 510, he initially fled to a friendly city in the north of Asia Minor, but he eventually landed in the court of the Persian king Darius. Hippias then accompanied the Persian army on its expedition to Attica in 490, and the Persian leadership made it known that the former Athenian leader had joined the invading forces. Clearly the Great King intended to make Athens subject to Persia just as the *poleis* in Ionia were subject to tyrants and satraps. Perhaps Darius hoped Athenians would welcome Hippias back to power as tyrant rather than suffer the loss of Athenian lives on the battlefield and the possible destruction of their homeland. The Athenians were willing to face the risk. When the Persians were defeated in Attica at the plain of Marathon, it was an army of Athenians and Plataeans that beat them back to their ships in retreat. The Athenians, fighting on their home territory, bore the brunt of the casualties.

Darius died before he could launch a second invasion, but his successor to the throne had an equally good memory of the Athenians' impiety at Cybele's temple in Sardis. Darius's son Xerxes came to power in 486, and as the new Great King of the Persian Empire Xerxes started planning a second attack against Hellas. Meanwhile, with the memory of the Persians at Marathon still fresh among the Athenians, one Athenian general saw an opportunity to shape the direction of Athens' future. When the silver mines at Laurium produced a sizable surplus for the state coffers, the Athenian *dēmos* found itself confronting significant financial decisions. The typical procedure was to share the wealth equally among all citizens, but in 483/2 a general named Themistocles persuaded the Athenian *dēmos* to move in a new direction. Themistocles urged the *dēmos* to build some 200 triremes and become a naval power. The Athenians in the *ekklēsia* found Themistocles' innovative ideas persuasive, and they voted to follow his proposal.

The Athenians' decision to apply the funds from the silver mines to the construction of a navy stands in contrast to the Great King's attitude toward the natural world. When Xerxes launched an invasion that included both land and naval forces, he was faced with engineering challenges unknown to his father. The inclusion of major land forces required the Persians to build a bridge across the Hellespont, the narrow straits that separate Asia from Europe where the Black Sea empties into the Mediterranean. Throughout antiquity this floating bridge was remembered as a miraculous feat of human engineering and, in a famous story recorded by Herodotus, it also revealed the Great King's tendency for *hubris*. When the first attempt to bridge the Hellespont failed in a storm, Xerxes insisted on his mastery of the passage between Europe and Asia: he declared that the straits were his slave. Xerxes accordingly punished the slave, giving orders that the waters of the Hellespont receive 300 lashes and then be fettered and branded with hot irons. Herodotus reports that Xerxes even ordered his men to curse the straits, and instruct the waters that since no man worshiped them they would bend to the Great King's will (Herodotus 7.33–35). Though the anecdote may well be a fabrication, it does reveal to us the Greek imagination: the words and actions of an arrogant barbarian tyrant run counter to accepted Greek mores surrounding the gods, the natural world, and the political world of humans. While Xerxes cursed the waters and asserted his dominance, the Athenians used the resources of Attica to defend themselves and their gods.

Xerxes' assertion of his will at the Hellespont soon brought foreign domination and Persian religious customs to the doorstep of mainland Greece. After another structure was engineered (a floating bridge that used cables to lash together boats and pontoons), Xerxes led the Persian army into Europe, entering Hellas from the north in the spring of 480. Reports spread that massive Persian land forces had crossed the Hellespont and were marching south into Greece through Thrace and Macedonia. *Polis* after *polis* in the north immediately capitulated in the face of the overwhelming foreign army; these Greek cities negotiated treaties with the Persians, offering up earth and water to the invaders in a sign of subservience to the Great King. The treatment of this Persian rite in Herodotus clearly links international politics and the public cult of the gods: with a single ritual action, Greek civic leaders admitted the foreign army and foreign gods into their *poleis*. The voluntary collaboration became known as "medizing," a word derived from the Medes, a northern Persian tribe. Spartans and Athenians watched with anxiety as more *poleis* medized and it became increasingly apparent that they would soon be battling the Persians somewhere on their home territory. With Sparta situated in the Peloponnesian Peninsula south of the Isthmus of Corinth, the Athenians suspected that their time was running out.

APOLLO, POLITICS, AND THE OUTCOME OF THE WAR

This news of invading barbarians and medizing Greeks sent the Athenians into a crisis. Again it was Themistocles who influenced decisions, as did traditional Greek religious practices related to *polis* finances, the ancestral gods, divination, and sacrifice. As they did in all extraordinary circumstances, the Athenians sent *polis* representatives to the shrine of Apollo at

Delphi to inquire about the best course of action in the present dire circumstances. Located in the territory of Phocis just northwest of Attica, Delphi was one of the most important of the panhellenic shrines. Every four years the Pythian games were held there, but the most significant activities at Delphi centered on the prophetic powers associated with Apollo. Since at least the sixth century it had been a custom for Greek *poleis* to send ambassadors to Delphi to ask questions of Apollo's oracle in the remote, rural shrine on a steep mountainside. Delphi actually lies at the intersection of several geologic faults, and abundant seismic activity in the area (earthquakes, vapors escaping from the earth) may have given rise to a tradition that Delphi was connected to unseen powers below the earth's surface. In myth Delphi was considered the center of the world—a special rock called the *omphalos,* or navel, stood there. A temple of Apollo was constructed at Delphi in the seventh century, but evidence for shrines and dedications in this location stretch back to at least the ninth century.

The Delphic oracle gave thousands of responses over the centuries to both states and individuals—for example, directing *poleis* when they wished to establish foreign colonies or go to war, and helping individuals in matters of cultic observance and ritual purity. The shrine was also a place where Greeks, whether individual citizens offering thanks for personal good fortune or cities celebrating victory in war, came to give thanks to the gods and make commemorative offerings. Whoever consulted the oracle left gifts for the god—often quite lavish ones—and *poleis* built elaborate treasuries to store the dedications. Just as individual athletes competed for glory on the field every four years, so each *polis* vied with others in the splendor of their building projects at this panhellenic shrine. Prominent wealthy families served as sponsors; in the sixth century the Alcmaeonid family had a history of financing building projects at Delphi. A committee composed of members from all over Hellas called the Amphictiony oversaw the running of the sanctuary, and the Amphictiony had the authority to punish a *polis* for offending Apollo: it could either fine the city or declare a "sacred war." When disciplining a *polis,* the Amphictiony used the language of religious offense and cultic impurity. These religious concepts indicated something much more complex than simple superstition: language of offense and impiety expressed whether a *polis* was treating its citizens and its neighbors with all due respect in accordance with ancestral norms and *nomoi.* This ability to oversee and comment on how *poleis* treated each other gave Delphi an unusually powerful panhellenic voice, and one that was not necessarily free from bias or corruption.

In fifth-century practice the inquirer making a pilgrimage to Delphi purified himself with holy water before entering the temple of Apollo. The pilgrim purchased a costly sacred cake that in effect served as the consultation fee, and upon entering the temple he sacrificed a sheep or a goat at an interior hearth. He could then proceed from the sacrificial altar into the inner recesses, where he consulted with male priests and attendants of Apollo who framed the question put forward to the female ritual specialist called the Pythia. The Pythia was Apollo's instrument—a priestess who traditionally sat on a special seat in a hidden corner of the sanctuary. She possessed the unusual ability to communicate directly with the god, and some scholars think that she fell into some sort of a trance state, perhaps after chewing special leaves or inhaling fumes that emanated from cracks in the earth. The Pythia was believed to be possessed by the god, and her utterances were understood to be the response of Apollo himself, relayed perhaps first in gibberish and then in a highly stylized, versified form of poetic speech that was often quite ambiguous. The male attendants recorded the Pythia's utterances, and the pilgrim's task was to consult with Apollo's officials, male and female alike, who helped him make sense of the images and poetic figures in the god's response. Figure 8 depicts the Pythia seated on her tripod, holding Apollo's laurel in one hand and a libation bowl in the other, while a bearded man (a priest or an inquirer) looks on.

On the eve of the Persian invasion of Attica in 480, the initial response seemed perfectly clear: flee to the ends of the earth. Such clarity dismayed the Athenian ambassadors, but they tried again. When they supplicated the god and inquired a second time, they received answers that seemed more helpful: "the wooden wall" that will not fall would save the Athenians, who should not await Persian land forces but withdraw and prepare for a confrontation since "divine Salamis will bring death" to many (Herodotus 7.141). The ambassadors took hope in these words, and they returned home. Back in Athens the Athenians debated the meaning of the curious wooden wall. Some men believed they should defend the Acropolis behind strengthened wooden fortification walls. But at this key moment, Themistocles stepped in. The traditional civic rites of the Athenians granted all male citizens the right to officiate at sacrificial procedures and interpret oracles and omens from the gods; Herodotus relates how Themistocles, contrary to the professional oracle interpreters, argued that the "wooden walls" were the sides of the ships in Athens' brand-new navy, and "divine Salamis" was the place where the decisive naval battle should take place. Athens would best defend itself against the invading Persians by planning for a naval battle and meeting the Persians

Figure 8. Consulting with the Pythia. Attic red-figure
cup by the Codrus Painter, ca. 450–430 BCE. Berlin,
Staatliche Museen Antikensammlung F2538.

in the most advantageous place: at sea. The Athenians agreed to follow the
advice of Themistocles: they would abandon the defenses of the city and attempt to engage the Persians in battle at Salamis (Herodotus 7.140–43).

As the Persian army marched south, non-medizing Greek *poleis* united to
defend their autonomy and traditional *nomoi*. The Greeks first engaged the
Persians in battles north of Athens at Artemisium and Thermopylae, but
they had mixed results. The Spartans held the narrow pass at Thermopylae
as long as they could and suffered great losses, while the Athenian naval
forces engaged the Persians' ships in an indecisive battle at nearby Artemisium. Xerxes' army marched on toward Attica; meanwhile the Athenians
prepared themselves and their navy. At that time a priestess of Athena on
the Acropolis reported that the goddess's sacred snake had disappeared
from the ancient citadel's temple (Herodotus 8.41). This final bit of news
persuaded the Athenians to evacuate the city and move the women and
children to Argos or onto nearby islands just off the coast of Attica. In
Athens a few holdouts defended the Acropolis and the sanctuary of Athena,
but they were easily defeated once the Persians arrived. Persian soldiers

slaughtered them within the sanctuary, stripped the temple of any remaining treasures, and burned the entire Acropolis, including a new temple of Athena that was under construction. And so the city of Athens fell to the Great King of Persia. In this way Darius's son Xerxes finally remembered the Athenians and got revenge for the Athenians' burning of Sardis almost twenty years earlier. Yet Xerxes' first official order as ruler of Athens reveals an uneasy conscience attuned to the vicissitudes of civic impiety. A small group of Athenian exiles were advising him on this campaign, and Xerxes ordered these exiles to ascend the Acropolis and offer sacrifices according to Athenian *nomoi* (Herodotus 8.49–55). Even under the rule of Persian occupiers, Athenian citizens observed the civic rites of their city.

Although they had followed Delphi's advice by abandoning the city, removing all the city's residents, and placing all hope in the wooden walls of their navy, the Athenians' chances for victory over the Persians were still not good. The Persian fleet far outnumbered the Greek. The Athenians put their new ships under command of the best and most experienced generals, including ostracized men recalled from exile. A Spartan general commanded the whole contingent. The Greek allies hesitated at this moment, unable to decide where to fight the Persians—in the open sea near Corinth or in the narrow passage between the island of Salamis and the mainland of Attica. While the allied Greeks vacillated, Persian commanders brought their ships down near Athens. Xerxes was so sure of his impending victory that, tradition has it, he pitched a camp on the slope of an adjoining mountainside that could provide the best view of the naval battle as it unfolded. But his hopes were dashed at Salamis when the Greeks were able to outmaneuver the Persians by relying on their familiarity with the narrow waters and unseen currents. The Persian naval forces were soundly defeated. Xerxes withdrew to Asia Minor, leaving his cousin and brother-in-law Mardonius in command of the Persian forces now stationed in Thebes, northwest of Athens. The Athenians returned to their devastated city and prepared for the land engagement they knew would come.

The final outcome of the war was decided the following year in a contest at Plataea, a plain just northwest of Athens. Under Mardonius the Persians had negotiated favorable terms with some Greek cities, offering protection in return for collaboration. Those cities in Boeotia that medized and accepted the Persian offer were spared destruction at the hands of the rampaging Persian forces. But Boeotia's neighbor to the south, Attica, again did not accept any Persian offer to cooperate, and as a result the villages and farms of Attica were invaded by the foreign army for a second time. Even with their countryside in ruins, the people of Attica and Athens turned away any renewed efforts to medize and accept a tyrant who answered to the Great King. For the second time the Athenians abandoned their homes in the city and fled to neighboring islands while their leaders prepared for a final, decisive land battle. Mardonius and the Persians continued their march through Attica and they utterly destroyed Athens again (Herodotus 9.3). But although the Persians may have won another battle at Athens, in the end they still lost the war. When the Persian army finally engaged the combined Greek forces at Plataea in 479, they were defeated. The renowned Persian general Mardonius fell in this battle along with many of his men.

At the end of the war the urban center of Athens was largely destroyed. One historian records that the only houses that remained standing were ones that Persian commanders had lived in during the occupation. Only a small portion of the great Persian army was left to retreat from Greece after the battle of Plataea. Thereafter the Greeks lived with the knowledge that the Persians could regroup and again invade their homeland in order to impose a Persian imperial structure upon the autonomous *poleis* of Hellas. Perhaps the Greeks feared this. The Athenians may have felt an anxiety sharpened by experience—after all, they had seen their city destroyed twice, while the Spartans and their Peloponnesian allies remained relatively safe behind the Isthmus of Corinth. In retrospect we can see that such fear of a third Persian invasion was ungrounded, but for the fifth-century Greeks it must have been very real.

At the same time the Greek peoples felt a new confidence that was reinforced by their common ritual background. The Greek *poleis* had always been divided to some degree by geography, customs, and dialect. Before the arrival of the Persians, there had been little common understanding of what it meant to be Greek. There had been no Greek political identity, even though the Greeks all shared cultural, religious and literary traditions. But after a few small, autonomous Greek *poleis* united to defeat a mighty barbarian empire from the east, suddenly a different self-awareness came to the fore. Later traditions report that the allied Greeks took a common oath before the crucial battle of Plataea, and swore they would not rebuild shrines and holy places destroyed by the invading Persians (Lycurgus *Against Leocrates* 81). Overall the Greeks became more conscious of their desire for freedom and autonomy, and of their commitment to their *nomoi*—both civil laws and religious customs. Despite regional differences in traditional rituals, there was agreement about one thing: Greek *nomoi* did not allow for servile obedience to a mortal king. Persian custom demanded *proskynēsis*, full prostration on one's knees before the Great King. Following the lead of Athens and Sparta, the *poleis* of Hellas declared that they would serve only their ancestral gods in accordance with their *nomoi*.

This new self-awareness convinced the Greeks that their way of life had to be defended in the face of a barbarian empire. They accordingly maintained an alliance after the victory at Plataea, and the Spartans were placed at the head of this confederation. The avowed goal was retribution for the recent war, but some on the mainland wished to regain territory and *poleis* that had fallen under Persian domination, especially cities across the Aegean Sea in Ionia. There may have been some hope that a continuing alliance would create a deterrent; if a confederation of *poleis* could unite and beat back the Persian Empire, then perhaps in the future the Great King would let them all be free and treat them as political and cultural equals. The Greek confederation pursued the Persians into Asia Minor to support *poleis* there that were still under Persian rule.

Although the city of Athens lay shattered, Athenian citizens showed great resilience and they immediately busied themselves rebuilding their city. Themistocles, whose vision of the city as a naval power had proven so successful, persuaded the Athenians in 479 to rebuild the walls and fortify the city center and harbor even before rebuilding their homes and temples. This activity made the Spartans suspicious, especially when viewed in the context of the Athenians' commitment to their new navy and the continuing alliance. Following naval campaigns in the Aegean and Ionia in 478, Sparta handed the leadership of the confederation over to Athens. Modern historians call this naval alliance under Athenian leadership the Delian League. The name reflects the establishment of an administrative center for the alliance on Delos, an island sanctuary in the middle of the Aegean Sea that was sacred to the god Apollo. Meanwhile Sparta did its best to persuade Themistocles and the Athenians to take down the walls and rely on the promise of Spartan military strength in the event of another foreign invasion. But the Athenians looked at their city that lay in ruins and decided otherwise. Athens' new standing, new navy, and emerging confidence were about to come into conflict with Sparta.

APOLLO, THESEUS, AND THE TRANSFORMATION OF THE ALLIANCE

The defeats at Salamis and Plataea did not necessarily mean the end of the Great King's desire to subjugate the independent *poleis* of Hellas. After all, Darius's defeat at Marathon in 490 did not stop the second invasion undertaken by his son Xerxes in 480. The Athenians had no way of knowing that in fact the Persians would not invade again. As the Greeks *poleis* anticipated another invasion from the east and deepened their commitment to their Hellenic alliance, other unforeseen issues emerged. The Hellenic allies soon found themselves facing not a continuation of the struggle with barbarians from the east but a more protracted and painful series of regional tensions and open conflicts among the Greek *poleis* themselves.

At first these struggles manifested themselves in leadership issues among the members of the alliance that had fought off Persia. After Athens assumed a leadership role the Delian League met with success, especially in Ionia and the Aegean. And while the alliance was initially formed in response to a perceived Persian threat, the new Delian League soon took an interest in policing the shipping lanes around the Hellespont that brought grain and timber to Athens' main port of Piraeus. Grain and timber imports were needed to rebuild the Athenian economy—timber for shipbuilding, and grain to feed the growing population of urban workers. Athens was also eager to control other natural resources that its allies could supply, like the precious metals mined on Thasos, a wealthy island in the northern Aegean along the trade routes leading to the Black Sea.

The island of Delos became a focal point for the cities that followed Athens. For several centuries Delos had been recognized as an important cult site for the Ionian Greeks, whether they lived on the mainland, in the Aegean islands, or on the Ionian coastline of Asia Minor. Whole families went to Delos together—women and children along with the men. An annual festival to Apollo was celebrated there, complete with feasting, singing, dancing, and musical and athletic competitions. Even women and girls competed for prizes in traditional dances, and singers came from all over the Aegean to vie with each other in the recitation of traditional oral verse. But Sparta was a Dorian community and not an Ionian one, and the decision to organize the league around an Ionian festival site on Delos underscored a new orientation for the alliance that quite consciously marginalized Sparta and other *poleis* that did not observe Ionian rites and religious festivals. Because leadership was transferred from a Dorian to an Ionian *polis,* Sparta withdrew from the league's naval interests.

The creation of a Delian League under Athenian leadership and the dissolution of the Spartan-led alliance eventually prompted the re-formation of an earlier confederation of Hellenic states, many from the Peloponnesian Peninsula. Historians today sometimes call this alliance headed by

Sparta the Peloponnesian League. The coexistence of two competing alliances headed by the two most powerful Greek *poleis* led in turn to the polarization of many other Greek states. Over time it became nearly impossible for independent *poleis* to maintain neutrality, and every state was forced to choose sides: an alliance headed by Athens or an alliance headed by Sparta. The choice was not always clear.

Unlike previous coalitions the Delian League was primarily a naval alliance that required major capital investments of ships and money. The traditional Greek army was made up of self-supporting hoplites who provided their own armor and sometimes even their own food. The reestablished Peloponnesian League continued to operate this way. But the new naval alliance headed by Athens required ships, men to power the ships, and resources to provision and support the men aboard the ships. The Delian League required each member *polis* to supply either a complement of fully manned and seaworthy ships, in proportion to its size and wealth, or an annual contribution to the treasury that maintained the allied navy. Athens had the most ships by far, and only a small fraction of the alliance members—Samos, Lesbos, and Chios—had the wealth and manpower to supply numerous ships and men, so most members came to Delos with cash. This annual tax was called tribute or *phoros,* and the treasurers who administered the tributary funds for the league at the treasury on Delos were always Athenian.

The naval league centered on Delos was conceived as an alliance that would confront the Persians, and members may have considered their tribute an investment that would soon bring them greater returns when the Persians were pushed out of Ionia and alliance members brought home the spoils of war. The Persian Empire was wealthy, and the potential spoils would have been almost beyond reckoning from a Greek's perspective. As the Delian League pursued this policy, some commanders in fact did acquire great wealth during these years—above all the Athenian statesman and naval commander Cimon. It was Cimon who led the allied Ionian *poleis* to a double victory over Persian land and naval forces in 466 at Eurymedon, on the southern coast of Asia Minor. This engagement momentarily put a stop to the Persians' designs on the Ionian cities of the Aegean and Asia Minor.

Even with the Persian threat suppressed, the Delian League remained under the compulsion of Athenian leadership. Athens managed the alliance's finances, and Athens became rather exacting in its demands and in the unity it forced on the allies. Gradually, the allied cities lost their status as equals in the alliance and became subject-allies in an Athenian *archē*, "rule," or empire. Subject-allies could be compelled to remain in the empire and contribute their *phoros*—even against their will. Resistant subject-allies who attempted to leave the alliance, as Naxos did around 470, were subjugated and had their ships taken away. In 465 the citizens of Thasos resisted Athens' takeover of their metal and timber resources, and they tried to back out from the Delian League and renounce their annual contribution of *phoros*. The Athenian response to this resistance was immediate. The navy, under the leadership of Cimon, laid siege to the city of Thasos. More than two years later, the Thasians were finally subdued and forcibly brought back into the league. Such costly expenditures of time, resources, and manpower did not hamper the Athenians in maintaining their authority. The revolt at Thasos in 465 and the Athenian response to it would be repeated many times over the course of the next five decades as members of the Delian League had to be coerced into remaining in—or even joining—the imperial alliance. Any resistance, much less open revolt, brought on penalties that grew ever harsher over time.

The aristocratic general Cimon led the Athenians and the Delian League during 470s and 460s, and it was Cimon as much as anyone else who laid the foundations for an Athenian empire. The son of another famous general—Miltiades, an Athenian commander at Marathon—Cimon had first achieved fame as a young man for his courage at the battle of Salamis. After this battle the Athenian *dēmos* often elected him *stratēgos;* he commanded most of the major operations for the Delian League between 476 and 463, and brought back to Athens great wealth from the spoils of war in the Aegean and Ionia. During his career he opposed policies that gave new powers to the *dēmos,* while supporting the interests of the Athenian nobility through his family connections with Sparta. At the same time Cimon proved to be a friend of the Athenian people: he sponsored costly state feasts for them. He was an aristocrat who understood the value of civic rites that benefited the *polis*.

Cimon made a significant contribution to Athenian cult practice at the very start of his career: around 475 he helped institute the civic worship of Theseus in Athens. The Athenians were at a bit of a loss after consulting Apollo at Delphi and learning they should recover the bones of Theseus, the mythical hero credited with the unification of Attica. How could they possibly rediscover bones of a long-lost king mysteriously murdered while in exile, hundreds of years before? But after a particularly significant naval victory in the northern Aegean in 476 Cimon made it a priority to investigate the death of Theseus. While on the island of Scyros he was inspired to follow the lead of an eagle who led him directly to the grave of Theseus, and when Cimon returned home from his first naval campaign in triumph he brought with him Theseus's remains. Cimon reportedly paraded into the city with great pomp and ceremony, and the Athenians feasted and celebrated at the foot of the Acropolis, where they dedicated a new sanctuary to the hero who would in time be viewed as the paradigmatic Athenian leader whose success in uniting Attica and defending it from invading barbarians prepared the way for later Athenian democracy.

Indeed, images of Theseus proliferated in Athens during the fifth century, and sometimes these images were linked to the family of Cimon. When the Athenians built an expensive new portico in the Agora early in the 460s—the Stoa Poikile, or Painted Stoa—two of the main panels depicted the Athenians' victory over invading barbarians. The first showed Theseus leading the fight against the Amazons, and the second showed the Athenians battling the Persians at Marathon in 490. Cimon's father Miltiades had served as general in this famous engagement, and a tradition arose that Theseus returned from the underworld and appeared on the battlefield to lead Miltiades and the Athenians in their fight for freedom. It is entirely possible that this stoa was built using funds brought back to Athens by Cimon after his campaigns in Asia Minor. When Cimon returned the bones of Theseus to Athens and instituted new festivals and civic rites for the hero, he did not let the Athenian *dēmos* forget that an aristocrat like him was pursuing a policy of empire in an effort to keep Athenians free. Civic rituals that celebrated Theseus and the unification of Attica in the distant past became linked to the defeat of the Persians and the preservation of Athenian autonomy in the present.

PERICLES REFORMS THE DEMOCRACY AND CONSOLIDATES AN EMPIRE

The last episode of the Persian Wars as recorded by Herodotus described the Greek fleet driving the Persians from cities in central Ionia, and then sailing north to the Straits of the Hellespont to dispel the Persian overlords from Greek cities there. The Greeks also wished to capture what was left of Xerxes' floating bridge so that they could take home pieces of the infamous cables and dedicate them as thank offerings in the temples of their gods (Herodotus 9.114, 121). The Athenian naval commander during these final operations in 479/8 was the once-ostracized leader Xanthippus, the father of Pericles. Pericles, a young adult at this time, would later become a talented general in his own right. If this anecdote from Herodotus about Xanthippus and the cables from Xerxes' bridge at the Hellespont is at all accurate, it would appear that Pericles at an early age learned about the complex and invaluable ties between the *polis*, its navy, and public expressions of civic piety in Athens.

Pericles the son of Xanthippus came from two old and noble Athenian families. It was his mother, Agariste, who was born into the family of the Alcmaeonidae. Agariste's father, Hippocrates, was the brother of Cleisthenes, thus making Cleisthenes the great-uncle of Pericles. Although family lines of descent in ancient Athens were not typically traced through the maternal line, sources consistently show that Pericles was still considered one of the Alcmaeonidae tainted by that family's curse. In moments of civic doubt the language of civic piety and impiety, benefit and curse, clearly articulated the citizens' awareness of political forces that linked the present to the past. As the symbolic heir to Cleisthenes, Pericles would in time carry on the tradition of political reforms that gave increasing political voice to the Athenian *dēmos*, even at the expense of traditional aristocratic institutions. He and the Athenians would also be reminded of the curse.

We don't know exactly how long Pericles' father Xanthippus lived after the Persian Wars, but he was no longer active in 472 when Pericles made his first appearance in Athenian public life. Then in his early 20s, Pericles had the wealth, authority and confidence to take on the responsibility of funding a civic religious celebration for his fellow citizens. This type of public service was called a liturgy—from the Greek *leitourgia*, "work for the people." It was the custom in Athens for wealthy nobles to vie with each other in sponsoring civic rites and religious festivals for the gods. In this case Pericles dipped into his own family's wealth and produced a trilogy of plays by Aeschylus at one of Athens' annual festivals of Dionysus. One of the plays Pericles produced was a tragedy about Xerxes' upset at Salamis called the *Persians*—told from the point of view of the defeated Persians themselves. This play is one of the few Aeschylean tragedies extant, and it is the single example from the thirty-three remaining Athenian tragedies that actually treats a historical subject—the rest all center on characters and episodes from the Greek mythological tradition.

The successful production of Aeschylus's *Persians* demonstrates the Athenians' continued deep interest in Persia. When a young Pericles produced this tragedy in 472 the people of Athens were still reflecting on their victory over the Persian Empire. After this first foray into Athenian public life, Pericles disappears from the extant records for a time. When he reemerged into a position of leadership some ten years later, he entered onto a political scene where the allied navy and its policy of Aegean dominance had a hold on many Athenians, most notably the wealthy and powerful Cimon. It was the practice in many Greek *poleis* for a board of magistrates to review the accounts and activities of public officials when they left office; in 463 Pericles was appointed to be the public examiner for Cimon, who as outgoing general had been accused of enriching himself by accepting bribes while in Macedonia. Although Pericles' prosecution of Cimon resulted in Cimon's acquittal (and later reelection to the office of *stratēgos*), managing the trial of a prominent Athenian public figure did place Pericles in the public eye, and he remained at the center of civic life until his death thirty-four years later.

Under Pericles' leadership the *nomoi* of Athens continued to change; the city grew in wealth, power, and prestige while the *dēmos* seized economic opportunities in the markets and sought access to decision making within the *polis* itself. Among the most important reforms that would be put forward by Pericles during his long career was a controversial policy that paid citizen jurors for their service in the Athenian law courts, thereby making participation in the judicial system more attractive to men of modest means. Equally significant were the citizenship laws of 451 that redefined and limited who was eligible to claim the privileges of Athenian citizenship. Civic rites would change under Pericles, too, as Athenian citizens publicly celebrated their patron goddess Athena and displayed their wealth and power at major festivals.

The first steps toward new status for the *dēmos* came when Pericles became associated with a reform-minded civic leader named Ephialtes. We know little about this Ephialtes, but what we do know attaches him, and possibly Pericles, to a reorganization of the Athenian court system—reforms that brought new power to the Athenian *dēmos*. Traditionally the council of the Areopagus held a good deal of power: as a body of ex-archons who were granted lifetime membership upon leaving office, the Areopagus had duties that probably ranged from advising current archons to maintaining legislative and administrative oversight to wielding judicial authority in certain cases with cultic implications, especially homicide. The Areopagus's custom of trying cases and considering their religious impact on the political community provides further evidence for the Athenians' custom of intertwining matters of civil law and religious practice. After Ephialtes' reforms in 462, the council of the Areopagus was left mainly with the task of trying cases involving religious offenses, while the *dēmos* exercised expanded powers in the assembly, the council, and the law courts. Responsibility for oversight (e.g., examining outgoing officeholders, as Pericles had tried Cimon) was moved from the Areopagus and given to the *dēmos* at large. These changes to the governance of the *polis* were highly charged: shortly after the passage of these reforms to the Areopagus, Cimon (who opposed the reforms) was ostracized, and Ephialtes himself mysteriously murdered. But Pericles survived and learned how to harness the new power invested in the Athenian *dēmos*.

The members of the *dēmos* who benefited from Ephialtes' reforms were inhabiting a social and economic landscape that was changing rapidly after two decades of Cimon's guidance. During the decades before the Persian Wars, Athens had fundamentally resembled other Greek *poleis*. The economy of Attica had been essentially an agricultural one, and its army was traditionally composed of ordinary citizen farmers who served as infantrymen in the hoplite phalanx. While Athens' prosperity had always relied to some extent on sea trade, the key decision under Themistocles to expand the Athenian navy, combined with its ensuing success at sea in the battle of Salamis, persuaded Athenians to develop their sea power further while also maintaining their army of hoplites. Consequently, during the heyday of Cimon's career in the 470s and 460s—well before Pericles' entry into civic life—the economies of Athens and its port city of Piraeus had turned to trade, banking, ship building, and weapons manufacturing.

These two urban centers of Attica grew faster than ever as Athenians repaired the damage done by the occupying Persian army and prepared for another war with the barbarians whom they expected would eventually return. All sectors of the Athenian *dēmos* grew quickly in response to decisions to continue funding the navy and building ships, but the lowest class of landless citizens, called *thētes*, benefited in a new way as they labored alongside slaves in the shipyards and workshops in urban Piraeus and Athens. Economic opportunities opened up not just for Athenians of the lower classes but for foreigners, too. Entrepreneurs from all over Hellas came to Athens to trade and start businesses related to the navy and defense industries. These foreigners were called metics, and although they were not citizens many of them became quite wealthy and powerful.

The continuing interest in naval development also prompted Athenians to design new ships and develop new strategies for battle at sea. The principal vessel at their disposal was the trireme, a long, slender, and unusually fast ship that was powered by banks of oarsmen. The typical Athenian trireme had 200 men on board—about 170 men at the oars, plus the sailors navigating the ship and armed marines who fought in hand-to-hand combat. Most of the oarsmen were recruited from the poorer *thētes*, but occasionally foreigners and much more rarely slaves served. While the traditional Greek army of hoplites relied on the limited wealth and resources of landholding citizen farmers, the Athenian navy embraced these lower classes. Training the men to work together to power ships and move them about in tight quarters was a long, arduous, and expensive task, but one at which the Athenians came to excel. Overall the shift in military focus from hoplite to naval warfare first put forward by Themistocles in the 480s, and continued under Cimon in the 470s and '60s, helped urban citizens and landless *thētes* take on additional and significant roles in the *polis* reformed by Ephialtes.

The new powers that Ephialtes granted to the *dēmos* reflected these social and economic changes. By 462 Athens was an empire that had twice used the navy to put down revolts within the Delian League; the *dēmos*, both the landowning hoplites and the urban *thētes*, apparently wanted more of a voice in decision making. Ephialtes gave them this voice with the reforms of the Areopagus. One of the first decisions the *dēmos* then made involved the city's defenses. In 478 the Athenians had shored up their fortifications first before rebuilding their homes and temples. But then between 461 and 456 they extended the city walls all the way to the harbors at Phaleron and Piraeus. By 445 a third wall built alongside the Piraeus wall connected Athens and its harbor with a 4-mile-long fortified corridor that was 200 yards wide. These walls, known as the Long Walls, enclosed a highway that could carry food and supplies from the harbor to the urban center of Athens. The increased fortification of Piraeus and the construction of the Long Walls now enabled Athenians to withstand any traditional siege for as long as the *polis* could afford to import necessities. Athens became, in effect, an island.

While making these changes at home Athens also renegotiated relations with its immediate neighbors, Megara and Thebes. As regional tensions waxed and waned the Corinthians and Spartans became nervous, and eventually the situation escalated into what scholars call the First Peloponnesian War. Victories in a few small regional conflicts after 460 allowed the Delian League to grow even more and gain some Dorian territory, including the island of Aegina, which lies immediately off the coast of Attica to the south. Aegina, like an increasing number of subject-allies, was forced to join the league in 458 only after prolonged pressure. As the Delian League was gaining strength under Athenian direction, alliance leaders in 459 made a crucial decision to extend their policy toward Persia in a slightly new direction. After successes in the Aegean and Ionia, the Athenians and their allies came to the aid of Egyptians who were trying to shake off the Persian yoke. The five years spent fighting in Egypt turned out to be very costly for the league, and entirely unsuccessful.

The expansion of Athenian rule, combined with completion of the fortified walls between Athens and Piraeus, created anxiety in the *poleis* of the Peloponnese, and even Athens' allies had second thoughts about Athenian management of the Delian League following the pivotal defeat in Egypt. The Peloponnesians' fears would be temporarily allayed when a peace was brokered between Athens and Sparta (446) and the two powers agreed to a thirty-year truce, but a major development in the Athenian empire— which used traditional religious practices to express Athens' power—took place before that truce was negotiated. In 454 decimated Delian League forces left Egypt in defeat, and the Athenians moved the alliance treasury from its home at the Apollo sanctuary on the island of Delos to a new home in Athens. Allies' suspicions about the Athenians' intention to use the league as a means to dominate other member states were thereby fully realized.

The shift made in 454 from Delos to Athens marks a key moment in Athenian self-definition, as traditional cult practices were used to express Athens' new economic status and the Athenians' changing identity. Apollo had long been worshipped by the Ionians at the sanctuary on Delos. Ionians from the mainland, the Aegean islands, and Ionia alike celebrated *nomoi* and commonly held customs that embraced sacrifice, prophecy, and athletic and poetic competitions. The goddess Athena was recognized by all Ionian *poleis,* but it was clear that she was a goddess especially connected to the people of Athens. While alliance monies had customarily been controlled by Athenian treasurers only, the transfer of the Delian League's treasury to Athens showed the Athenians openly embracing their role as imperial leader of other nominally independent *poleis.* The Athenians first ritualized this transformation, and then they memorialized it: starting in 454 they recorded and publicly displayed lists of the *aparchai,* or first fruits offerings, separated out from the tribute payments annually presented by the subject-allies. The dedication of *aparchai* to the gods was one of the most ancient and widespread traditional practices in the Mediterranean, common among Romans, Greeks, and Semitic peoples. Typically, a chosen sample of an offering was given to the appropriate deity—for example, grain for Demeter or grapes to Dionysus. At an animal sacrifice a small portion of the victim was consecrated in the fire before humans enjoyed the rest. *Aparchai* were symbolically presented to the gods first; *aparchai* literally means "things from the start." Beginning in 454 the goddess Athena annually received her due portion of *aparchai* at a civic festival in Athens when the Athenians designated a portion of the tribute paid by *poleis* in the Delian League. Instead of giving a portion of an animal victim or agricultural produce to the goddess, the Athenians dedicated money: specifically, one-sixtieth of the allies' *phoros.*

Never before had membership in the Delian League combined with Athenian citizenship promised so much power and prestige to Athena and the *dēmos* of Athens. Democratic institutions and practices continued to open up for all sectors of the *dēmos,* as the political reforms to the courts that Ephialtes advanced in 462/1 were followed by another policy change in the late 450s. Whereas service in the law courts had in the past been a voluntary service that citizens offered the *polis,* under Pericles the *dēmos* instituted pay for jurors. The daily salary of 2 obols (later raised to 3) was not great, but it was roughly equivalent to a day's wage for laborers like the citizen *thētes* who toiled in the workshops and factories of Athens and Piraeus. Providing pay for citizens to serve in the law courts proved to be a controversial move, one that the aristocracy especially loathed. But by supporting this change to Athenian *nomoi* Pericles showed his continuing commitment to sharing power among all members of the *dēmos,* not just those with sufficient wealth. Such a radical change in the city's customs could not have been anticipated in the reforms of Pericles' ancestor Cleisthenes.

The reforms of Ephialtes and the institution of pay for jury service provide the political background for some key citizenship laws that were then passed in Athens in 451. These laws, often credited to Pericles, limited the rights of Athenian citizenship to those whose parents—father and mother alike—were both Athenian. The passage of this law implies that the *nomoi* surrounding citizenship in the past had been more fluid, perhaps allowing metics, former slaves, and their children to achieve citizen status. Earlier customs had also acknowledged the citizenship of children of Athenian men married to non-Athenian but ethnically Greek wives from neighboring *poleis*—a custom that was especially common among old aristocratic families of Hellas. The reshaping of governance under the leadership of Pericles and his political allies made Athenian citizenship more attractive than ever. The combination of an Athenian-led tributary alliance with the revenue that alliance annually brought to this *polis,* now led by the people, transformed many civic customs—including the traditional worship of the gods. Democracy and empire were mingling powers in ways never before imagined.

THE PANATHENAEA REMADE

Under Pericles' three decades of leadership, the Athenian *dēmos* instituted controversial democratic reforms while consolidating an empire that was growing in wealth and power. Monumental changes in civic festivals accompanied these political developments, and the changes in Athenian civic rites were grounded in the citizens' changing understanding of their own economic and political power. The transferal of the Delian League's treasury to Athens in 454 ushered in the final stage in the development of an Athenian empire. During this stage the financial, political, and religious aspects of empire wove together and their synergistic interlocking propelled Athenians toward new relationships with each other, while it transformed the relationships between Athens and other cities in the empire. In the Athenians' eyes the new relationships had divine sanction, and the citizens of Athens visibly expressed their cultural dominance with religious rituals and cult practices that celebrated their city's patron deity, Athena.

Once the treasury of the Delian League was transferred to Athens and the *dēmos* had new powers, Athenian customs of governance and decision making took off in a new direction. While precise details of the Athenian budget during these years of Pericles' leadership are lost, historical sources record that heated discussions arose about how to use the money—Pericles representing the interests of the *dēmos* and aristocrats like Thucydides son of Melesias representing the old guard that opposed many of the democratic reforms. Athenians took out loans from treasuries sacred to Athena and to the other gods to finance military operations. Extant financial records and decrees indicate how Delian League funds were used for projects not related to the navy. Access to this revenue enabled Athenians to fund new programs and finance public works. Direct access to the Delian League treasury may even be the very thing that persuaded the *dēmos* that it could afford to fund the service of jurors. Even if league funds were not directly used to pay the jurors, access to the funds relieved other areas of the budget and freed up monies for such pay. More notably, after much debate the assembly voted to use Delian League funds to help rebuild the monuments on the Acropolis—the temples to Athena and the other gods that had been destroyed by the Persians during the two periods of occupation in 480 and 479.

In the decades immediately following the defeat of the Persians at Plataea, the Athenians had decided to not rebuild the archaic temple of Athena: the temple was left in ruins as a reminder of what invading forces could accomplish. A later (fourth century and highly controversial) inscriptional source records that Athenian soldiers took a vow to this effect at Plataea immediately following the second fall of Athens in 479. Right after the war Athenians cleared the Acropolis and dug a trench in which they deposited sculptures and ceremonial objects that had been damaged beyond repair when the Persians overran the sanctuary. This artwork from the Archaic period was uncovered by archaeologists in the late nineteenth century and now is displayed in the museums of modern Athens. Pieces of buildings and temples destroyed by the Persians were reused as building stones in repairing the ramparts of the Acropolis; even today, column drums and other architectural elements are visible in the north face of the Acropolis walls. The Acropolis itself remained a sacred *temenos,* or precinct, and a place where civic sacrifices was performed at public altars; there must have been a simple temple of some sort to house the ancient wooden image of Athena. Meanwhile the *dēmos* voted to spend its money for other public works projects, especially those related to the defense of the city.

But sometime shortly following the transfer of the Delian League treasury from Delos to Athens the Athenians moved in a different direction, choosing to use Athena's share of the tributary funds to rebuild the Acropolis more gloriously than ever. Perhaps the *dēmos* justified the decision to fund the rebuilding with Delian League funds by saying that Athens had been singled out for destruction over other *poleis* during the struggle with Persia; perhaps the threat of Persia had receded and the Athenians argued that the other *poleis* owed it to them for saving Greece from barbarian overlords. However they justified it, the Propylaea, Parthenon, and Erechtheum— architectural masterpieces sacred to Athena that artists, poets, and tourists have marveled at and that are being preserved on the Acropolis today—were built not only with monies paid by Athenian citizens but also with tribute money collected from Athens' subject-allies in the Athenian empire. Much of this building program was funded and begun during the mid-440s, and although there was opposition, the leadership skills of men like Pericles persuaded Athenians that the *dēmos* would be best served at that moment by reinvigorating the worship of the patron goddess Athena, now that the city and the harbor had been rebuilt and fortified.

The traditional Athenian celebration of the Panathenaea was subtly changed during these decades following the transfer of the Delian League treasury to Athens, and the changes reflected the status of the Delian League's recognized leader. All segments of Athenian society were visible in the procession, and eventually this meant that the procession made room for visiting foreigners and for resident metics, their wives, and their daughters. While metics and foreigners did not share the same status as citizens, especially after the citizenship laws of 451, they did play an integral role in the *polis* and the empire. Starting in the late 450s, allied member *poleis* in the Delian League were required to send ambassadors to take part in the great procession that began at the city's gates and wound through the Agora and up the Acropolis. Subject-allies were also required to supply a cow for the procession and the sacrifice afterward, as well as a full set of armor called a panoply. During the fifth century, some wagons in the procession were decorated and transformed into ships on wheels, and the great birthday robe of Athena that was the centerpiece of the festival was displayed as a sail on a ship that glided through the city to the foot of the Acropolis. The sail recalled the Athenians' critical naval victory over the Persians at Salamis: the transformed civic rites of Athens demonstrated the links between Athens' navy, its empire, and its goddess.

The procession with ship-carts started at the Dipylon gate in the Kerameikos neighborhood and passed by the most important major civic monuments: the altar of the twelve gods; the Royal Stoa, which had displayed the law tablets of Solon since at least the time of Ephialtes; the heroic bronze images of the Tyrannicides; and the new Painted Stoa, with its patriotic paintings of Theseus leading the Athenians to victory at Marathon. Athenians processed past these monuments that celebrated the legacy and trajectory of Athenian democracy as they wished to portray it to themselves and to the others in attendance. During the festival subject-allies learned from Athenian civic magistrates what their assessed *phoros* would be for the coming year, and the tribute list detailing each member's *aparchai* offerings for Athena was published. It has even been suggested that secure rooms in the Parthenon or immediately below the Acropolis were designed to be a safe place for depositing and storing Athenian treasure. In this way one of Athens' most important religious festivals celebrated the paradox of democratic and imperial ideologies.

It was the new Parthenon itself that came to project most visibly the striking image of Athenian superiority and transcendence. An earlier construction phase for a new temple sacred to Athena had been interrupted in 480 when occupying Persian forces knocked down whatever partially completed structure had been standing. The design and construction of an entirely new temple then resumed under Pericles in 447 as the Athenian empire was reaching its peak of wealth and influence. The Parthenon was completed in two phases—the structure itself was finished in 438 and the full program of artwork in 432. When the Parthenon and all its artwork and sculptural friezes were dedicated in 432, the Athenians could finally see the completed images they were presenting to the Greek world. The art on the Acropolis celebrated Athena's victories over chaos and foreigners: the Amazons, the Giants, the Centaurs. A long, continuous frieze in honor of Athens' patroness that ran along the top of the interior porch of the temple was finished last. It may have been an afterthought, but the frieze broke new artistic ground: instead of depicting the gods, the great frieze pictured the Athenians themselves in their orderly Panathenaic procession, leading animal victims destined for the goddess's altar. Today a part of this frieze is housed among the Elgin Marbles in London's British Museum.

The overall architectural design for the Acropolis included rebuilding other sacred structures destroyed by the Persians. Following the completion of the Parthenon the Athenians built the Propylaea (436–432), the monumental gateway at the top of the stairs leading up the Acropolis. This complex structure that symbolically marked the entrance to the sanctuary was built in a great hurry and, because of the war, never fully completed. The gallery on its north side is believed to have been used as a dining room for honored guests and civic magistrates who officiated at sacrificial rites. The location of the great altar remained where it had been before the Persian invasion, namely in front of the east entrance of the archaic temple of Athena, even though this placement meant that the altar was out of line with the new Parthenon. Finally, work on the Erechtheum, the Acropolis's most complex sacred structure, was begun in 421 and completed, after a lapse in construction, in 407. This unusual building probably stood on the foundations of an older structure that contained shrines to many gods and heroes sacred to the Athenians—not just Athena but also Zeus, Hephaestus, Poseidon, and Erechtheus, a mythical king who gave his life serving the *dēmos* in the struggle for the unification of Attica.

Under Pericles the glory of Athena and the *polis* of Athens reached an apex of influence and grandeur. Athens was acknowledged as the sole leader of the Delian League; it was a wealthy and powerful empire, unafraid to use this power over its allies or at home. The Athenian *dēmos* confidently moved forward with new religious customs and democratic institutions. The modified civic rites of the city reflected the glory of Athena and created the image of a democratic Athens as superior among Greek *poleis*—Athena's city became the divinely sanctioned leader of Hellas. The culmination of the Panathenaic procession was the great altar situated between the Parthenon and the Erechtheum, where civic officials sacrificed sheep and cows and distributed the meat to the citizens and guests in attendance. At the Panathenaea the traditional civic rituals of *thysia* were altered to bring together citizens, slaves, foreigners, and allies who together celebrated the wealth and power of Athenian rule. Subject-allies were made to feel their subordination even while observing common cult practices. The civic rites of this *polis* were transformed to suit the needs of an empire.

INTELLECTUAL MOVEMENTS IN THE CITY OF ATHENA

At the same time that the Athenians were celebrating ancestral practices and traditions with unprecedented cost and ceremony, imperial Athens in the 440s and 430s was also attracting intellectual figures from around the Mediterranean. Famed philosophers and natural scientists came to Athens to teach new ideas, and Pericles was known to welcome these figures and financially support them during their visits to the city. One Ionian foreigner who reportedly came to Athens during these years was a woman who would acquire great fame in the city, Aspasia of Miletus. In the Athenian public milieu—in the gossip of the Agora and in plays produced on the stage—Aspasia acquired a wildly varied reputation, credited with being a great beauty and intellect who taught rhetoric, a madam who kept an up-scale brothel and whose influence on public figures was more intimate, and everything in between. Ancient biographical traditions are notoriously unreliable and most if not all of these ancient reports may be false speculation and rumor. Still, some facts about Aspasia are certain: when Pericles' first marriage ended in failure, Aspasia became Pericles' life partner; together they had at least one child, a son also named Pericles. Ironically, the terms of the Periclean citizenship laws of 451 ensured that this son of an Athenian father and Ionian Greek mother could not be considered a citizen, though a special decree was later passed in the Assembly recognizing the full citizen status of the younger Pericles.

Pericles also befriended a number of other foreigners who found Athens to be a favorable place to pursue their careers. Anaxagoras, a philosopher and scientist from Ionia, settled in Athens in perhaps the 450s. Indeed, he is the first philosopher known to have made Athens his home, and he taught there for at least twenty years. Anaxagoras was one of the teachers known in antiquity as the *physiologoi* or the *physikoi*—those who teach about the natural world. The subtlety and innovation of his teaching made a great stir among Athenians, and many eagerly became his pupils. They took great pleasure in discussing his scientific theories about eclipses and his radical new idea that the sun was actually a great rotating, fiery rock. Such revolutionary views were not welcomed by all Athenians; some religious conservatives deemed it impious for mortal men to construct scientific theories about the sun and the heavens, entities considered divine in more traditional Greek cosmologies. While the conservatives did not stop Pericles from studying with the Ionian philosopher, they did punish both men. One later source reports that Anaxagoras was successfully prosecuted for impiety in the courts of Athens, and the scientist was compelled to live out the remainder of his life back in Ionia. Pericles' support for Anaxagoras and his new scientific ideas came at a dear price.

Pericles' love for innovation did not end with scientific inquiry—he also appreciated pioneers in art, architecture, and design. One of Pericles' confidants was the artist Phidias, a fellow Athenian. His reputation throughout antiquity was of the first order, and he was acknowledged as the artist responsible for much of the art on the rebuilt Acropolis, including a colossal bronze image of Athena that was visible from the sea as ships approached Athens and the Piraeus. He likewise fashioned a gold and ivory cult image of Athena that stood within the Parthenon itself. The engineering and art design for the buildings that Phidias oversaw suggest that sculptors and architects were applying new mathematical concepts about proportion and harmony. But Phidias may have suffered the same fate as Anaxagoras: he too was reportedly charged with impiety just as the temple of Athena Parthenos was nearing completion. The charge centered on the claim that Phidias had sculpted his own image and that of Pericles in details on the base of the cult statue of Athena. Another tradition reports that the artist embezzled some of the gold and ivory intended for the statue of the goddess. Whether or not he was put on trial, the fact remains that by the end of the 430s Phidias had left Athens and was working in the Peloponnese, fashioning the great cult image of Zeus that would dominate a new temple in the panhellenic sanctuary at Olympia.

The historical tradition surrounding the impiety trials of Anaxagoras and Phidias during the late 440s and '30s was the subject of much debate among scholars in the twentieth century. Adding to the uncertainty were further reports alleging that Pericles' common-law wife Aspasia, too, was charged with impiety in the 430s. While later sources from the Hellenistic and Roman periods are nearly unanimous in assigning these three impiety trials to this decade, there is no evidence from the fifth century that any such trials ever occurred. Perhaps the safest thing to conclude is that during these years of his leadership Pericles had his critics in Athens, and Greek writers a century later found it compelling to imagine these critics attacking Pericles through his friends. The attacks as described involve charges of civic impiety—behaviors that run counter to the prevailing modes and customs of worshipping the gods. Yet Pericles' visible commitment to Athena spoke in his favor: he apparently saw no contradiction between the new ideas being advanced and the traditional civic cult of the Olympian gods as practiced in Athens. *Thysia* remained one of the foundations of civic life. For Pericles, worshipping Athena in a restored sacred precinct that embodied the new mathematics was a celebration of traditional civic rites. Most Athenians apparently agreed with him: he enjoyed the support of the Athenian *dēmos*, who elected him to the office of *stratēgos* every single year between 444 and 429. Pericles' popularity during these decades waned for only a moment in 430/29 when he was deposed from office. But the *dēmos* reelected him again later that same year.

WAR'S CASUALTIES AND FUNERAL RITES IN PERICLES' ATHENS

Sparta and its allies on the Peloponnesian Peninsula did not fail to notice the growing power of Athens. Corinth, situated on the strategic bridge of land between Sparta and Attica, felt the pressure keenly. Although Athens and Sparta arbitrated their differences and negotiated a thirty-year peace treaty in 446/5, this peace in fact barely lasted fourteen years. By the late 430s the tension between Attica and the Peloponnesian League had focused on Corinth in two separate incidents. One related to Athenian involvement with Corinth and two colonies in northwest Hellas, the Corinthian colony Corcyra and Corcyra's colony Epidamnus. There Athenian and Corinthian ships engaged directly in a minor naval skirmish. Around the same time another conflict arose between Athens and Corinth over the Corinthian colony of Potidaea, a well-fortified port city in the northern Aegean. Potidaea was close to the forests of Macedon, a source of timber for Athenian ships, and it was on the major trade route to the Black Sea. Its strategic location made it an attractive ally for the Athenians, who had earlier forced it into the Delian League. But by 432 the Potidaeans grew dissatisfied with the increasing demands for tribute from the alliance with Athens; when they desired to pull out of the Delian League the Corinthians gladly offered help. After a two-year siege of the colony (432–430), with Athens facing combined Potidaean and Peloponnesian forces, the Athenians achieved victory. They established their own colonists in Potidaea and compelled the city to remain in the Delian League.

When the Corinthians confronted the Athenian navy late in the 430s at Corcyra and Potidaea, they did so on the northern and the western edges of Hellas. In one sense these were minor conflicts in marginal places, and the political differences could have been easily negotiated. But some members of the Peloponnesian League felt they saw a pattern emerging. Although Sparta had so far stayed outside the center of action, it still feared the growing dominance of Athenian rule. Pericles remained a steadfast proponent of the Athenian empire, and the *dēmos* followed him. Meanwhile Corinth and Sparta suspected that the two minor disputes at Corcyra and Potidaea had less to do with relations between the Delian League and the Peloponnesian League than with the ability of any Greek *polis* to govern itself and manage relations with its colonies and neighbors. Continued Corinthian appeals to the Spartan leaders of the Peloponnesian League prompted Sparta to issue a series of three ultimatums to the Athenians. Their final demand was simple: let the Greeks be free. Pericles advised the Athenians to make no concessions to the Peloponnesians (Thucydides 1.139–44).

Much of our understanding of the causes of the war and the motivations of the Athenians and Spartans has come to us through the writings of one particular historian: Thucydides. A capable Athenian general who exercised command over a naval vessel until 424/3, Thucydides exhibited an acute awareness of himself as a historian. Like Herodotus, who recorded what he saw as the epic confrontation of Hellas with a major imperial Asian power in the past, Thucydides early on recognized the larger significance of the current war between Athens and Sparta. But while Herodotus's moral compass warned of an inevitable divine response (*nemesis*) to humans' denial of their mortal limitations (*hubris*), Thucydides largely discounted the role played by the gods' justice in human affairs. Thucydides' views on political power and the decision-making process within human communities—and the limitations on this power—are put forth independently of the gods, and independently of older religious traditions and theologies. The war that Thucydides chronicled ultimately brought an end to the Athenian empire. Twenty-seven years later, in 404, Athens lay in utter defeat. Athens' allies had been liberated by the Peloponnesian League and the empire was broken. Some of Athens' enemies even called for the death of all its citizens and the enslavement of Athenian women and children, a tactic the Athenians had come to use on especially resistant subject-allies during the course of the war. The Spartans, recalling the sacrifices of the Athenians and Athens' total destruction during the Persian Wars seventy-five years earlier, exercised mercy. They opted for terms of peace stipulating that Athens never again be allowed to build a navy. But they did allow the civic monuments and the political and religious *nomoi* of Athens to remain unchanged. Even in defeat, the civic rites of the Athenians persisted.

This outcome—that the Spartans would be such clear winners—could never have been predicted from the ebb and flow of the early phases of the war. The first decade of fighting, from 431 to 421, cost a great deal, both in lives lost and resources spent, and yet it ended in a stalemate. This first phase of the conflict, known as the Archidamian War, was a calculated face-off between two entirely mismatched forces. From the start of the war, with their first invasion of Attica in the spring of 431, the Spartans relied on their famous and formidable hoplite infantry. The army of Peloponnesian hoplites was trained as Greek armies had always been trained, and they planned to wage a traditional war against the Athenians, invading the countryside of Attica during the early summer and laying waste to agricultural lands before retreating back to Sparta. The Spartan strategy assumed that no community of Greek citizens would tolerate this sort of devastation for very long.

The Athenians, on the other hand, under the leadership of Pericles continued to develop their navy as they had been doing since the days of Themistocles and the second Persian invasion in 480. Athenian offensive tactics entailed sailing to the Peloponnese and landing armed forces that made incursions into Spartan territory and wreaked havoc before retreating back to their ships. But the defense of Attica was far more innovative. Pericles had long supported the strategy that made the city of Athens into a virtual island, and he urged the Athenians to abandon the countryside of Attica and move their families within the city walls. The *dēmos* followed his recommendations—even though doing so entailed great hardship and economic loss. With the reinforced city fortifications of Athens and the Piraeus, and with newer walls linking the two, Athenians could withstand any siege the Spartans might lay.

Pericles' plan relied on defensive fortifications that had been rebuilt and substantially enlarged in the decades following the Persian Wars. As long as the citizens were inside the city and as long as the Long Walls held, the navy could bring provisions to Piraeus and feed the people enclosed within the urban centers. Subject-allies would continue to bring their annual tribute and the seat of empire would remain intact. The Spartans were stunned that the Athenians, or any Greek people for that matter, could adopt a policy that forced them to abandon their farms and sacrifice the countryside in order to maintain a naval empire. But the Athenians did precisely this during the early phases of the conflict, surprising the Spartans and creating the conditions for stalemate. Even after changes made to the defenses of Attica in the war's later phases, the fortifications held until the capitulation of Athens in 404.

There were, however, unforeseeable and immediate consequences to this Athenian defensive strategy: a plague broke out. The devastating epidemic hit Athens not once but twice during the opening years of the war, a major outbreak from 430 to 428 and a smaller one in 427. No one was quite sure where the disease came from. Perhaps it traveled to Piraeus from Ethiopia or Egypt, as Thucydides proposed, carried on infected rodents that infested shipments of imported grain, or possibly it was an outbreak of epidemic typhus or smallpox. Regardless of its origins, the illness was deadly and killed thousands of victims. Thucydides himself survived a bout with this plague, and his famous account of the disease described the gruesome and fatal symptoms that did not discriminate among victims. Rich and poor, men and women died alike, as did citizens, slaves, and resident foreigners (Thucydides 2.47–54).

Some historians have estimated the number of dead at 50,000—an astounding number, given that the total population of Attica at the start of the war was perhaps 250,000, of whom 40,000 were citizens. Since the overcrowded walled city was sheltering refugees from the countryside of Attica, living conditions deteriorated and even aggravated the disease rate and death toll. At the height of the outbreak Thucydides described a complete social and moral breakdown not unlike what was later reported during plague outbreaks in fourteenth-century Europe. All *nomoi* that held together civic society were forgotten in the panic of disease: the sick went uncared for and corpses lay rotting in homes, streets, and public areas.

When they did bury the dead, residents did not have the time or resources to conduct burials according to *nomos*. The sanctuaries of the gods were overrun with refugees from the countryside who had put up tents and temporary huts there, and soon even temples were polluted with corpses. In the face of indiscriminate suffering and death, citizens behaved without any consideration for law, whether divine or human.

Among the victims of the plague was the Athenian leader Pericles. He was about 65 when he fell ill alongside thousands of his fellow citizens and died the same excruciating death. We do not know who mourned the passing of Pericles. Even though most scholars consider Thucydides to have been a strong supporter of Pericles and his policies, his history barely mentions the death of Pericles. Instead of narrating this dark moment in Athenian history at the start of the Peloponnesian War, Thucydides twice shows Pericles at his proudest. The two passages that surround the description of the plague reveal the Athenians' feelings of confidence and superiority at the start of the conflict, and they also showcase Pericles' powers as a public speaker whose brilliance so inspired the Athenian *dēmos*. A speech following the description of the plague gives Pericles' final words of encouragement after Attica was invaded for the second time in the summer of 430, just as the plague was first breaking out and the residents of Athens were really starting to suffer (Thucydides 2.59–64). Pericles reminds Athenians of the greatness of their naval empire, and he cautions them against becoming lesser men than their fathers: they must fight for freedom, and fight to uphold the honor that empire brings to the city.

In the passage immediately before he mentions the plague, Thucydides presents Pericles giving his famous funeral oration for those who fell fighting for Athens (Thucydides 2.34–46). In this passage we see Pericles in the winter of 431/0. It is the end of the first year of the war, and Pericles the *stratēgos* memorializes the fallen dead with an *epitaphios*, a eulogy for those who have fallen in battle. In accordance with democratic tradition the Athenians held a great civic funeral to honor the dead. Public funerals were occasionally depicted in literary sources; for example, in Homer's *Iliad* fallen warriors were honored with funerary rites that included libations, sacrifices, a communal meal, and athletic games. In the historical period, funerary customs varied by *polis*. Cemeteries were generally located alongside major roads outside a city's walls, as the graves in Athens' Kerameikos district lined both sides of the Sacred Way just north of the Themistoclean fortification walls built following the Persian Wars.

The state funeral, with its *epitaphios* speech and the Epitaphia festival that followed, appears to be a uniquely Athenian custom that dates perhaps from the 460s and the period of Athenian ascendancy. All members of the community, citizens and foreigners alike, processed to the state cemetery in the Kerameikos, where a leading citizen spoke in praise of the fallen dead and compared these men to those who had died defending Athens in the past. Athletic and poetic competitions followed the burial. The civic funeral was also one of the few occasions when Athenian women participated in the shared public ceremonies. As the Athenian custom unfolded over time it diverged notably from the practice described in Homer: in the *Iliad* only aristocrats received a magnificent burial, but in Athens every man who died in battle received the same honors. The bones of the lowly *thētes* and oarsmen on the ships were gathered and buried together with those of the richest aristocrats. In this civic rite awareness of human mortality was placed in a larger context that included both the ancestors and the immortal gods; the community gathered to reflect on its past victory over the Persian Empire and to reaffirm its current commitments.

Just as Pericles' final speech given later in book 2 (2.59–64) recalls the glorious accomplishments of the Athenians' forefathers and urges citizens to look to the honor of their empire, so Pericles' funeral oration links the recent deaths of soldiers with the deaths of honorable men from prior generations, and it celebrates their contributions to the continuing glory and ultimate victory of Athens. Thucydides' placement of the funeral oration right before the plague narrative underscores the tragedy not only of the lives lost in that first year of fighting but also of those who would soon perish on the home front—including Pericles himself. The surviving family members and friends that Pericles addressed in the state cemetery in the Kerameikos in 430 were the very Athenians who were about to succumb to the plague and suffer needless, horrific deaths.

Thucydides' report of Pericles' funeral oration illustrates one of the major themes in his history: how humans are motivated by power and honor. A close reading of the passage also shows how religious rituals play a role in the unfolding of that power. Thucydides clearly indicates the political context of the funeral ceremony, and pointedly refers to the foundational Athenian democratic institution of the ten Cleisthenic tribes. Underneath a tent, the ashes and bones of those who had fallen in battle were arranged according to the tribe the dead belonged to. One empty bier symbolically honored the unknown soldiers whose remains were unable to be recovered or identified. Then all the remains of each tribe were gathered together and placed in a coffin; at the state funeral ten coffins were interred (Thucydides 2.34). When Pericles delivered his words of praise, he spoke facing the Athenian people and alongside the ten tribal coffins of the dead.

The bones of the ancestors had long carried a powerful political meaning for all the Greeks. Two hundred years had passed since the Athenians had cursed Megacles and his descendants the Alcmaeonidae, and it had been perhaps a hundred years since Athenians (with Spartan encouragement) had expelled bones of the accursed Alcmaeonidae from Attica. Although the Alcmaeonids did return to Athens and two descendants (Cleisthenes and Pericles) even succeeded in bringing democratic reforms to the *polis,* the memory of the curse was not forgotten. Following the episodes at Corcyra and Potidaea in 432/1, when Sparta and its allies were considering how to respond to the overwhelming power of the Athenian empire, the Spartans had tried to force the Athenians to exile Pericles, the leader who was most energetically urging the Athenian *dēmos* toward war. The Spartans sent negotiators to Athens who called down the curse of the goddess: they reminded the Athenians that Athena herself had been wronged long ago when men were impiously killed in her sanctuary (Thucydides 1.126). The taint of the curse that rested on Pericles, a descendant of the impious murderers, could bring harm to Athens, the Spartans claimed. Thucydides' report of this diplomatic move explicitly states that the Spartans did not expect that the Athenians would actually expel Pericles—they hoped only that the reminder of the curse would implicate Pericles, and then the curse would come to be considered a cause for the conflict. There is some evidence that Athenians viewed the curse similarly, and in the coming years no one would doubt that Athens suffered under the accursed plague of war.

FOUR

Demeter

Civic Worship, Women's Rites, and the Eleusinian Mysteries

ATHENS WAS SACRED TO ATHENA, goddess of the olive, of handcrafts, and of wisdom, but Athenians were of course polytheistic, and for many generations they had also worshipped Demeter, the goddess whose power was manifest in abundant sheaves of wheat. The plains of Attica could provide only a limited supply of wheat, barley, and rye—certainly not enough to feed all the citizens and residents of the *polis;* over time Athens became dependent on imported grain to feed the population in the main city and the Piraeus. The Athenian navy ensured the empire's continuing access to foreign markets by protecting merchant ships and trade routes. The devastation of the plague that hit Athens at the start of the Peloponnesian War only served to remind Athenians of the importance of a reliable and safe food supply. After 428, Athens needed the blessings of Demeter more than ever to maintain its empire.

It was Demeter's great power over the fertility of the land that connected her to the cultivation of crops. She was worshipped all over the Greek world, and indeed throughout much of the Mediterranean basin. Demeter had important cult centers in Attica, Asia Minor, and Sicily; later on, the Romans in Italy called her Ceres, the goddess of cereal crops. The worship of another agricultural god was likewise ancient and deeply rooted throughout the wider Greek world. Dionysus, too, held a position of power in ancient Hellenic societies. Greeks considered Dionysus the god of the grapevine and its cultivation, and therefore also the god of wine. With bread and wine at the very heart of the most rudimentary Mediterranean diet, Demeter and Dionysus were present in the daily lives of all Hellenic peoples in antiquity.

Both Dionysus and Demeter occupied prominent places in the civic calendars and mythologies of Greek *poleis*. Many cities had their own particular story of how Demeter once visited and taught their ancestors to cultivate grain. In Attica Demeter was said to have given the gift of agriculture to all humankind when she once lived near Athens in the town of Eleusis; likewise Dionysus chose to give his unique gifts to Athenians in the long-ago mythological past. To commemorate these divine gifts Athenians celebrated Demeter festivals such as the Eleusinian Mysteries and the Thesmophoria in the late summer and fall, and Dionysian festivals such as the Lenaea, the Anthesteria, and the Dionysia in the winter and spring. These civic festivals with their sacrifices and feasts were publicly financed and widely attended by both citizens and other residents of Attica. The Thesmophoria was open only to citizen wives; other festivals attracted foreigners as well as citizens and residents.

In ancient Athens, social activities not recognized today as religious were deeply connected to the gods and to the state: publicly funded worship of the gods provided the *dēmos* with opportunities for feasting and drinking, and these civic rites linked humans and the gods as collaborators in the Athenian *polis*. In fundamental ways the worship of Demeter and Dionysus was no different than the customs of war as it was waged in Greece. Warfare too involved the gods at every step, from battlefield sacrifices performed before fighting commenced to peace treaties as it ended. The gods were invoked when Persian invaded Attica in 490 and 480, and when an alliance was forged at Apollo's sanctuary on Delos. Whenever any alliance or treaty was negotiated, *spondai* sealed the agreement: libations of wine dedicated to the gods were poured directly onto the ground. The terms of treaties required Olympian gods such as Zeus, Athena, or Apollo to witness their annual renewal at local festivals where prayers, civic sacrifices and communal feasting would follow the libations that soaked into the soil.

While the earth and soil were not considered holy per se, traditional customs did link certain immortals to the earth and its powers that supported life and protected the dead. Public libations were made to Zeus, who oversaw oaths and protected the stranger who traveled far from his homeland; to Hades the Lord of the Dead, who lived under the earth with his queen; and to the ancient female deities Gaia and Demeter, whose influence extended over the fertility of the land. But not all offerings to these gods were as public as libations poured by generals negotiating peace, and not all sacrifices made at public expense required worshippers to approach the altars of the gods primarily in their roles as citizens or warriors belonging to a particular political community. Rites that took little account of worshippers' social identities or political status in the *polis* enabled individuals to experience the power of the divine in less visible ways. Some practices sacred to Demeter and Dionysus were among this latter class of rites, practices frequently called "the mysteries."

This chapter will explore the worship of Demeter in Periclean Athens—the civic festivals, the women's rites, and the Eleusinian mystery cult; chapter 6 will examine the related phenomena of Dionysian civic festivals and mystery rites. Unlike Athena, whose monumental temples and public altars crowned the height of the Acropolis, Demeter was not always worshipped in the open. At her most important festivals, worshippers gathered behind closed doors or in exclusive groups far from the prying eyes of the unsympathetic and ill-informed. Familiarity with Demeter's civic cults and mystery rites will make possible a deeper understanding of some of the more dramatic events that occurred during the second half of the Peloponnesian War. Alleged desecrations of Demeter's rites and accusations of *asebeia* led to public trials, guilty verdicts, and the Athenian general Alcibiades' betrayal of his native city. The full account of this episode and its aftermath will be discussed in chapters 5 and 7 below.

Studying the worship of Demeter offers yet another route for tracing the growth of power in Athens. Traditional ancestral cults that started out as agrarian festivals grew in cultural and political importance over the generations. Annual rites celebrated by citizen wives and sacred to the female goddess of fertility were transformed to include all residents of the *polis;* eventually anyone could attend regardless of their origins. Changing patterns of worship in Demeter's cults first reflected the synoecism of Attica; later, her rites marked the development of the Athenian empire. The revenue that the Delian League and the Athenian empire brought to the citizens of Athens transformed many civic rites in the fifth century; as democracy and empire mingled together the *dēmos* came to worship Athena in new ways at the Panathenaea, and the same holds true for festivals of Demeter as well.

OLYMPIAN MYTHS AND HUMAN FAMILIES

Understanding Athenian democracy and civic rites starts from a familiarity with traditional tales of families and power. Myths about the Olympian gods in some ways reflected social relationships among humans and helped outline familiar gender roles and power dynamics. The Succession Myth points to one pattern, while stories of Demeter reveal another pattern of possible interaction. But the images reflected in the mythological tradition did not provide consistent models for human society, and viewed together ancestral tales can indicate the rough seams and internal contradictions within Greek culture. Athenian women were politically powerless, but in other ways surprisingly powerful. This ambiguity was preserved in both the myths and the civic cults of the divine grain mother Demeter.

Fatherhood occupied an elevated position in these tales about the complex divine family on Mount Olympus. There could be only one "father of gods and men," the just and forceful heavenly patriarch who ruled over all, and this was Zeus. Divine motherhood was constructed in a different and somewhat fragmented way. While Zeus was depicted as the principal divine male consort with multiple wives and lovers who bore him countless progeny, there were numerous goddesses who symbolically embodied the culturally defined feminine functions of sexuality, fertility, reproduction, and motherhood. The archaic poet Hesiod wrote about the primordial goddess Earth, called Gaia or Ge, and how her authority was handed over to Rhea when Cronus defeated Uranus in the first episode of the Succession Myth. In the third generation of immortals, ruled by Zeus, the goddess of sexuality, Aphrodite, was completely separate from Hera and Eileithyia, the goddesses of marriage and birth respectively. The goddess who protected infants and young children, Artemis, was yet again separate from these, and moreover she was an eternal maiden, at home in the wild but ever ignorant of erotic love. And all four of these goddesses were quite distinct from the principal Olympian goddess of female fertility, Demeter. There was no single "mother of gods and men" who corresponded to Zeus, the divine father figure.

While Zeus the father of gods and men was imagined as married, his two most commonly recognized marriages were not particularly happy ones. He annihilated his first consort, Metis (Cunning), when he learned of a prophecy foretelling that she would give birth to Athena and then to a son destined to be greater than his father. Wise Zeus outwitted the prophecy by swallowing the pregnant Metis. Metis's presence within Zeus prompted him to give birth to only one child—the favored daughter Athena, who burst forth from the head of her father fully grown and fully armed. Athena combined the cunning power of both her parents, and she cleverly remained unmarried and thus unable to betray her loyalty to the father of gods by pledging herself to another male and leaving her father's household.

Zeus's more permanent consort, Hera, embodied the culturally defined qualities of the demanding and jealous wife. Given his countless affairs with numerous divine, semi-divine, and human partners (both male and female), Zeus gave Hera plenty of opportunities to express her jealous rage. Many of the more youthful Olympian deities, including Apollo, Artemis, and Dionysus, were the result of Zeus's liaisons with especially beautiful mortal women. Hera the jealous wife was no model mother. She was only rarely celebrated and honored for her maternal qualities. In Homer she was known to ridicule her son Hephaestus, but the poets Homer and Hesiod were at odds as to whether Zeus was Hephaestus's biological father. The only uniformly recognized male offspring of Zeus and Hera was Ares. It is perhaps not surprising that the famed god of war was the only certain legitimate son of the troubled marriage of Zeus and Hera. Ares was harsh and fierce to the point of being considered nearly barbarian. He was thoroughly hated by the other Olympians, and posed no threat to his father's authority.

While Hera needed her husband Zeus to receive honors as divine consort, Demeter apparently had no need for a lawful husband to receive her worship as the divine and maternal giver of fertility. The very name Demeter appears to combine the Indo-European roots for "give" (*dō-*) and "mother" (*māter-*), the latter related to the Greek *mētēr* and Latin *mater*. Some linguists have also suggested associating *dē-* with the word for earth, *gē*, making Demeter literally mean "Earth Mother." Demeter was in fact the prototype of the protective, selfless, and self-reliant single mother. Though she did share a child with Zeus, Zeus played only a marginal role in his daughter's upbringing. This daughter was named Persephone, or more often simply Kore: the Maiden. The divine mother and maiden were so closely associated with each other that in Athenian inscriptions and legal decrees they were referred to as "the Two Goddesses" or, even more briefly, "the Two." Likewise, in their plays tragic poets referred to Demeter and Kore together as "the Two."

Long before the fifth century and the decrees of democratic Athens, the Greeks told myths that credited Demeter with teaching humans the civilizing gift of tilling the earth. Knowing how to cultivate cereal crops—barley, rye, and wheat—set humans apart from other animals and allowed men and women to live together in settled communities. Human society in the organized towns and small cities of Greek antiquity relied on the gifts of Demeter, made visible through the fertility of the land and the abundance of the grain crops. Human society would decline and fall apart if the cereal crops were not harvested and stored so that they could sustain the population at a later time.

The most famous myth about Demeter, goddess of grain, was told in the *Homeric Hymn to Demeter.* Nearly as old as the *Iliad* and *Odyssey* and written in the same style and meter as the famous epics, this shorter poem describes how the divine mother went into mourning when her young daughter Kore was abducted by Hades, the god of the dead. Hades intended to take Kore as his wife with the full knowledge and consent of his brother Zeus, who was also Kore's father. Demeter was left in the dark about these plans for her daughter's future, and in the poem Kore herself was entirely unwilling to be separated from her young playmates and her mother.

Neither Demeter nor Kore could die—they were after all deathless Olympian deities—but after this betrayal at the hands of Zeus, each goddess experienced a different sort of social, symbolic death. While Kore languished in the underworld alongside Hades and refused to eat, Demeter cast aside her identity as an immortal, and along with it all the proper honors and sacrificial gifts that belonged to Olympian gods and goddesses. Demeter mourned her loss by taking on the identity of a homeless old woman named Doso. Doso wandered into the town of Eleusis and sat down next to the town well, where she found the only employment available to someone of her social status and position in life. She became a nurse—in this case the nurse of the king's infant son Demophoön. At night in secret the nurse Doso/Demeter placed the royal baby in a sacred fire, knowing that this action over time could transform the human child into an ageless and immortal god. Then she would have another child to replace her lost daughter. The baby flourished in the care of his new divine nurse.

Metanira, the queen of Eleusis and the child's mother, soon wondered what the new nurse Doso was doing to make her child so healthy, so she spied on them one evening. Metanira caught the old woman placing the infant Demophoön in the flames. In her alarm and anxiety the mortal mother rushed in and withdrew her son from the hearth. Demeter's plans to make the human child immortal were thus thwarted, and she became enraged. She revealed her awesome divinity to Metanira and the people of Eleusis, and commanded them to build her a temple and worship her forever. The anger and frustration of the mother Demeter now reached their full expression, and the goddess of fertility withheld her gifts from everybody she could, even from the deathless gods. Plants and fruits withered, famine fell upon the land, humans no longer honored the immortals with offerings at temples and altars. Man and beast both perished, and the Olympian gods grew concerned about their own future and the future of the earth.

Zeus took action only when he realized how desperate the situation was growing. He agreed to negotiate with Demeter, who demanded the return of her daughter, even though he had already reached an agreement with Hades. Zeus eventually brokered a new compromise between Hades and Demeter: Kore would spend part of the year with her mother, and the remaining part with her husband in the underworld. Finally Demeter relented. The return of Kore and the reunion of the divine mother and daughter at the temple in Eleusis brought fertility back to the earth and joy back to the gods. Demeter celebrated in Eleusis by giving gifts to the Eleusinian people, who had suffered alongside her during her time of great loss. Demeter taught the young nobleman Triptolemus and other Eleusinian leaders how to celebrate her rites and mysteries, rites that would make all initiates blessed and favored in the afterlife (figure 9). Demeter's mysteries would instruct mortals, taking the terror out of death by guaranteeing initiates their share of good things in the underworld after they died.

This myth demonstrates Demeter's great power over the earth and indeed the whole cosmos; the immortal gods depended on her continuing good graces to bestow fertility and abundance upon them, too. When drought and famine fell upon the earth in the *Homeric Hymn to Demeter,* humans no longer had the resources to worship the Olympian deities. The lack of sacrificial offerings made by humans threatened the very existence of the gods. Zeus and the other immortals could thrive only when humans regularly offered them sacrifices and honors at public altars. As the myth of Demeter and Kore showed, the civic rites of *thysia* relied on the gifts of Demeter: humans fed surpluses of grain to their domesticated cows, which then were sacrificed at altars. Zeus may have been the father of gods and men, but his position of heavenly leadership required the full cooperation and blessings of Demeter.

In this traditional tale of the divine grain mother mourning her maiden daughter, the goddess set aside her true form and put on a social identity mirroring that of real, mortal women. According to normal Athenian social customs, citizen women were expected to remain at home under the protection and care of a male guardian, usually their father or husband. As the nurse Doso, Demeter came under the authority of the king of Eleusis. At home in the company of other household women, citizen wives and

Figure 9. Fifth-century marble relief sculpture found at Eleusis showing Demeter and Persephone with a young Triptolemus. National Archaeological Museum, Athens, votive relief 126.

daughters were occupied with the labor-intensive task of making textiles. Girls and women prepared the wool, spun it, and toiled at the loom. Like Metanira, the good and responsible citizen wife also managed household slaves and servants, and oversaw the mundane tasks of housekeeping, child care, shopping, and food preparation. Women kept the household running smoothly, while the men met together and managed the public realm of the *polis*.

The daily life of most citizen women in Greece revealed a contradiction at the heart of this ancient society: although women possessed great power in the family they were simultaneously denied access to the institutions that managed the larger community. On the one hand, Athenian women were expected to be largely invisible in public and political life; they remained at home while male citizens managed the *polis*. They were not citizens with voting rights in the *ekklēsia* and the courtrooms. On the other hand, women were necessary to bear and nurture the next generation of legitimate citizens, as Metanira bore the prince Demophoön. The integrity of family lineage and the rightful transfer of wealth and resources along male lines of descent depended on women, and on husbands' confidence in their wives' sexual fidelity.

This circumstance gave women a kind of hidden power in the structured society of classical Athens, and that power became even more significant during the fifth century. The Periclean citizenship laws passed in 451/0 required of all Athenian citizens that both their father and mother be recognized Athenian citizens. This law gave Athenian women a new status in the *polis,* and presented male citizens with new incentives for marrying well. The stability of Athenian society rested on the security of the family and the trustworthiness of its female citizens—unmarried maiden daughters as well as lawful, childbearing wives. Women were considered full citizens when it came to civic rites celebrating fertility, motherhood, and the family, and in this way women had a share in the common life of the *polis.* Even women past their childbearing years continued to shoulder the responsibility of keeping Athens stable by helping to raise the next generation of Athenian citizens, as the nurse Doso nurtured the child in the myth.

But the elevated status of citizen women in Athens after 451/0 highlighted deeper divisions embedded in the practices of civic cult. When male citizens of the *polis* gathered together for public occasions such as assemblies, meetings, civic sacrifices, and feasts, women may not have been present in significant numbers, if at all. The ancestral traditions of *thysia* and civic feasts were intended to cement male bonds of citizenship, helping to create the male world of political community and social continuity. Even today scholars cannot agree at all on how often women appeared in public in ancient Athens—the evidence goes both ways. When the procession at the annual Panathenaea celebrated the public self-image of the Athenian *dēmos,* citizens, foreigners, and animals filed through the heart of the city and ascended the steps of the Acropolis. There male priests and magistrates performed the central public rituals and dedicated gifts from the *polis* at the altar of Athena next to the Parthenon, and there male magistrates slaughtered bulls for the civic banquet. Meat was distributed in their demes among male citizens, who then shared their portions with their households. Though images on Attic vases and the Parthenon frieze do depict young women in the procession carrying the sacred basket, women are not visually represented as often as men, and our literary sources do not clearly and consistently indicate whether women were present at public civic feasts in large numbers. Analysis of skeletal bones found in graves provides evidence that females suffered from malnutrition more frequently than men. A few select girls and young women at the Panathenaea may have manufactured the *peplos* of Athena and presented it to her, but the story commemorated by the *peplos* itself recalled the subordinate position of women in Athenian society. The images woven into Athena's robe celebrated the Olympians' decisive victory over the forces of chaos—a victory led by the paradigmatic male and paternal figure, Zeus. Even when the commanding female figure Athena was at the center of attention, as she was at the Panathenaea, her power served to support the male patriarch. Athena's festival enshrined the standard social order of Athens.

Some festivals of Demeter did not fit this model. Like the Panathenaea, the chief civic festivals of Demeter were organized and funded by the *polis,* but their celebrations completely suspended the normal social order and the political and social hierarchies that defined typical Athenian society. Athenian women mirrored Demeter and Metanira in the myth when they celebrated the Demeter festival called the Thesmophoria. Women suddenly became more than simply visible in the public sphere; they exercised considerable power in the *polis.* At the Eleusinian Mysteries, Athenian wives, together with foreigners and slaves of both sexes, were treated much the same as Athenian-born citizen males. The civic rites of Demeter were as startlingly different from the worship of other Olympian gods as they were popular. Demeter's rites reveal another side of fifth-century Athenian democracy.

DEMETER AND THE ATHENIAN 'DĒMOS'
AT THE THESMOPHORIA

As the time for sowing grain in fall grew near, residents of Attica witnessed unusual things taking place. The women grew busy and excited, and then one afternoon they all left their homes carrying packs and bundles. In Athens they gathered on a hillside overlooking the Agora. The women elected female officials of their own; the governing male citizens disbanded and were forced to suspend all public business. There on the open grassy slope beneath the Acropolis, Athenian women set up camp for themselves and conducted their own civic rites of the Thesmophoria. What happened during these rites was left to the imaginations of Athenian men, who over the years conjured up some pretty wild goings-on among their wives: dirty jokes, lewd behavior at drunken parties, and plots to overthrow the government. While it is true that the government of Athens did suffer two coups in the late fifth century, neither was carried out by women. All evidence indicates that the official proceedings of the women gathered together in the autumn near the Agora were much tamer than the men supposed.

This same scene of women leaving home and congregating at all-female festival sites was repeated in demes all over Attica, and indeed in cities and towns all over the Greek world. The civic festival called the Thesmophoria celebrated the goddess Demeter and her gift to humankind: the knowledge of how to cultivate the earth and sow grain. The Thesmophoria was in fact the single most widespread of all Greek festivals, and probably one of the oldest. Among the common threads for the ancestral communal rites was the uniform exclusion of men. The heart of this civic festival took place in caves and alongside crevices and holes dug deep into the earth. These pits called *megara* are today still found in many of the Demeter sanctuaries in the eastern Mediterranean basin. Throughout Hellas priestesses of Demeter stood at the edge of the pits, and as other women looked on they lowered terra-cotta pots down into them to scoop out the holy contents: fertile soil mixed with plant matter and bloody, decomposing piglets. After the sacred compost was combined with seed and deposited on two altars, one for Demeter and the other for her daughter Persephone, the women sat down to a great state-funded feast.

The ancient customs of the Thesmophoria provide further evidence for how activities that in today's world are typically labeled religious lay at the heart of civic life in Socrates' and Pericles' Athens. Some today might even call the civic rituals involving seed, soil, and pig's blood "primitive" or "magical," but those terms do not adequately capture the social dynamics that created real meaning for those who honored and maintained the age-old rites of Demeter. The official Athenian calendar noted at least a dozen civic festivals in honor of Demeter every year. One cluster of these festivals, attested especially in the calendars of rural demes, revolved around the cultivation of the grain crops: the Chloia, the Antheia, the Kalamaia, the Proerosia, and the Procharisteria. These five relatively minor festivals were spread throughout the agricultural year, from autumn pre-plowing rites (the Proerosia) to festivals that marked the gradual maturing of the crops in the spring (the Chloia, the Antheia, the Procharisteria, and the Kalamaia). The cultivation of the fields from sowing to reaping occupied the men of rural Attica, and male priests appear to have played a big role in these festivals for Demeter in her role as corn mother.

But the worship of Demeter the fertility goddess carried further meaning for women throughout the Greek world. While men participated in those festivals that corresponded to their labor in the fields, ancestral *nomoi* explicitly excluded male citizens from attending other civic rites sacred to Demeter, including the Haloa, the Scira, the Stenia, and the Thesmophoria. At the Haloa in midwinter, women and men were pointedly segregated for their great feasts: the women celebrated all night long inside a temple, and the men celebrated in a courtyard outdoors. The Scira in early summer and Stenia in the autumn likewise required citizen women to offer sacrifices to Demeter and Kore in rites that excluded the male *dēmos*. In Attica the women's festival of the Thesmophoria was celebrated in Pyanopsion, roughly corresponding to October; other *poleis* nearby observed the festival a few weeks earlier, in Boedromion. During this part of the autumn the weather was still warm and fine, and the seasonal tasks in the rural countryside were not too demanding for either women or men.

In Athens the Thesmophoria was the most important of the civic festivals for Demeter that excluded the male *dēmos*. Because it was an official state holiday all the regular assemblies and courts of male citizens were canceled, and all official state business was suspended until the end of the third day. Archaeologists have not yet unearthed a particular Athenian sanctuary called the Thesmophorion; in the city, citizen wives could have met near the Eleusinion, a hillside sanctuary along the Sacred Way between the Agora and the Acropolis. Another theory holds that the Thesmophorion was located on the slopes of the hill called the Pnyx, a prominent landmark in the southwest quarter of the city that normally served as the outdoor meeting place for the regular Assembly of male citizens, the *ekklēsia*. For three days the women met together and camped outdoors, worshipping the goddess of fertility and enjoying each other's company. From all accounts it was an occasion that the citizen women looked forward to all year.

The myth of the Two Goddesses played a central role in the rituals of the Thesmophoria. The main narrative that records the rape and marriage of Kore, the grief of Demeter, and the eventual reunion of mother and daughter corresponded to the final two days of the three-day Thesmophoria, while the opening day had a strong political and civic meaning. The first day of rites was called the Anodos, or the Path Up, presumably because on this day the women of Athens left their homes and took a path up to the hillside sanctuary where the civic rites would take place. They brought along with them any equipment they would need for the next few days—food, cooking utensils, and bedding. They slept in huts or shelters that they built themselves, so we can imagine them also toting along whatever materials they would need to construct their camps. Because the weather was still warm and dry at that time of year, there would have been no great need for sturdy or waterproof shelter. The whole process of encampment required a good deal of organization, and two women from each deme were elected "leaders," *archousai*, to manage the complex three-day festival. The rare feminine form of this title imitates the more common masculine word *archontes*, the male magistrates and leaders of the Athenian *dēmos*. The designation *archousai* in effect made the annual all-female Thesmophoria an alternative assembly—an officially sanctioned gathering that mirrored the activities of the normal male political gatherings.

The second day was a day of mourning and fasting, the Nesteia. Some of the more significant rituals apparently took place on this day. Keeping in mind the story of the Two Goddesses, the women in essence imitated the mourning of Demeter, who according to myth came to live in Attica after learning that her maiden daughter Kore had been abducted by Hades. In the *Homeric Hymn,* as noted above, Demeter disguised herself and took on the form of Doso, the older mortal woman who came to Eleusis and found employment as a servant in the house of a local noble. Since even in her mortal disguise the goddess Demeter was still privately mourning the loss of her immortal daughter, she observed the human customs of mourning; in the *Hymn* Demeter wore shabby clothing, fasted, and sat on a simple stool low to the ground that indicated her inferior status in the household of her new human masters. The Athenian women at the Thesmophoria likewise mourned and fasted, sitting directly on the earth. Some sources indicate that worshippers sat on woven mats made of plants thought to dampen the female sexual drive and restrict a woman's fertility. These ritual actions were done in a spirit of gloom and sadness, like that of Demeter mourning the loss of her daughter at Eleusis.

In the myth Demeter was eventually reunited with her daughter and she then joyfully restored fertility to the earth. The restoration of the relationship between Mother and Daughter was commemorated on the third day of the Thesmophoria—the Kalligeneia, the day of Beautiful Birth. On this final day of the festival, Athenian women broke their fast and made special offerings to the goddess at altars in her sanctuary. Pigs and piglets were Demeter's favorite animal votive, and piglet offerings played an essential role here. Earlier in the summer the city's priestesses of Demeter had prepared for the Thesmophoria by placing offerings in a nearby cave sacred to the goddesses. Whole piglets were sacrificed and deposited in *megara* near the cave well in advance of the Thesmophoria, along with plant matter from pine trees. Special cakes formed in the shape of phalluses and snakes were thrown into the pits along with the piglets, and the whole mixture was left to rot. Snakes and phalluses had clear connotations of male fertility; by adding them to the bloody piglets, the priestesses symbolically restored the fertility of the soil after Demeter's loss, mourning, and withdrawal from life. On the day of Kalligeneia, women designated as "bailers" returned to the *megara* chambers and bailed out the decomposed but fertile goop from the pits. The mixture was then placed on the altars of Demeter and Kore in the sanctuary and dedicated to them. The power of the goddess of fertility made the muck extra fertile, and later in the fall the sanctified compost was mixed with seed, then sown with the winter wheat in a separate civic ritual.

The association between female reproductive sexuality and the fertility of the soil was celebrated almost concretely in Athens at the Thesmophoria. Demeter was a female goddess, the goddess of grain and the fertility of the earth; the Western tradition still speaks of the earth as feminine and motherly rather than paternal and protective (i.e., culturally identifiable as masculine). To this day the earth is anthropomorphized as Mother Earth and Mother Nature, as though it were a human mother common to us all. The cultivation of the earth had additional associations that were considered culturally feminine among the peoples living in Greece and the ancient Mediterranean basin, who were not long removed from the great shift in human history from nomadic subsistence to settled communities. Ancient Mediterranean mythologies and rituals often reflected the effects of this change on their societies, and the dynamics captured in myth used gender to express larger social changes in familiar and concrete terms. The more domestic pursuits of agriculture became culturally feminine, while the rougher lifestyle of the nomadic hunter who ranged over a wild and untamed wilderness was considered culturally masculine; thus as unmarried goddess of the hunt, Artemis had power that was culturally defined as masculine.

Some memory of these transitions to settled farming persisted symbolically in the worship of Demeter among the Athenians and other Greek peoples. The Greeks looked to their own experience of the human life cycle, and mapped their experiences of cultivating the soil onto their understanding of human fertility. The earth was thought to be like a woman's womb: it nurtured the seed necessary for life. Ancient peoples saw farmers broadcasting seed—*sperma*—over the rich soil of ancestral lands just as a man cast his seed in the productive womb of his lawful wife. In both instances the farmer expected a return that would support him in the future. Harvested grain could either be ground immediately for bread or be stored—even for many years—and used later to support the community during a famine. Likewise children would grow up to shoulder the responsibility of caring for aging parents. As the seed absorbed a culturally defined masculine resonance, the soil cultivated for growing grain came to have explicit feminine, sexual meanings. Oedipus in Sophocles' *Oedipus the King* famously lamented that he had plowed the same furrows that his father had, and one formula attested for betrothals in Athens explicitly made the connection between soil and women: "I give you her (my daughter) for the plowing of legitimate children" (Menander *Perikeiromene* 1013 and *Dyskolos* 842).

Working from these hints in the mythic tradition and drawing from other fragmentary evidence, scholars speculate about what happened at the Thesmophoria. But their guesses can only go so far, and the fact remains that most aspects of the women's worship of Demeter at the Thesmophoria remained secret from the men of Athens. Men in antiquity were always suspicious of any meeting that excluded them, and their ideas about what happened at the Thesmophoria illustrate this suspicion. Some of Aristophanes' comedies produced in Athens in the late fifth century mention the alleged wild drunkenness and sexual promiscuity of female citizens in their worship of Demeter during the three-day festival of the Thesmophoria. Such a prurient image may simply reflect the overactive imaginations of Athenian men. One of the more plausible and reliable historical accounts of women's behavior at this festival relates that the citizen wives sat with their genitals directly in contact with the earth. In such a sympathetic rite, Athenian women were apparently hoping to absorb into their own bodies the fertility of Demeter and the earth itself. Or perhaps their human fertility helped restore Demeter when she was in mourning.

The persistent suspicions of Athenian men point to one of the more curious aspects of the Thesmophoria: Athenian residents probably viewed and experienced the festival very differently, depending on their own sex and social location. The three-day autumn festival may well have constituted a hardship for the adult men of Athens. Without their mothers, wives, and daughters to run the household, men were left home alone to look after the children and slaves and keep things running smoothly. Perhaps this is another reason why all public state business, including the courts and the Assembly of male citizens, was suspended for the duration of the festival. Men, who were quite accustomed to living, working, and socializing with their citizen peers in the public realm of the *polis*, had a taste of their wives' more restricted domestic existence for a few days. Meanwhile, Athenian wives had a break from the routines of housework and enjoyed each other's company at state expense. They probably returned home from the day of Beautiful Birth relaxed and cheerful. It is little wonder, then, that the men, unable to pursue their normal occupations and perhaps cooped up in the house for three days, imagined their wives drinking and otherwise living it up.

The celebration of the Thesmophoria throughout Greece existed long before the reforms of Cleisthenes and well before the unification of Attica, and over time it achieved an esteemed place in the *polis* calendar of fifth-century Athenian festivals. These ancient rites honoring the fertility of the earth demanded the complete separation of male and female, and they privileged the knowledge that women carried in this culture. Although the Thesmophoria was not a mystery rite, it did share something important with the mystery religion at Eleusis: namely, the particular focus on being female in ancient Hellas. The Eleusinian Mysteries also acknowledged the deep connections to the earth's resources maintained by females—divine and human—in Greek culture. Ritual customs recognized the renewal of life in the cultivated fields of grain and in the family. Ancestral traditions constructed a homology between the land and the human body, and then extended it to the fate of the individual. The Greek idea of the soul differed significantly from what it would become following the development of Christianity. The afterlife of the soul was not tied to an individual's moral behavior, but there was interest in the fate of the person in the underworld. From its humble beginnings in the rural landscape of Greece, the powerful rites of Demeter would soon attract worshippers from throughout the Mediterranean.

THE ELEUSINIAN MYSTERIES

The rituals of *polis* sacrifice and *thysia* described in chapter 2 nourished the citizen body, but the mystery rites of Demeter articulated other more hidden aspects of lived human experience. Participation in civic rites that honored the ancestral Olympian gods and bound humans together in the political community was an essential aspect of being a citizen in an ancient Mediterranean society. Citizens and foreigners alike were expected to take part in civic festivals that featured prominent rituals of animal sacrifice and the subsequent feasting at public expense, as in Athens everyone attended the Panathenaea during the summer and Athenian women attended the Thesmophoria in the fall. While the civic rites of *thysia* and cultic democracy celebrated those relationships that sustained the *polis* and its citizens as a collective group, the polytheistic traditions of ancient Greece also included another type of civic rite that supported worshippers as individuals who can experience fear, awe, wonder, and joy. These sorts of rites were voluntary: men and women chose to become initiates. Such elective rites illustrated one way that ancestral *nomoi* made room for the interests of the person within the larger *polis* community. Even when the institution of the classical *polis* later gave way to the Hellenistic and Roman empires, initiatory cults remained a powerful force in ancient Mediterranean societies.

Fifth-century Athenians worshipped Demeter in both ways: at public civic festivals and with rites of initiates. The voluntary rites sacred to Demeter were celebrated out of the public eye—behind closed doors and under the cover of night. In modern times these forms of elective worship have come to be grouped together into what scholars often misleadingly call "the mystery religions." The mystery religions of Greco-Roman antiquity were not obscure, strange, or puzzling, and their rituals were hardly distinct from those associated with other civic rites and festivals. Mystery rites were actually quite common and popular forms of voluntary religious practice in the ancient world. Attendance at public feasts was required for citizens in any ancient Greek *polis,* for participating in *thysia* signaled membership in the body politic. But a citizen or indeed any resident of a *polis* could make the deeply personal decision to undergo an initiation ceremony and join a voluntary group dedicated to the worship of Demeter or Dionysus. These mystery rites, called *orgia,* supplemented the obligatory traditions of civic sacrifice to the Olympian gods; choosing to participate in the mystery cults of Demeter and Dionysus sent a different social and political message.

In the cultural context of fifth-century Athens, the term "mysteries" very often referred to one particular group of elective rites sacred to Demeter in Attica: the ancient *mystēria* of Eleusis. Those who chose to participate in this worship were initiated into the mysteries; an initiate into Demeter's elective rites was called a *mystēs.* Our sources make it clear that throughout the centuries, countless Greeks and foreigners came to Attica to be initiated into the mysteries of Demeter at Eleusis. By the time of Pericles and Socrates, anyone who spoke the Greek language and was not a murderer was allowed to participate in the annual mystic rites—"mystic" from *mystikos,* related to Demeter's *mystēria.* Although the Eleusinian rites were the most famous in Greek and Roman antiquity, Attica was not the only *polis* with mysteries sacred to Demeter, and voluntary associations sacred to other deities also inducted initiates into their ranks of worshippers. Mystic rites holy to Dionysus were celebrated throughout Hellas, and mysteries sacred to all the Olympians were also observed on the island of Samothrace.

The rites of Demeter and Dionysus remained influential throughout antiquity, far outliving Athens and its fifth-century empire. The popularity of the Greek-style mystery cults continued to grow steadily during the Hellenistic and Roman periods. At the height of Roman imperial dominance of the Mediterranean in the first and second centuries CE, mysteries were celebrated for other gods, too: non-Greek deities such as the Egyptian goddess Isis, the Anatolian goddess Cybele, and the semi-Persian god Mithras. Most instances of Greco-Roman "mystery religions" at their core resembled the famous Eleusinian mysteries of Demeter, and the later Hellenistic and Roman mystery rites were loosely patterned after the traditional Athenian rites of Demeter and Dionysus as celebrated in Attica in the fifth century. Personal experiences of mystery rites were so common in the first and second centuries CE that the earliest Greek-speaking authors of the Christian Gospels and New Testament letters chose to write about the "mysteries" of their own new movement when they addressed their audience of potential converts—Greek-speaking inhabitants in the eastern end of the Mediterranean basin.

The actual town of Eleusis lay 14 miles to the northwest of Athens. Today Eleusis is situated near oil refineries, industrial depots, and a concrete plant, but in the fifth century Eleusis was a small coastal town on the bay of Salamis near Attica's border with Megara, midway between the commercial centers of Athens and Corinth. The town had a small defensible hill or acropolis called the Akris, and in antiquity the town was built up along an elevated ridge just west of it. The fertile plain below the ridge and acropolis had been under cultivation for many centuries. The settlement of Eleusis had been walled, possibly in the Mycenaean period, and certainly it was well fortified after it became an Attic border town. Fortifications continued to be enlarged throughout antiquity. The sanctuary of

Demeter lay within the walls of Eleusis toward the base of the acropolis, and it occupied man-made terraces that hugged the eastern end of the Akris.

Eleusis had been an independent town in the more distant past of the eighth century before the *polis* of Attica was unified. By the seventh century, Attica had organized itself under the leadership of Athens and the town of Eleusis was absorbed into the larger *polis*. The Mysteries of Demeter were already taking place at this time in the small hillside sanctuary. The earliest secure archaeological record for a sanctuary at the site dates perhaps to the Geometric period of the eighth century; although some scholars maintain that the cult of Demeter was celebrated as early as the twelfth century, we have no clear evidence that any of the Mycenaean remains are related to the worship of Demeter. In the seventh and early sixth centuries the Mysteries were a largely local celebration of Demeter organized by two local priestly families, the Kerykes and the Eumolpidae. The earliest known temple was modest, to say the least: a walled shrine enclosing a courtyard and a small roofed temple building with an open portico across the front.

Once the town of Eleusis was absorbed into the *polis* of Attica, the Athenians strengthened the town's defenses and took control of the local cults, too. Although the details are not clear to modern scholars, Athenian leaders made the local Eleusinian rites of Demeter an official part of the civic calendar while keeping the local priesthoods intact in Eleusis. The earliest Athenian law code, the code of Solon from the early sixth century, mentions the role of the *boulē* in the oversight of the official civic cult of Eleusinian Demeter. Following the synoecism of Attica, the Athenians chose not to move the temple and the entire annual festival to Athens itself—after all, the myth recounted how Demeter had once visited the town of Eleusis and instructed the locals to build her temple there on the hillside. The residents of Athens instead did the next best thing: they established a sanctuary in Athens called the Eleusinion, and appointed Athenian priests and magistrates in the main city while Eleusinian priests remained in control at the shrine in Eleusis. Like the original precinct in Eleusis, the Athenian sanctuary of the Eleusinion was situated on a hillside—on the north shoulder of the Athenian Acropolis, between the Acropolis and the Agora.

After the Mysteries of Demeter became an official festival in the Athenian civic calendar, the Athenians needed to enlarge the temple and sanctuary in Eleusis to accommodate the increasing number of worshippers.

Starting in the seventh century we can trace the steady development of the sanctuary and the main temple, which came to be called the Telesterion, or Hall of Initiation. Their size was increased once in the seventh century, and twice in the sixth century. The tyrant Pisistratus took a strong interest in the cult, and he was responsible for a significant expansion of the Telesterion that required further enlargements of the man-made terrace, as well as the construction of new walls that surrounded the Telesterion, courtyards, and other buildings that came to be included in the sanctuary. Pisistratus also reoriented the main gate of the sanctuary, moving it from southeast (facing the sea) to the northeast, where it joined the Sacred Way—the road to Athens.

Twice more in the fifth century the *polis* undertook improvements at Eleusis; the first of these fifth-century renovations was never completed, though, since construction coincided with the Persian Wars and the Persian army broke through a section of the walls in 480. Once the Persians were defeated and had retreated from Attica, the Athenians returned to Eleusis to repair the walls and make them even taller and thicker. They also took this opportunity to move some of the defensive walls and extend the terraces in front of the ruined Telesterion. The financial pressures of rebuilding the city of Athens after the Persian invasions caused a delay in the reconstruction of the Telesterion, but the renovations were eventually completed. The final restoration was accomplished around 435 under the leadership of Pericles, at the very height of Athens' imperial aspirations.

The archaeological record indicates that in every period, the heart of the Eleusinian sanctuary remained a small building called the Anaktoron, probably the original roofed building in the earliest walled sanctuary. The Anaktoron was contained within the temple: each successive enlargement of the temple kept this one small room as its focal point. By the time the *polis* had finished the renovations under Pericles, the Eleusinian Telesterion was the largest roofed building in the Greek world. It was a square building (about 165 by 165 feet) with a modest exterior and a simple portico across the front looking out over a large courtyard to the east. The inside of the Telesterion was most unusual: at the very center in a wide and open space stood the smaller Anaktoron. Along all four interior walls of the Telesterion ascending rows of benches were built parallel to the walls, like bleachers in a gymnasium or rows of seats in a theater-in-the-round. The whole Telesterion was covered with a high roof; since Greek engineers had not yet figured out how to design structures using an arch or dome, the roof had to be supported by rows of pillars—forty-two in all.

Archaeologists who study this building have estimated that upwards of 8,000 people could have fit inside it. This Periclean Telesterion was never enlarged again, although additions were made to the sanctuary as late as the Roman era in the second and third centuries CE.

There are many things that modern scholars do not know about the actual celebration of the Eleusinian Mysteries. Because Eleusinian initiates were forbidden to talk about what they did, saw, or heard during the celebration of the mysteries, precisely what they experienced and learned while inside the Telesterion and the Anaktoron remains secret. Some scholars have linked the nouns *myēsis* (initiation) and *mystēria* (the mysteries) with the verb *myein,* "to close" the mouth or eyes. Initiates who didn't keep their mouths properly shut might disclose the secrets of the holy rites. Those who did disclose the secrets could be charged with impiety, *asebeia,* and prosecuted in court. Some ancient sources record that famous figures from the fifth century, among them the philosopher Diagoras of Melos and the Athenian playwright Aeschylus, defended themselves on impiety charges after being accused of revealing the mysteries to the uninitiated.

Although the written records from ancient Athens do not document the proceedings at Eleusis, scholars can establish some facts about the fifth-century Eleusinian Mysteries by analyzing the archaeological record: the plan of the sanctuary, inscriptions, and iconographic evidence from sculpture and vase painting. We know, for instance, that the festival was held in the early autumn, in the middle of the month of Boedromion about a month before the Thesmophoria was celebrated in Athens. The Mysteries lasted an unusually long time for a Greek festival: a full seven days, from the 15th to the 21st of Boedromion. We also know that men, women, slaves, and foreigners were initiated together in the Telesterion, making the cult's tradition unusually egalitarian.

Before the seven-day festival of the Mysteries began in Boedromion, other preliminary rituals prepared initiates for the festival. Individuals who intended to be initiated at the Eleusinian Telesterion in the fall were required to take part in rites called the Lesser Mysteries in the late spring. The Lesser Mysteries seem to have involved some sort of ritual of purification, but we know little about them. At the collective level there were also important civic preparations in Athens and abroad: *spondophoroi,* representatives from the priestly Eleusinian families of the Eumolpidae and the Kerykes, traveled as diplomats to Greek cities throughout the Mediterranean to invite all people to take part in the rites and to announce the sacred truce (*spondai*) that went into effect for the festival. This sacred truce lasted nearly two months—enough time for men and women from all over Hellas to safely travel to Eleusis and back home again. By tradition the sacred truce also marked the cessation of any ongoing military campaigns.

The number of people who chose to attend the Eleusinian Mysteries in any given year was substantial. Herodotus, for instance, reports 30,000, but his numbers are often grossly inflated. According to ancestral tradition, a person had to attend the Eleusinian Mysteries only once during his or her lifetime to receive the full benefit of Demeter's blessing. But we know that some people did go more than once. Each initiate or *mystēs* was escorted on the journey to Eleusis by an experienced guide called a *mystagōgos*, or mystagogue. A mystagogue was someone who had already been initiated at least once before, and she or he would remain with the new initiate to explain and guide him or her through all the rituals. Also taking part in the Mysteries were initiates who had attended at least once before and were going again as *epoptai*, or "watchers," who would be initiated into the higher level of the Mysteries. The crowd had to have been quite large, composed as it was of first-time initiates, their mystagogue escorts, and finally the *epoptai* and any others who chose for their own personal reasons to attend again.

Because Athens and Eleusis were located at a distance from each other and because the priests involved were in both towns, the Athenian civic festival of the Eleusinian Mysteries entailed a certain amount of traveling back and forth across the countryside of Attica. Before the official start of the festival, a civic procession wended its way from Eleusis to Athens on the 14th of Boedromion. A group of ephebes, the Athenian young men training in the military, was selected to ride on horseback alongside a wagon that brought the priests and priestesses of Demeter to Athens. Sacred cult objects that normally resided in Eleusis, presumably in the Anaktoron, had to be transferred to Athens for the start of the festival, and it was the responsibility of Eleusinian priestesses to carry special baskets called *kistai* that contained the sacred objects to the Eleusinion in the center of Athens. The ephebes kept everyone and everything safe. Once the procession reached the walls of the Eleusinion in Athens, the officials from Eleusis were welcomed by the local Athenian civic-religious officials. A sacred messenger was dispatched from the Eleusinion to the Acropolis, where he informed the priestess of Athena that the priests and priestesses of Demeter had arrived. In this way Eleusinian Demeter was welcomed into the city of Athena.

The festival officially began on the 15th of Boedromion, the day of the month that marked the full moon (every month in the Athenian calendar began with the new moon). The extra light provided by the moon must have made possible festive public celebrations that extended into the warm autumn nights. This day when all the participants convened in Athens was called the day of Gathering. The *archōn basileus,* the Athenian civic official responsible for all matters of cult and worship, accompanied the Eleusinian officials to the Painted Stoa in the Agora. There the Eleusinian sacred herald made the official proclamation inviting people to take part in the Mysteries. Eligibility was taken seriously, but the criteria were not demanding: to take part in the initiations you had to be able to understand Greek, and you had to have pure hands—that is, be free from the taint of murder. Perhaps initiates registered on this day, and paid the required fee that went to the various priests and covered the purchase of sacrificial animals. In the fifth century the fee was 15 drachmas, which amounted to about fifteen days' wages for the average laborer or craftsman. This fee was high in comparison to other civic festivals, but the Eleusinian initiation was a voluntary association and not a festival required of all citizens. And, as noted above, initiates needed to go only once during their lifetime to achieve the desired benefit.

Because being initiated into Demeter's Mysteries was considered an unusually sacred event, initiates were required to undergo special rituals of purification, and they took care of these on the next several days of the festival. The 16th was called Elasis, the day of the "drive" or the "ride." Each initiate was given a piglet, and together the initiates took their piglets on a ritual outing to the ocean. Ancestral tradition required initiates to purify themselves and their sacrificial victims in the sea. Athens was of course not far from the Aegean, and initiates walked or rode in carriages and wagons to one of several beaches located near Athens—usually to the Bay of Phaleron, south of the city. This had to have been a day of fun and merrymaking as thousands of men and women purified themselves and their piglets at the ocean. Special officials were assigned the task of directing traffic, which on this day would fill the roads between Athens and the coast beyond capacity. After the purification rituals the initiates and their escorts returned to the city, where they sacrificed their piglets and dined on a meal of tender roast pork.

The 17th was likewise a day of purification and preparation, but on the collective rather than the individual level. Back in Athens the state priests and officials met with the official foreign delegations, and they made the great civic sacrifice at the altar of Demeter and Kore in the Eleusinion. The *archōn basileus* also prayed for the *boulē* and the *dēmos* of Athens on this day. The 18th was one final quiet day of preparation called both the Asclepieia and the Epidauria. Initiates were required to remain at home; this was an unusual restriction in a city like Athens where most of one's civic and religious life was lived out of doors in public and in the company of other citizens. Meanwhile in the Eleusinion the eponymous archon and other civic officials made the last-minute arrangements for any latecomers to the festival. The day was named in honor of the god Asclepius, who, according to myth, came to Athens to be initiated into the Mysteries but arrived a few days after all the preliminary purification ceremonies had taken place. This myth of the tardy Asclepius actually masks a more complicated political situation that emerged during the Peloponnesian War. In 420/19, immediately after Nicias had negotiated a truce with Sparta, Athens strengthened its political and religious relationship with Epidaurus by officially importing the cult of the healing god Asclepius. The god's arrival in the city happened in Boedromion just as the celebrations of the Mysteries were starting in Athens. The tragic poet Sophocles was said to have played a public role in welcoming the new god to Athens, and Asclepius's cult was temporarily housed in the city Eleusinion until a more permanent sanctuary could be built. By connecting the new god from Epidaurus with the Demeter festival that was being observed, Athenians could assign to Demeter the same sort of protective role that Athens imagined for itself as it managed its empire and alliances.

Finally, on the 19th of Boedromion there was the grand *pompē*, the religious procession of all the participants with their wagons and pack animals. The entire body of priests, magistrates, foreign delegations, ephebes, *epoptai,* first-time initiates, and their mystagogue escorts assembled in Athens at the Sacred Gate in the Kerameikos district. Hundreds and hundreds of initiates, many of them crowned with myrtle or carrying branches and staffs bound with myrtle, walked and rode along the Sacred Way out of the city and into the countryside of Attica. Again the ephebes protected the Athenian and Eleusinian officials as they rode along; priestesses again accompanied the sacred cult objects borne in the *kistai* baskets. The 14-mile journey took them through rolling farmlands, along the foot of the local mountains, and finally along the sea to Eleusis. The entire procession moved slowly uphill over the first half of the journey to the pass where the monastery of Daphni stands today, and from there down onto the fertile Thriasian plain. It reached Eleusis in the evening, and stopped at a public courtyard outside the sanctuary walls at the end of the Sacred Way. In this broad open area stood civic altars sacred to all the gods of Athens, and a well said to be the one by which Demeter sat when she first reached Eleusis disguised as the old women Doso.

A gate in the walls of the Eleusinian sanctuary separated the public space with the civic altars and a well on the outside from the space sacred to Demeter on the inside. Only initiates were allowed through the gates and into the interior courtyards and spaces that surrounded the Telesterion. After the procession arrived in the evening the party atmosphere continued, with singing and dancing by torchlight under the moon. Those who had procured lodging in the area settled in, while the rest of the crowd pitched camps in the area outside the walls of the sanctuary. The party undoubtedly lasted long into the night under the bright waning moon.

During the day of the 20th of Boedromion, participants rested after their long walk and their arrival celebrations, and they may well have fasted or observed at least a partial fast. The initiates undoubtedly took it easy, if rest was possible in their state of excitement and anticipation, for the main initiation happened after sunset and the revelation of the Mysteries of Demeter went late into the night. Come evening, when the torches had been lit, the mystagogues led the way and escorted the initiates through the gates of the sanctuary and into the Telesterion. The *epoptai* (watchers) entered, too, and once inside the great Telesterion the Mysteries unfolded.

What exactly happened during the night of the Mysteries has remained for centuries precisely that: one of the great mysteries of antiquity. Scholars can glean hints here and there from the sources, but for much they must rely on conjecture and speculation. For instance, we know that the content of the Mysteries was imparted in three different ways: there were "things done," "things said," and "things shown." The head priest from the family of the Eumolpidae was called the hierophant, or "the one who reveals the sacred things." He was perhaps seated on a throne situated next to the door to the Anaktoron, where the most sacred objects were likely stored. Some scholars have even proposed that the hierophant was seated on top of the Anaktoron, which could have served as a sort of stage. Other priests and priestesses must have helped him during the course of the evening. One child initiate was honored each year as the "child at the hearth," perhaps a symbolic substitute for Demophoön at Eleusis, or perhaps a representative of the rite that took place at the public hearth in the Prytaneion in Athens. The Telesterion itself is a unique building, and it certainly was designed (and enlarged over the years) to allow all worshippers to watch what was happening at the center of the massive room. At the very climax of the Mysteries there was said to have been a great flash of blinding light.

Another known bit of information about the rites in the Telesterion is that early in the evening worshippers drank a special drink called the *kykeōn*, a thick concoction made of water, meal, mint, and other herbs. A few scholars have speculated that the meal used in the drink might have been tainted with ergot, a fungus that grows naturally on stored cereal products that become damp. Ergot can be fatal when ingested in large doses, but in small doses it can facilitate mild hallucinogenic experiences. No direct evidence proves that *epoptai* and initiates did consume ergot or other drugs, but scholars have not entirely ruled out that possibility.

Scholars can be sure of other facts, too, when they study the Eleusinian Mysteries. The Mysteries were first and foremost sacred to Demeter. Perhaps the initiates felt that they experienced the same things that Demeter went through when she first lost and then was reunited with her daughter. If we assume that some motifs present in the myth and the *Homeric Hymn to Demeter* somehow corresponded to the initiation rite, then myth and mystery together reveal an ancient Greek foundational narrative for a human being's experience of the divine. Demeter was at one time living among the other divinities, but then separated herself from them after Death, or the god Hades, forcibly took her daughter Kore away to live with him in the underworld. She nursed the child Demophoön, perhaps represented in cult by the child initiate "at the hearth." The divine mother became enraged, and then she mourned, but in the end she rejoined her beloved daughter. Kore accepted her dual role as the maiden daughter of Demeter and the wife of Hades. Some have speculated that the Mysteries included a ritual of sacred marriage (*hieros gamos*) between Kore and the god of death. The myth, the *Hymn*, and the rites all illustrate a human journey of separation from and eventual reunion with the divine, as Demeter and Kore are reunited with each other and with the deities on Mount Olympus after Persephone's return from the underworld. To commemorate the reunion with her daughter, Demeter taught Triptolemus and the humans at Eleusis how to sow crops, as well as how to celebrate her Mysteries. Knowledge of these mystic rites could give solace to humans as they worshipped the Two, gave thanks for the gifts of Demeter, and accepted their own mortality and eventual union with Hades and the divine. Completing the Mysteries made initiates blessed.

A broad range of the female experience was represented in the mythology surrounding Demeter and Kore: girls, young brides, spirited mothers, and older nurses all figured prominently in the narrative. The full spectrum of social status was also present in the myth, from the lowest (homeless slave and foreign servant) to the highest (queen and goddess). Gendered power relationships are evident, and clearly inverted: the female takes the leading role both in the household and in the cosmos. Aristotle wrote that initiates went to Eleusis not in order to learn something, as if memorizing facts or the words to a song, but to experience something personally (Aristotle fr. 15). His observation suggests that the Mysteries of Demeter were akin to drama; initiates witnessed the story of the mother Demeter and experienced the suffering of Demeter and Kore within the walled sanctuary and the Telesterion. And whatever the sequence of things they witnessed, suffered, and experienced, testimony from the ancient world documents the feeling of joy and happiness of the initiates as they left Eleusis. For centuries the Greeks and Romans were forbidden to reveal the actual content of the Mysteries themselves, but they did write about the personal effect that the celebration of the Mysteries had on them. They uniformly reported that the Eleusinian Mysteries taught them something that removed their dread of death.

The festival of the Mysteries officially ended the day after the revelation in the Telesterion, and the final celebrations returned to the public courtyard outside the gates of the sanctuary. There were civic sacrifices of bulls, as well as general celebratory feasting, drinking, and dancing. Special vessels called *plēmochoai* were used to make libations and offerings for the dead. Initiates repeated a ritual formula while spilling the contents of the *plēmochoai* to the earth, first facing east and then facing west. After these last celebrations ended there was no organized procession back to Athens; the initiates simply disbanded their temporary community, and each went her or his own way. The sacred objects remained safe for another year in the Anaktoron, Eleusinian officials remained in Eleusis, and Athenian officials went back to Athens. The 24th of Boedromion was reserved in Athens for an official report made by a ritual oversight committee which reported back to the *boulē* on the conduct of that year's civic festival of Eleusinian Demeter. This final report was issued in accordance with an ancient law of Solon.

DEMETER IN THE EMPIRE: THE FIRST FRUITS OFFERING

The myth found in the *Homeric Hymn to Demeter* and likely celebrated at Eleusis was common to all Greeks, but during the late sixth and early fifth century Athenians refashioned the tradition about the Eleusinian noble-man Triptolemus to emphasize the cultural importance of Athens and Eleusis. The myth about Demeter at Eleusis came to fill significant politi-cal functions; in the new telling, Demeter not only taught the Eleusinians her mystery rites but also taught Triptolemus the basics about the cultiva-tion of grain. Triptolemus then set off from Eleusis in a winged carriage to visit all the cities of Hellas, teaching Demeter's art of cultivation as he traveled. In Attic art from the mid-sixth century onward, Triptolemus is often depicted in this flying carriage. The new Athenian variant of the myth created in Triptolemus humankind's first cereal farmer; he became one of the principal heroes of Greek culture, and he was from Eleusis. Since Eleusis by the sixth century been had absorbed into the *polis* of Athens, Athens could be seen as the seat of all human civilization. It was an ancestor of the Athenians who had bestowed upon all Greeks this es-sential knowledge. Under the Pisistratid tyrants in the sixth century, the Athenians even built a small temple for Triptolemus in the city Eleusinion on the north slope of the Acropolis.

During the period of the Athenian empire in the fifth century, the Athenian *dēmos* exploited the details of the refashioned myth, and then used the myth to shape rituals that suited its ideological position as the leader of a Hellenic empire. A decree passed by the Athenian *dēmos* prob-ably in the late 420s (Fornara 140) and preserved in an inscription known as the First Fruits Decree mandated that all cities subject to the Athenian empire bring annual tribute in honor of Demeter. The tribute of grain was to be presented at a festival in Eleusis—possibly at the Proerosia, a pre-plowing festival celebrated shortly after the Eleusinian Mysteries. Cities not subject to the empire were likewise strongly urged to bring their portions in honor of the goddess who provided the gift of grain to hu-mankind. Just as the Athenians annually dedicated to Athena a portion of the tribute that their subject-allies had paid them, so too we have evidence that allies paid an annual tribute to Demeter at Eleusis. The annual tax came in the form of a tithe of barley and wheat.

When the Eleusinian religious officials called *spondophoroi* traveled around Greece to announce the sacred truce, they also asked each city to send a delegation of officials to celebrate Demeter with their own first fruits, or *aparchai*. Offering the initial portion of an agricultural harvest or animal sacrifice—an *aparchē*—was among the most ancient of ancestral customs commonly observed throughout Greece. With this gift humans honored the gods first before they enjoyed the harvest themselves. The Eleusinian

First Fruits Decree implied that it had been a long-standing ancestral custom for communities in Attica to honor Demeter with first fruits offerings at Eleusis; after the synoecism of Attica, each deme annually brought its *aparchai* and dedicated them to the goddess. But the reality of empire changed the ritual practice, and what had been proper for demes now became required for subject-allies. This same inscription also stipulated the precise type of animal sacrifice that should accompany the annual first fruits offerings in Eleusis: after the *pelanos* offering (a cake made from the choicest wheat and barley), the priests of Eleusis were to offer three bulls with gilt horns to the Eleusinian trio of Demeter, Kore, and Triptolemus; Athena too, the patroness of the empire, received a bull. With so many animals sacrificed, those present must have dined on a grand feast.

The sum of money that Athens realized from Demeter's *aparchai* at Eleusis could not have been trivial. The inscription required the *polis* to construct great storage pits at Eleusis to receive the grain contributions, which, once collected, were sent by Eleusinian priestly officials to Athens, where it was sold. Funds from the sale were stored in Demeter's treasury in Athens. It appears that Eleusinian civic officials maintained control over these funds, and kept treasuries both in Eleusis and in Athens. Related inscriptions concerning the finances of Eleusis and Athens that are dated to later in the fifth century show how the *polis* took out loans from Demeter's treasury in an effort to finance the Peloponnesian War. These loans drew directly from the wealth of the subject-allies. The First Fruits Decree reveals how Athens justified its hegemony over its allies, and even tried to extend it over other states. While the Athenians claimed that they had selflessly passed on the gifts of the goddess Demeter to the rest of humankind, the allies knew that it was their tribute that helped fund the war and kept the Athenian empire strong.

DEMETER'S POWER IN ATHENIAN RELIGION

The Eleusinian Mysteries, with their complex history as a local celebration incorporated into the official *polis* calendar of Athens, present illuminating contrasts to the obligatory practices of Athenian civic cult as observed in the Agora and on the Acropolis. Priests and public officials performed civic sacrificial rites at Eleusis, just as they did at the civic festivals that regularly took place in the urban center in Athens. But contrary to the customs of *polis* animal sacrifice, at the Mysteries it was not priests and magistrates alone who communicated with the divine at the altar on behalf of the group. Animal sacrifices officiated by priests were part of this festival of Demeter, but apparently played no role in the central ritual in the Telesterion that revealed Demeter's mysteries. In fact the altars where public sacrifice took place were located in courtyards outside the sacred precinct at Eleusis. In place of the communal rituals of civic sacrifice stood a different experience of the gods inside the Telesterion. Each individual among the initiates—female and male, foreign and Greek, slave and free—dedicated piglets to Demeter, watched the sacred drama, and obtained knowledge of the divine directly through the power of his or her own senses. While admission to the Eleusinian Mysteries came at some cost, ancient sources show over and over again that women and slaves regularly attended alongside citizen men. Its breadth of participants makes the Mysteries the most inclusive and egalitarian of Athenian religious institutions. The Eleusinian Mysteries, a traditional ritual practice existing alongside other *polis* sacrifices and rites, allowed men and women alike to experience a type of communication between divinity and humanity that the traditional civic cult of *thysia* could not match.

The Eleusinian rites were also unusual in the full system of Athenian polytheism because their focus remained fixed on the experience of the female, in this case a divine mother and her daughter as the young woman comes of age and marries, maintaining a relationship with her mother all the while. Unlike the civic festivals of the powerful duo of Zeus and Athena, which ensured social stability and the fixed political hierarchy within the *polis,* the mystery rites of Demeter had the ability to balance tensions in Athenian society that were not easily reconciled. The symbolic power of Demeter emerged at the intersection of the very categories whose creation was deemed necessary for the proper functioning of a stable civic society: the socially defined norms that separated male from female, citizen from noncitizen, and Greek from foreigner. The worship of Demeter looked beyond the importance of conventional hierarchical political values to celebrate native and foreign elements, free and slave members of society, male and female experiences. The privileged social status of the adult citizen male so evident in the Greek rites of *thysia* mattered little in the ancestral practices sacred to Demeter and her daughter.

In this way the Eleusinian Mysteries resembled the female-only rites of the Thesmophoria. Some scholars have suggested that the mystery rites at Eleusis started off as a local Thesmophoria ritual. At a time when Eleusis was still an independent entity, the men of Eleusis were apparently welcomed at the rites that their wives celebrated, and they too learned the lesson taught by Demeter and Persephone. Following the synoecism of Attica the rites of Eleusinian Demeter were made available to all residents of Attica. With the unification of Athens the festival grew bigger than ever. In the sixth century the Pisistratids enlarged the Eleusinian sanctuary and oriented it toward Athens, and in Athens they constructed the first temple in the city Eleusinion. The Eleusinion in Athens linked the city to the border town by requiring priests and rites in both places, and rituals reinforced the connections between the two locales. The construction of a truly monumental building under Pericles opened up the Mysteries to Greeks from far beyond Athens. At the same time, Athenians required subject-allies in the empire to contribute first fruits to the goddess of Eleusis, and with their contributions acknowledge the self-proclaimed cultural superiority of Athens.

Yet while Demeter's festivals in Attica reflected the political changes in democracy and empire in the fifth century, the people who actually worshipped Demeter perhaps felt less concern for the *polis* than for their own personal well-being. The citizen wives at the Thesmophoria celebrated the fertility of the earth that nurtured everyone, and the people from all walks of life who traveled to Eleusis in the autumn stood side by side to receive blessings from the goddess who could change their understanding of death. In the fourth century, Plato used Eleusinian language and imagery in some of his dialogues as a metaphor to describe the soul's experience of transcendent reality. There was something uniquely powerful about Demeter's secret, nocturnal rites. Although the Mysteries developed alongside the civic religion of the *polis* in the seventh, sixth, and fifth centuries, they actually survived the decline of the *polis* in the fourth century. The sanctuary at Eleusis remained a center of cult activity for more than 800 years after the fall of Athens in 404. It even endured the rapid growth of Christianity in the eastern half of the Roman Empire until its destruction by rampaging Visigoths in 396 CE. The rites themselves remain a mystery, but the power that Demeter offered her worshippers left many traces in history. In the late fifth century the lure of this power even altered the course of the Peloponnesian War, when politics and the observance of ancestral cult again captured the attention of the Athenians.

FIVE

Alcibiades

Politics, Religion, and the Cult of Personality

THUCYDIDES' LAST REPORTED SPEECH OF Pericles in book 2 depicts the
dynamic Athenian leader encouraging the people of Athens to be patient
and maintain their naval empire. Above all Pericles warned against expanding the empire while at war. This plan might well have worked, had
the Athenians stuck to it. But Thucydides' narrative clearly states that after Pericles' death the Athenians did just the opposite: eventually private
ambition and the desire for honor and wealth won out over the interests of
the city. When Alcibiades, a member of Pericles' extended family, took a
leading role in Athenian affairs, his regard for ancestral religious customs
brought him both blame and praise. Civic rites—both the rituals of democracy celebrated in the open and the more secretive traditions surrounding Demeter, goddess of grain—continued to be celebrated in the *polis,*
and under Alcibiades their observance had a decisive impact on the lives of
all Athenians.

MAINTAINING THE EMPIRE AFTER THE PLAGUE

The loss of so many civilian lives within the city of Athens at the start of
the war was something nobody could have predicted, not even Pericles.
Athenian allies, subjects, and rivals all took note. Several attempted revolts
from the empire in *poleis* to the north followed the outbreak of the plague,

and in 428 a major rebellion arose in the eastern Aegean. The large island of Lesbos off the coast of Ionia contained several *poleis* that had long desired to combine forces and free themselves from the Athenian *archē*. Mytilene, the main city of Lesbos and leader of the uprising, was negotiating for aid from Sparta and Boeotia. The revolt that unfolded shows just how relentless the Athenians' response could be, and it anticipated some of the uglier chapters of the war soon to come.

Thucydides' narrative of the Mytilene episode reveals how *poleis* other than Athens also worked within civic calendars of religious festivals to support residents and plan for a city's defense. The Athenians realized that Mytilene was determined to revolt, and so they sent forty ships. When the citizens of Mytilene realized that they were not fully prepared for a revolt they canceled their annual festival to Apollo in the Apple Country (Apollo Malea) so that they could complete repairs to the city's fortifications (Thucydides 3.3). Soon afterward the Mytileneans were invited to send ambassadors along with athletes to the Olympic games in the Peloponnese. The renowned panhellenic festival that celebrated the physical strength and skill of young athletes also set aside time for the leaders of Hellenic *poleis* to consider political affairs. During this festival of Zeus in 428, Sparta and its allies heard the Mytileneans' case for war—ironically, while they met together under a truce. The negotiations between Lesbos and Sparta at the festival of Zeus were initially successful: the Spartans agreed to gather their allies and invade Attica directly by land and sea. This action would force the Athenians to fight major campaigns on two fronts: both at home in Attica and on Lesbos.

As hard-pressed as the Athenians were after the plague, they still put together a firm response to the Spartan plans and manned 100 additional ships by calling on available citizens and metics. These ships and men sailed south to the Peloponnese and plundered the countryside near Sparta while the navy handled the situation on Lesbos as it did most revolts: it laid siege to Mytilene. This unexpected show of Athenian strength surprised the Spartans, who then abandoned their campaign in Attica to defend the Peloponnese. They did send a few token ships to Lesbos in belated support of the uprising. Meanwhile the heavy expenditures of the war's first years and the cost of besieging Mytilene forced Athens to levy a stiff new property tax on its own citizens. It was the first time the previously tribute-rich Athenians had been compelled to take such measures.

With Mytilene blockaded and with the promised Spartan aid arriving too late, the revolt on Lesbos soon faltered. Now the *dēmos* back in Athens discussed how best to respond to the revolt. Many Athenians grew alarmed to see once-trusted allies turning to Sparta for aid, and their thoughts turned to punishment. Though the course of the war had pushed Greeks to treat each other inhumanely and even brutally, harsh treatment was usually reserved for opponents on the battlefield. But now in lengthy and impassioned meetings of the Assembly the *dēmos* did something it had never done before: it voted to punish its rebellious allies in Mytilene by putting to death all the citizens and enslaving all the women and children. A trireme was dispatched to Lesbos with the grim news.

The very next morning the Athenian *dēmos* had second thoughts, and public debate was resumed. It was the rising politician Cleon who continued to support the harsh measures, arguing that a uniformly severe punishment would deter other subject-allies from revolting and leaving the empire. In a close vote it was decided that the sweeping destruction of an entire city was too cruel: the *dēmos* voted to rescind the initial order. A second trireme carrying the new decree was sent off a full day and a half after the first, and the rowers were offered rich rewards if they arrived in time. Thucydides reports that the men ate while rowing and took turns sleeping; they managed to reach Mytilene just as the fatal decree was being read—but before it had been enacted. In this way the people of Lesbos were spared such a harsh fate, although 1,000 men said to be responsible for the revolt were executed. Thereafter the autonomy of Mytilene was severely limited: the Athenians tore down the city's walls, disbanded its navy, and redistributed the land on Lesbos. Ten percent of the land was set aside for the gods, and the remainder allotted to Athenian citizens who served as landlords charged with leasing the land back to the natives. In the future, other allies who revolted from the Athenian *archē* would not be so fortunate.

Beyond the crisis with Mytilene and Sparta, the devastation of the plague had another immediate effect on the fortunes of the Athenians. The unexpected death of Pericles, the main architect of the war's strategy, left Athens without its accustomed general and trusted counselor. The leadership vacuum in Athens produced no immediate heir to Pericles, and during the next eight years the *dēmos* followed several men. Among these were the impulsive Cleon—the speaker who had advocated the harshest penalty for the Mytileneans—and an older and more cautious aristocrat by the name of Nicias.

No two Athenian politicians could have been more dissimilar: Cleon was a rash and energetic man whose family had apparently achieved new wealth in the boom years of manufacturing in Athens and Piraeus. His rise to prominence in the *polis* was fueled by his persuasive speaking abilities at public forums and not by any prior experience in state office. He was among the first of a new generation of leaders sometimes called demagogues, literally "leaders of the *dēmos*." His unwavering support for the empire led to increases in tribute paid by the allies, while his domestic initiatives appealed to many in the *dēmos,* especially after he successfully advocated for an increase in the daily pay for jury service. Nicias, on the other hand, had less interest in expanding the empire than in reaching favorable terms for a viable peace between Athens and Sparta. His military experience and cautious competence on the battlefield resulted in numerous elections to the office of *stratēgos.* An extremely wealthy and moderate aristocrat, Nicias was widely respected for living by the highest standards of public service and old-fashioned *aretē* (virtue), and for his observance of traditional ritual practices. But Nicias shared with Cimon one important trait: both used their considerable wealth to sponsor civic feasts, dramatic and athletic festivals, and other forms of public service for the Athenian *dēmos.*

Nicias's leadership following the crisis with Mytilene and Sparta highlights the place that observing traditional cult practices played in his public career. The winter of 427/6 saw a second resurgence of the plague, when rampant death and illness again tore through Athens. Perhaps taking a cue from the opening of Homer's *Iliad* (where Greek military leaders appeased Apollo after he let loose a plague to punish them for insulting one of his priests), or perhaps following the advice of an oracle, the Athenians determined that they had inadvertently offended Apollo at his sanctuary on the island of Delos, the original seat of their naval alliance. If the god was angered, there was only one remedy: purification of the sanctuary (Thucydides 3.104). Athens had a history of involvement at the sanctuary of Delos independent of the Delian League. During a period of building and development at the Ionian festival spot in the sixth century, Pisistratus had purified the sanctuary by moving any graves that were within sight of Apollo's temple on Delos. Now the Athenians purified the island again, this time by transferring all the graves they could find on Delos to the neighboring island of Rheneia. They then decreed that no one might pollute the island sacred to the god of prophecy by either dying or giving birth there. Our sources do not indicate precisely who it was who oversaw and administered the repurification of Delos, but certainly Nicias represented the kind of pious citizen leader who would have supported a policy like this.

What lay behind this plan to repurify Delos is less a theology of belief grounded in empty superstition than a common commitment to maintaining the powerful separateness of certain places. Sites historically frequented by Greeks from different *poleis* had deep connections to a shared past and shared *patrioi nomoi*. By sacrificing and celebrating in these joint sanctuaries, Greeks maintained that connection to the past. Piety and proper worship of the gods required collaboration and communication among human communities in the present; maintaining these patterns of cooperation that culminated in a shared feast afterward ensured the common good for the future.

One ancient idea shared by all Greeks was the notion of *miasma,* or ritual pollution. The repurification of Delos illustrates the workings of *miasma* in two separate but related areas. First, traditional rites of *thysia* included commonly observed rituals aimed at containing the blood spilled in animal sacrifice: blood properly handled by priests according to ancestral custom facilitated worship and communication between human and the divine, but improperly handled blood became polluted—a source of *miasma* and contagion for all who came in contact with it.

But there were additional sources of *miasma* beyond the blood of sacrifice, and these included the natural and very human phenomena of birth and death. These essential life-cycle events changed and indeed defined human society in powerful and fundamental ways. Death especially, the loss that immortal gods by definition could not experience, created disruption and temporary disorder in society. Sexual activity did so too, though to a lesser extent, and therefore the customary precautions against *miasma* created by sexual activity were not as strict. The psychological anxiety that arose in critical moments of birth and death were translated into action, namely the rituals surrounding *miasma* that required humans to control blood, the stuff of life. Since the gods represented order in the cosmos, human society had the responsibility to contain whatever might potentially disturb that order; from this emerged rituals of avoiding pollution, clearly illustrated by birth and death rituals, as well as by rituals of *thysia.*

At the shared sanctuary on Delos, Ionians worshipped the immortal god Apollo by performing rites of *thysia* and celebrating feasts afterward. The Ionians' tradition of worshipping Apollo at the common festival site articulated the group's commitment to respect each other and their common past; repurifying the island of Delos and the sanctuary of Apollo constituted an action that again demonstrated the Delian League's respect for the pan-Ionian deity Apollo, and by extension for shared ancestral *nomoi.*

Although we don't know the exact role Nicias played in the repurification of Delos in 426, one source does describe him leading a grand sacrificial procession to Apollo's shrine there at the dedication of a new temple a few years later in 417. This traditional—and perhaps even unspoken—notion that a *polis* and its leaders were responsible for maintaining the proper alignment of divine and human was the sort of thing that many Athenians probably respected in Nicias.

Nicias's respect for the *nomoi* and the Athenians' decision to purify Delos represent one response of the Athenians to the stress and devastation of plague. The leadership of Cleon during the debate over Mytilene shows another, very different reaction. While the actions of Nicias confirmed common Ionian worship and the foundational traditions of the *polis,* both of which channeled anxiety through civic rituals that controlled *miasma,* Cleon's rhetoric of empire and superiority pushed for the harsh treatment of subject-allies. This extreme stance had some historical precedent within the Delian League, and, as Thucydides tells us, both Spartans and Athenians would regularly continue to abuse their enemies during wartime.

Thucydides' account of the war and the compelling personalities behind it is famous for its subtle understanding of human motives and psychology. In extreme circumstances men can make horrific decisions: torture of prisoners, wholesale extermination of entire communities, and even cannibalism all make their appearance in Thucydides' account of the conflict between Athens and Sparta. For him human nature was constant and predictable: when circumstances allow for it, mortal men will try to exercise power over others, and then increase this power when they can. At the same time the pursuit of power can become oppressive, and when this happens the driving need to maintain power leads to collapse. In essence, the Thucydidean view of power replays the ancient pattern of the Succession Myth in which divine sons are destined to drive their oppressive fathers from power before becoming oppressive themselves and succumbing to their own sons. It also echoes Herodotus's theory of human *hubris* and divine retribution, although Thucydides might well not admit that he saw any continuity between himself and the other historian, who wrote openly about the impact of the gods in human affairs. Throughout the eight books of his history, Thucydides avoids attributing human behavior to direct or even indirect influence of the gods, though he does consistently acknowledge the role that religious festivals played in the course of the war. For Thucydides men are motivated by fear, honor, and self-interest; patterns of piety (and impiety, as the case may be) in the traditional worship of the gods do not function independently of the human desire for power.

Thucydides' articulation of Cleon's position in the Mytilene debate supplies ample evidence for how the Athenians' will to power and *archē* was moving them away from their ancestral *nomoi* and customs that established how others should be treated during wartime. Another example of the gradual departure from traditional *nomoi* of conventional warfare became evident in 424 with the Athenian invasion of Boeotia, immediately to the north of Attica and now an important Spartan ally. There was factional strife within Boeotia itself—some citizens supported Athens and others Sparta—and Athens formed a complex plan that took advantage of the Boeotian civil conflict. As part of the strategy to compel Boeotian cities to adopt Athenian-style democracies and join the Delian League, a significant contingent of Athenian hoplites and metics occupied and fortified a Boeotian temple of Apollo located at Delion. The Athenians adopted this strategy even though forcibly taking possession of a god's sanctuary and transforming it into a military fort violated shared Greek *nomoi* about activities appropriate on sacred ground within any *polis* (Thucydides 4.92). In the end the Athenians botched the coordinated timing of the offensive. Boeotian and Theban forces allied with Sparta dealt the Athenian hoplites a crushing blow at Delion, and this battle lived on vividly in Greek historical consciousness—not least of all because Socrates fought there and would later speak of the desperate struggle that almost cost him his life as he fled Apollo's sanctuary (Thucydides 4.76–77, 89–101; Plato *Symposium* 220b, *Apology* 28e, *Laches* 181b).

At the same time that the Athenians were struggling at Delion, they were also fighting important battles further to the north in coastal Macedonia and Thrace. The Spartan army under the commander Brasidas adopted a policy of supporting cities in that region that wished to revolt from the Athenian *archē*. In 424 Brasidas took control of Amphipolis, an important city in the Delian League that commanded access to trade, timber, and mines (Thucydides 4.102–7). Over the next few years the Athenians fought hard to regain the strategic city. While they never succeeded, the extended campaign on the northern edges of the Athenian empire did see a good deal of dramatic action. For failing to save the city when Brasidas and the Spartans attacked it, one respected Athenian naval general who served at Amphipolis was sentenced to twenty years of exile—namely, Thucydides the historian (Thucydides 4.104, 5.26). The twenty years Thucydides spent in exile allowed him to travel freely, and he recorded the events of war sometimes while living among the Peloponnesians.

Following the fall of Amphipolis, Scione, another Athenian subject-ally in Thrace, welcomed the Spartan general Brasidas. They honored him as a heroic liberator and crowned him with a victor's golden crown at public expense (Thucydides 4.121). The Athenian *dēmos,* urged on by Cleon, voted to recapture the city—and kill all the adult male citizens and enslave the women and children. It took more than a year for a naval blockade to fully reduce Scione, but this time the Athenians had no second thoughts. They were successful. The men were killed, and the women and children enslaved. The land was turned over to settlers from Plataea (Thucydides 4.121–12, 5.32). At the same time a second protracted and bloody conflict was taking place near Amphipolis, as the Athenian navy attempted to win back the strategic port. The final battle at Amphipolis in 422 brought the deaths of Brasidas and Cleon, the principal generals leading the Spartan and Athenian forces (Thucydides 5.8–10). Chance accomplished what generals and strategies could not: with Cleon dead, Nicias and the Athenians eager for peace with Sparta could pursue policies aimed at bringing the conflict to a close.

Meanwhile the residents of Amphipolis buried Brasidas with every honor in their city's Agora (Thucydides 5.10). In time they came to view him not only as their liberator but even as their founder. Although Athenians had colonized the city just a few decades earlier, the citizens of Amphipolis transferred their allegiance from Athens to Sparta with the death of Brasidas. In death Brasidas became a hero whose accomplishments were memorialized with annual athletic competitions. Citizens worshipped him at public feasts with animal sacrifices performed at an altar by his grave. A Spartan general became the savior of this former Athenian colony that now rejected imperial rule, and civic rites celebrated the rejection of Athens.

PEACE, POLITICS, AND FESTIVALS

The first ten years of the war, which scholars often call the Archidamian War after the Spartan king Archidamas, had resulted in a stalemate: repeated Spartan incursions into Attica were followed by Athenian naval attacks on the Peloponnese. The purpose of these seasonal invasions every summer was the destruction of crops, estates, and farmland and, perhaps equally important, the psychological effects created by the annual attacks. While residents of Attica and Sparta were suffering under the continuing psychological stress, conflicts raged throughout the Athenian *archē.* Sparta did not take full advantage of the changes in the Athens' fortunes following the plagues that hit in 429 and 427, and the war dragged on. Heavy hoplite losses at Delion (424) and Amphipolis (422) left Athenian morale even lower than it had been after the plague outbreaks. Fiscal problems in the empire loomed as the funds in the treasury were beginning to run low, even after the new levies implemented by Cleon. The Athenians feared that more cities within the empire would revolt.

The deaths of Cleon and Brasidas at Amphipolis pointed the way to an exit from the conflict, especially because the demise of Cleon, the demagogue who had aggressively pursued war, left no vocal leader in Athens who opposed peace with Sparta. Without a clear winner in a struggle that now engulfed much of Hellas, the Athenians and the Spartans seized the moment and negotiated a fifty-year truce, sometimes called the Peace of Nicias, in 421.

Under Nicias's leadership, during the next year Athens and Sparta actually struck two separate agreements: the peace treaty in 421, and a mutual defense pact a little later (Thucydides 5.18, 23). Nicias believed that a negotiated truce offered the best course for the future of the Athenian empire. Like all peace treaties in ancient Greece, this agreement called upon the gods. As we have seen, the Greek word for truce, *spondai,* actually refers to a civic religious ritual. Athenian and Spartan leaders agreed to the terms and swore vows to each other while pouring libations, *spondai,* of wine onto the ground. Thucydides records the agreement verbatim, and the very first items in the agreement involve the worship of panhellenic gods: both parties swore to allow free access to common shrines "in accordance with ancestral custom": *kata ta patria.* The oracle of Apollo at Delphi was mentioned by name, and it was to remain autonomous. Each side vowed to return lands taken from the other in the course of the war (which raised some objections, especially among Sparta's allies), and to exchange prisoners. Above all, the treaty of 421 explicitly allowed the Greeks to continue making pilgrimages to shrines commonly recognized by all Hellenes (e.g., Delphi, Eleusis, Olympia), where they could all worship the gods and offer sacrifices without fear of harm. The mutual importance of these panhellenic shrines was underscored by a clause stipulating that the Athenians and Spartans both set up public inscriptions that recorded the oaths at Delphi and Olympia, as well as in Athens (presumably in the temple of Athena) and in a temple of Apollo in Sparta. For the later alliance the gods themselves, in addition to the citizens of Athens and Sparta, would bear witness to the promises each side made when the agreements were annually renewed at civic festivals in Athens and Sparta.

As well-intentioned as the treaties may have been on both sides, they did not last. Already in 420 Sparta found itself in a conflict with neighboring *poleis;* as a result Sparta was blocked from taking part in the panhellenic festival of Zeus at Olympia when Elis, the *polis* that governed the sanctuary, accused the Spartans of violating the truce (Thucydides 5.49–50). The Elians forbade the Spartans from entering the temple and sacrificing to Zeus; their actions effectively blocked the Spartans from competing in the athletic games and attending any scheduled negotiations. One Spartan competitor who entered his chariot team under the Boeotian flag was whipped by Olympian officials when he tried to claim his prize. Meanwhile in Athens the death of Cleon did not bring an end to the war party. Nicias may have been a capable, though cautious, military commander and a diplomat able to recognize a good opportunity for negotiating peace, but his leadership could not sustain the *polis* once the peace libations had been poured. Nicias proved to be ineffectual when another man arose who placed power before peace. A remarkable Athenian aristocrat emerged to fill the gap created by the deaths of Pericles and Cleon; he led the Athenians back to war, and persuaded them to further develop their naval *archē.* The name of this aristocrat was Alcibiades.

Alcibiades was the product of two well-connected and aristocratic Athenian families. He was also Pericles' relative and legal ward. Alcibiades' father Cleinias was born into the noble clan of the Salaminioi, while his mother Deinomache, the daughter of Megacles and first cousin of Pericles, was born into the Alcmaeonid line. Cleinias, a longtime personal friend of Pericles and a supporter of the Athenian empire, may have fought on a ship that he personally funded as a liturgy during the Persian Wars. Cleinias showed his loyalty to the Athenian empire under Pericles when Athens came into conflict with neighboring states in the First Peloponnesian War of the 440s. When tense hostilities led to outright battles in 447, Cleinias was killed in combat at the battle of Coronea.

Alcibiades was then a small child and Pericles became the legal guardian for him and his brother, also named Cleinias. According to tradition Alcibiades was actually raised in Pericles' household and was a favorite of the Athenian leader. He received the best education, was a fine athlete, and became a gifted speaker. Alcibiades was reported to be unusually good-looking, and though he spoke with a noticeable lisp he managed to find a way to make that lisp a charming and persuasive asset. Alcibiades was Athens' golden boy who lived in the house of Pericles; he came of age during the earliest phases of the Peloponnesian War, and had the opportunity to witness daily how his guardian Pericles exercised power and influence. Alcibiades learned these lessons well. He exercised courage and strong leadership qualities during his 20s, and he reportedly won medals for bravery in the battles at Potidaea (probably in the winter of 430/1) and Delion in 424.

Alcibiades made his first big appearance on the Athenian political scene shortly following the Peace of 421. Taking advantage of his high social standing and some old family ties to Sparta, he secretly met with two separate groups of foreign envoys: the Spartans and a coalition of Sparta's neighbors from the Peloponnese, among them Argos (Thucydides 5.43). Athens had great interest in both groups, and Nicias was committed to maintaining good diplomatic relations in an effort to reinforce the peace of 421. But the young Alcibiades proved to be a daring opportunist who worked the diplomatic situation to his advantage. In a meeting of the Athenian Assembly he tricked the Spartan ambassadors into publicly misrepresenting their position, thereby betraying the Spartans and Nicias at the same time. Alcibiades spoke so convincingly that the *dēmos* agreed to form a new coalition with other Peloponnesian *poleis;* Argos welcomed this move, as its strong democratic faction was not eager to renew an old alliance with Sparta. Alcibiades argued that since this handful of Sparta's immediate neighbors (Mantinea, Elis, and Argos) no longer had confidence in Spartan leadership, it was the right moment for Athens to propose that they all band together and create a new partnership that excluded Sparta (Thucydides 5.47).

Even in this, Alcibiades' first entrance into Athenian public life, we can see a strong rivalry developing between Alcibiades and Nicias. Although his diplomatic strategy of rebuffing Sparta clearly violated the spirit if not the terms of the Peace of Nicias, and although Nicias opposed the proposed coalition, Alcibiades' eloquence and powers of persuasion swayed the Athenian *dēmos.* The Athenians made new allies—not subject-allies like those in the *archē,* but allies in the Peloponnese who, Alcibiades claimed, could help keep Spartan ambition in check. Alcibiades was then elected general and given command over a small expedition into the Peloponnese. But while he had the charisma to connect with the *dēmos* in the Assembly at home, his performance as a military leader in the field was poor. Sometimes he led his men to victory, but more often he arrived too late to help. His plans to help fortify cities in the new alliance were shrewd—but the projects were not always completed. When the Athenians next held elections for generals they overlooked Alcibiades and turned again to Nicias. The Athenians eventually abandoned Alcibiades' Peloponnesian plan altogether, but only after the Spartans defeated the weakened coalition headed by Argos and Athens at the battle of Mantinea in 418.

For the next few years the Athenian *dēmos* generally followed the polices of Nicias, but traces of the rivalry between Alcibiades and Nicias were still evident in both men's visibility in rituals during civic festivals for the gods. In 417 Athens celebrated the completion of a new Athenian temple dedicated to Apollo on Delos. Nicias undertook a civic liturgy at his own expense, and in a remarkably grand style he built a temporary floating bridge between Delos and the neighboring island of Rheneia; he then led a magnificent sacrificial procession across the bridge and to the altar in the Apollo sanctuary (Plutarch *Nicias* 3). Not to be outdone, Alcibiades countered by undertaking at great private expense a public project of his own by sponsoring not one but seven Athenian chariot teams at the Olympic festival of 416 (Plutarch *Alcibiades* 11; cf. Thucydides 6.16). No private individual had ever before attempted such a thing. Of these seven teams, three placed in the top five, and in the sanctuary of Zeus Alcibiades was able to suggest to the Hellenic world that the Athenians were mightier than ever.

Even in the rites performed for these festivals the Athenians could appreciate the different temperaments of the two men. Both the athletic festival at Olympia and the dedication of the temple on Delos showcased the Athenians' wealth and power, but to different audiences and through different means. While Nicias's display highlighted the public piety of the Athenian people and their renewed commitment to Apollo and the league of Ionian cities, Alcibiades intuited that not just the Ionians but all the Greeks would feel renewed respect for Athenian greatness when they witnessed the performance of his chariot teams. The grace and power of seven thundering four-horse chariots at a panhellenic festival brought unprecedented Olympic glory to Athens.

At the same time that Nicias and Alcibiades were at religious festivals vying for the love and support of the *dēmos,* the *dēmos* brazenly pursued the harshest of its imperial policies. With a series of decisions reminiscent of those involving Mytilene in 428 and Scione in 423, in 416 the Athenians moved against Melos, an island settled by Spartan colonists and one of the only islands in the Cyclades that remained neutral and outside the Athenian *archē.* The citizens of this *polis* in the southern Aegean had long resisted joining the Delian League, insisting on their autonomy when Athens had earlier tried to force them to join the alliance in 426/5. Finally in 416 the

Athenians sent ambassadors to Melos to persuade the Melians once and for all to surrender to the Athenian empire—or else. Given what had almost happened at Mytilene, and what had actually happened at Scione, the Melians must have been aware of what the Athenians were capable of. Yet the Melian leaders refused all offers, and their city was besieged. At the end of the siege the surviving men of Melos were killed, and the women and children sold into slavery.

Thucydides records the events on Melos at the end of book 5 of his history, and his detailed account of a private dialogue between Melian leaders and Athenian ambassadors has become famous for its clear articulation of a specific view of power: those who have power use it, while the weak are compelled to make compromises (Thucydides 5.84–116). Both sides invoked the gods in their arguments. When the Melians claimed they would not be defeated by the unjust Athenians because they were protected by the gods, the Athenians turned right around and claimed that their actions were in line with both human nature and the affairs of the gods. When looked at from the point of view of traditional Greek religious practice, both claims are accurate. The Melian position relied on a view of Zeus as the god who metes out justice among gods and men and who punishes those who transgress the laws of *xenia;* the Athenian position assumes that mortals worship this king of the gods who came to power by defeating those who were weaker and older (Cronus and the former generation of Titans from the Succession Myth), and then dominating the other Olympian gods in his own generation. Athenian insistence on the overwhelming compulsion of power was grounded in their particular understanding of relationships among the Olympian gods; the Melian commitment to observing traditional *nomoi* gave them confidence that the justice of Zeus would prevail in the end. Ritual practices of the Greek *polis* and ancestral traditions surrounding the gods helped fuel the drama of this episode on Melos.

The harsh imperial diplomacy of Cleon and his followers evident in the affairs at Mytilene and Scione was again realized at Melos, and Thucydides reports no hesitation on the part of the Athenian ambassadors and generals to exercise overpowering and brutal force against the Melians whom the Athenians had hoped to force into their alliance. After killing or enslaving any Melians who resisted, Athens repopulated the island by establishing a colony of Athenian citizens. The Athenian *archē* lived on, and the Athenians relied in part on their civic rites to increase this empire.

Alcibiades' victories at the Olympic games in 416 kept him in the public eye and ensured that the earlier failure of his Peloponnesian policy did not end his public career. In the next round of elections for *stratēgos* in 416 both Nicias and Alcibiades were elected. The election of the two men, one older and cautious and the other younger and ambitious, reflected the increasingly polarized divisions within the citizen body itself as Athenians contemplated how best to manage their empire while maintaining the truce with Sparta. Nicias urged the Athenians to keep the peace and strengthen the existing empire by turning their attention north again, where allied cities continued to threaten rebellion from the *archē*. This region was significant for the security of Athens since the *poleis* there supplied tribute to Athena and timber for ships in the empire's navy. In addition, the Athenians considered it essential to control these cities because they lay along the route to the Hellespont, the main shipping channel for much-needed supplies of grain.

But Alcibiades undercut Nicias's advice with his own idea. Alcibiades' real desire was to increase the reach of the Athenian *archē,* and he cast his gaze further west toward Sicily. The coasts of Sicily and southern Italy had long been home to Greek colonies. The fertile countryside of Sicily produced a good deal of grain; if it could offer an additional source of food for Athens then perhaps control of the northern Aegean and Hellespont would not be so crucial after all. In 416 ambassadors from the city of Segesta visited Athens and reported on a troubling situation in Sicily: Syracuse, a Dorian city with strong connections to Corinth and Sparta, was growing stronger and would soon control the entire island unless someone intervened. Already the Syracusans were aiding the city of Selinus in a border dispute with Segesta. The Segestans' dire predictions of the rising power of Syracuse raised the anxiety of the Athenians, who feared that the Dorian city of Syracuse could come to the aid of the Dorian Spartans and join in dismantling Athenian authority. As a first step, the Athenians sent a delegation to Sicily. Envoys returned to Athens with favorable reports about resources for war available from public temple funds and private sources in Sicily. This information encouraged the Assembly to do something that Pericles had cautioned the Athenians against at the start of the war with Sparta in 431: the *dēmos* voted to expand the conflict beyond the scope of the existing empire. The Athenians set about preparing a naval expedition to the west.

Thucydides describes the mood in Athens at that time as bold and eager; the city had finally recovered from the plague twelve years earlier, had trained a new generation of warriors and sailors, and was again in reasonable financial shape thanks to the increased tribute paid by subject-allies. The youthful and handsome Alcibiades, now about 35 years old, embodied Athenian feelings of confidence, and he projected a kind of dynamic strength that the older and pious Nicias lacked (Thucydides 6.15–18). While some Athenians did express confidence in Alcibiades' plans, others expressed reservations about an ambitious, expensive expedition to Sicily. In the Assembly Nicias articulated the position of the mission's opponents. He simply felt the Athenians were not thinking straight. He pointed out that it would be foolish to attack and subdue a people who would be hard to control once conquered; the resources needed for such a foreign campaign would be much better spent at home on the Athenians, who were still recovering from the plague and enjoying a respite from the war with Sparta (Thucydides 6.9–14, 20–23). But the *dēmos* was too much under the spell of the charming Alcibiades and his dreams for their empire, and the Athenians voted to prepare an expeditionary force with Alcibiades and Nicias serving as generals, along with a third man named Lamachus. Nicias was appointed against his will and against his better judgment (Thucydides 6.25–26).

The preparations for the expedition were fraught and complicated, and another public debate that soon followed only made matters more complex. Thucydides reports the speeches of Nicias and Alcibiades, detailing disagreements over how many ships would be needed, and how many heavily armed hoplites and lighter armed soldiers should be marshaled. Alcibiades anticipated a quick and easy victory in Sicily that would require a modest expenditure of resources. In his view conquering Sicily would naturally propel the Athenians even further into the central Mediterranean and lead them to make new alliances—for example, with the Phoenician city of Carthage, an important trading center in North Africa. Alcibiades saw great potential for enriching the Athenian empire, and himself too (Thucydides 6.15). Nicias was much more measured. He argued that victory in Sicily could be achieved only with great effort and careful planning. Nicias cautioned that the expeditionary force would require far more men, more ships, more resources, and much more luck than Alcibiades was making allowances for. Nicias did everything in his power to discourage the Athenian *dēmos* from moving forward; he even offered to resign his command.

As Thucydides reports it, Nicias's warning had the opposite of its intended effect. The Athenians voted to transform Alcibiades' limited expedition of sixty ships into an armada of one hundred triremes with a full complement of 5,000 heavily armed hoplites, plus lighter armed troops. And they remained steadfast in their decision to give command jointly to two men of such opposite bent, relying on Lamachus to temper the two conflicting personalities. The decision to invade Sicily on such a grand scale marks a major shift in Athenian strategy, and its significance cannot be overstated. Thucydides asserts that the Athenian-led armada bound for Sicily was the most magnificent—and most expensive—ever launched by a single Greek city (Thucydides 6.31). But it was also to have one of the most miserable endings of the war: in a matter of a few years the entire fleet and nearly all the men would be lost—killed or sold into slavery. No ships would return. But before the Athenians suffered this catastrophe abroad, they would know enormous turmoil at home. Alcibiades and the city's civic rites lay at the heart of these upheavals.

THE HERMS AND THE MYSTERIES
IN THE SUMMER OF 415

The mood of excitement and ambivalence in Athens was reflected in religious behaviors of the Athenians as the final preparations for the expedition were completed. One morning early in the summer of 415, in the very last days before the armada's spectacular departure to Sicily, the residents of Athens awoke to discover that in the night religious images and statues in the city had been knocked about (Thucydides 6.27). It had long been customary throughout Athens to set up statues called herms. These pillarlike images were considered sacred to the god Hermes, a deity whose authority extended over merchants and commerce and ensured the safety of all travelers. The squared-off pillars typically stood some 5 feet high, and they featured a sculpted bust of the bearded god Hermes at the top, knobs or handles on the side, and a large, erect phallus about halfway down. There were no other recognizable human or divine features. In figure 10 an Athenian workman places a herm in front of an altar. Herms were understood to protect the city; they stood at the frontier of the *polis,* alongside public highways, and at the crossroads of city streets; they were visible on the Acropolis, in the agora, and at the entrance to any sanctuary; they marked public boundaries and were set up outside of private homes. There were hundreds of the pillars throughout the city.

Figure 10. A workman sets a herm before an altar. Red-figure
Athenian *chous* (wine jug), ca. 440–430 BCE. Boston Museum
of Fine Arts. Gift of Edward Perry Warren, 13.100.

In fact fifth-century Athens was famous for its herms. The custom of
placing these pillars in highly visible places probably originated in the piles
of stones or cairns (*hermata*) that marked territory and stood beside roads
and paths. It was only later, when *hermata* took on anthropomorphic features, that they became associated with the god Hermes. While the earliest recognizable herms may have been wooden images, in Athens herms
were given their unique sculptural form during the sixth century. The first
stone herm was reportedly set up by the Pisistratid tyrant Hipparchus as a
milestone; other public officials also dedicated herms in public places, and
the figures soon took on strong political meanings. Some scholars have

even suggested the flat sides of the trunk of the pillar functioned as a surface for posting public notices. By the mid-fifth century, herms were a standard feature in the Athenian cityscape. They were sometimes objects of worship, and they also performed an important apotropaic function in the city as they aggressively warned travelers and foreigners that the Athenians had power and were willing to exercise it.

When the Athenians woke up that morning they discovered that the faces of virtually every herm had been damaged and the phalluses knocked off. Striking these images of Hermes was an act of impiety, *asebeia,* that constituted civic sacrilege. Given that Hermes was the god of travelers, and that the Athenian navy was about to embark on a major expedition across the sea, some interpreted the mutilation of the herms as a dark and ominous message. Even more shocking was the extent of the damage. It was not limited to just a few herms in one quarter of the city—hundreds of pillars throughout the urban center of Athens were destroyed.

These acts of public impiety at such a critical moment unnerved the Athenian *dēmos.* While some dismissed the vandalism as a youthful prank carried out by drunken youths, others feared that the destruction of the herms carried a message for the *polis.* The more pious understood the sacrilege against the images of Hermes to be an ill omen for the Athenian fleet as it set out on a major offensive carrying men to faraway Sicily. Some of the more politically minded in Athens felt a different anxiety, though. They believed that such wanton destruction was not the random work of a few drunken young men but an organized effort that foreboded revolution: they feared that the sacrilege had been committed by aristocrats who were threatening to overthrow the government and replace it with an oligarchy.

The fears of an aristocratic conspiracy were not entirely unfounded. It had long been an Athenian custom for groups of aristocratic citizens to meet in social groups called *hetaireiai*—voluntary private associations of comrades, *hetairoi.* Members in these clubs sacrificed and dined together, and perhaps also worshipped new gods or heroes not yet incorporated into the official state calendar of civic rites. Often *hetaireiai* included informal political activities that backed the civic ambitions of group members and offered assistance and support for members in the Athenian Assembly and law courts. The sacrilege against the herms on this night in June 415 suggested to some among the *dēmos* that aristocrats were conspiring in their clubs and sending a message to the Athenian people that the *polis* and its democracy were no longer safe. Mutilating the herms who protected the citizen body signaled that Athens was vulnerable to an attack from within.

The citizens of Athens felt the threat and immediately organized a thorough investigation. They voted to offer large rewards to anyone who witnessed the sacrilege, and immunity from prosecution to anyone personally involved who was willing to give evidence about this, or any other, act of civic impiety. Athenian customs so thoroughly infused religious activity into the arena of politics that an affront to the ancestral gods implied an affront to the *polis* itself.

Although no one came forward initially with information about the mutilation of the herms, allegations about other recent acts of *asebeia* did soon surface (Thucydides 6.28). In a last-minute meeting of the Assembly and naval commanders to discuss the Sicilian expedition, a citizen named Pythonicus rose up to denounce one of the three generals: Alcibiades. Pythonicus said he could produce a witness who would attest to serious acts of impiety involving Alcibiades and the Mysteries of Demeter. The witness who was brought forward, a slave named Andromachus, was given leave to address the Assembly—normally slaves gave testimony in Athenian courts only under torture, but in this case the Assembly bent the rules. The information that Andromachus had concerning the secret meetings was so sensitive that the *dēmos* was forced to reconvene after dismissing all those present who had not yet been initiated at Eleusis. Only citizens who had experienced the Eleusinian Mysteries were allowed to attend the meeting. Andromachus reported that he had attended his master at a gathering in a private home, and although he was not personally an Eleusinian initiate he was able to disclose the content of the Mysteries. He identified three citizens he had seen performing the sacred rites of Demeter at the home of Poulytion while others watched. Seven other citizens were present that night, plus four slaves. The three men Andromachus named as the leaders were Niciades, Meletus, and Alcibiades (Andocides *On the Mysteries* 11–14).

Alcibiades found himself cornered: he was directly implicated in one charge of impiety, and his political rivals took this new charge about the profanation of the Mysteries and linked it to the mutilation of the herms, and the threat of an oligarchic revolution. Given his charisma, charm, and skill at persuading the people, Alcibiades certainly had political enemies; Thucydides describes them as rivals who were jealous of his abilities to lead the Athenian *dēmos*. When Alcibiades' rivals linked the charge of the profanation of the Mysteries to the mutilation of the herms, they did so in the name of the *dēmos*. They claimed that these acts of impiety were an assault on the people led by a group of men bent on destroying the democracy (Thucydides 6.27).

This news stirred up the Athenians. In every way the accusers tried to depict Alcibiades as someone resolved to deviate from the norms of Athenian civic and religious traditions. Thucydides writes that Alcibiades' enemies hoped that they could use these acts of impiety as ground for exiling him, and thereby get rid of him once and for all. What moderns would consider public religion, private religion, and the supposed interests of the democracy were utterly intertwined in this affair. Any public act of civic impiety was a punishable offense with serious consequences for the perpetrator. Psychologically, these charges about the destruction of the herms and the desecration of the Mysteries took a great toll on the Athenians, who now were faced with two impious acts that they interpreted as bad omens for the imminent expedition to Sicily. The gods would punish the *polis* and its citizens if they did not bring to justice those responsible.

Before Alcibiades departed for Sicily he spoke before the Assembly and denied all the charges. He offered to stand trial immediately. He pointed out that it was in the interest of the Athenians to try him before the expedition departed: leaving the whole question of his alleged impiety unresolved might compromise the success of the mission. He even encouraged the people to kill him at once if they found him guilty of any wrong. However, Alcibiades' enemies wished to delay the trial. They knew that he would call upon his friends to give testimony on his behalf, and they feared that the army and the people would be moved to support him rather than to criticize his behavior. Alcibiades' detractors wanted time to conduct a thorough investigation, and they would do anything possible—even fabricate charges—to strengthen their case. The Assembly voted that the expedition headed by Alcibiades and Nicias should set sail immediately (Thucydides 6.28–30).

In midsummer the expedition was finally ready. The entire population of the city, citizens and foreigners alike, went down to see the launching and the ceremonies before the magnificent armada set sail. A flourish of trumpets quieted the crowds, and civic officials made the customary prayers. In every ship officers mixed wine and water and poured libations from cups made of gold and silver. All the ancestral civic rites were scrupulously observed for the departure of the fleet to Sicily (Thucydides 6.30–32).

Once Nicias, Alcibiades, and the armada had set sail the Athenians continued their investigations. Three informants came forward in rapid succession. First a metic named Teukros was given leave to speak in the Assembly and granted immunity from subsequent prosecution. In his damning testimony he admitted that he had himself celebrated the Mysteries in private homes alongside Athenian citizens. He denounced twelve by name, including a brother of Nicias. Teukros the metic was evidently so well-placed in Athenian society that he knew of other acts of *asebeia:* not only did his testimony denounce men who profaned the Mysteries, but he could also name eighteen citizens involved in the mutilation of the herms (Andocides *On the Mysteries* 15, 34–35).

Next a citizen wife named Agariste supplied information about another instance of citizens celebrating the sacred rites of Demeter in a private home, this time the home of Charmides. Although a woman could not give sworn testimony in the Athenian Assembly or courts, her citizen husband could speak for her. Agariste again named three who officiated in these rites, and again one of those named was Alcibiades (Andocides *On the Mysteries* 16). Then another slave named Lydus identified even more citizens who had been present at his master's (Pherekles') house on an occasion when the Mysteries were celebrated (Andocides *On the Mysteries* 17–18).

Finally an Athenian citizen spoke out. Diocleides reported that he had accidentally stumbled across the men who mutilated the herms (Andocides *On the Mysteries* 37–42). Diocleides described how he had set out on a journey one night to take care of some morning business 20 miles away. Walking by the light the full moon he passed the theater of Dionysus, where he said he saw more than 300 men gathering down in the orchestra. Of these 300 men he recognized many and was able to positively identify 42, and he denounced these men before the *boulē*. Some of the men Diocleides identified were themselves members of the Council, and others were aristocrats well known in public life, including another of the brothers of the general Nicias. Alcibiades was not named. But even this number was only a fraction of the 300 men Diocleides testified he had seen in the moonlight that night.

With the report of Diocleides the fears of the Athenians were magnified again, and they voted to suspend a previously existing law that forbade the torture of citizens (Andocides *On the Mysteries* 43–44). They were so afraid of revolution and tyranny that they would go to any lengths to obtain testimony that could resolve the issue, even if that testimony was clearly coerced and possibly falsified. In the meantime distinguished citizens charged with impiety by Diocleides were imprisoned. The level of fear in the city at this time was so high that innocent citizens fled the Agora in terror whenever the signal was given that announced the convening of the *boulē* (Andocides *On the Mysteries* 36). Many simply went into exile to avoid trial.

One prominent aristocrat named Andocides, identified by Diocleides and implicated in the herms affair, was taken from prison and granted immunity in exchange for his testimony. While carefully pointing out that a collarbone injury had kept him at home on the precise night in question, Andocides did testify that it was his own *hetaireia* of young noblemen that had planned and implemented the mutilation of the herms. Because the account of Andocides did not fully agree with Diocleides' first account, Diocleides was brought in again for further questioning. When faced with torture Diocleides now admitted that his earlier testimony had been entirely false, and that it was Alcibiades' cousin who had instructed him to give an unfaithful account. Diocleides was summarily executed, but only after the men he had slandered—including Andocides and his family members—were cleared of all charges (Andocides *On the Mysteries* 60–67).

Andocides' account confirmed the Athenians' fears of an oligarchic plot, and Diocleides' social connections to the aristocratic family of Alcibiades raised the anxiety of the Athenians even further. They recalled Alcibiades to Athens to stand trial and face the inquiries of the people. A fast ship was dispatched to fetch Alcibiades and other soldiers who were charged with mutilating the herms or profaning the Mysteries (Thucydides 6.53).

The Athenians now felt confident that religious crises were jeopardizing the expedition to Sicily, and one of the principal leaders of the naval forces was responsible for creating the danger. While Nicias remained widely respected for his public expressions of piety and his conservative religious stance, Alcibiades attracted even more attention for his outrageous, impious behavior. The most passionate reservations about the Sicilian expedition were now expressed in the *dēmos*'s official and unofficial responses to the unusual flouting of religious norms. In the witch hunt of the summer of 415, scores of Athenian citizens were denounced, imprisoned, tortured, and executed; friends and family members betrayed one another. The city was filled with suspicion, and citizens dreaded having to stand trial, especially since trials were not always conducted with complete fairness and citizens took to perjuring themselves to avoid being named by others. Those who were named in the affairs of the Mysteries and herms that summer either fled the city before they could be tried or were executed after standing trial and being found guilty. Those who were not present at their trials were tried in absentia; when found guilty they were condemned to death and their estates confiscated by the state. And at the center of the greatest civic and religious crisis perhaps ever in the history of Athens stood Alcibiades.

Today most scholars conclude that Alcibiades was probably guilty of profaning the Mysteries, but not necessarily involved in mutilating the herms. While none of the remaining historical accounts can clarify what happened when Alcibiades and his friends celebrated the rites of Demeter in the homes of Poulytion, Charmides, and Pherekles, there are some interesting similarities in the reports. The unlawful rites took place in private homes and among relatively small groups of friends—never more than a dozen were named. Two of the accounts specifically name three individuals (citizen men) who "did" the Mysteries while the others looked on. Two accounts note that slaves were present, and at least two identify metics. All these details square with what we know about the official Mysteries as celebrated annually in Eleusis. In the official civic rites inside the sanctuary at Eleusis, a handful of officials performed the Mysteries while initiates watched from their seats in the Telesterion. Women, slaves, and metics sat alongside Athenian citizens when the mystic rites were performed. And significantly, three special Eleusinian priests performed the nocturnal rites: the hierophant (revealer of sacred things), the *dadouchos* (torch-bearer), and the herald. Each time a witness testified in the summer of 415 to the presence of three ritual leaders, Alcibiades was named as one of the three.

Plutarch's report of Alcibiades' impious profanation of the Mysteries actually names Alcibiades as the hierophant and states that he wore the special robes of the Eleusinian priest, while others served with him as torch-bearer and herald (Plutarch *Alcibiades* 22). All three of these roles in the official *polis* cult were traditionally held by hereditary priests and magistrates who came from the old noble families of the Eumolpidae and the Kerykes. When Alcibiades and his friends took on these cultic roles for themselves, they assumed religious and civic authority not rightfully theirs. The Athenians understood the profanation of the Mysteries of Demeter to be a civic crime that simultaneously had serious religious and political implications; whatever happened was likely not drunken revelry or a silly parody, as some have claimed in the past. The patterns of the profanations instead disclosed a secret desire to subvert the authority of the *polis* and its civic priesthoods. Whether an oligarchic revolution lay behind the private and unlawful celebration of Demeter's civic rites is another matter.

In their desperate desire to get to the bottom of these acts of civic impiety, the Athenians took measures that were highly unusual for them. They not only suspended laws that prohibited the torture of citizens, they even accepted public testimony in the Assembly from slaves, women, metics, and foreigners. While some citizens did give testimony in the trials of the summer of 415, the witnesses who gave the most valuable information had the lowest political standing in the *polis*. The importance of the testimony of the disenfranchised—the slaves Andromachus and Lydus, the metic Teukros, and the citizen wife Agariste—provides further evidence for us today that the civic rites of Demeter did not privilege those worshippers who had high social status, namely citizen men.

As the difficult summer of 415 came to a close, the Athenians tried hard to set their city to rights. At the annual celebration of the Panathenaea that year the *dēmos* made good on its promises to award money from the public treasury to anyone who could identify the perpetrators of the civic impiety. On the Acropolis before the entire city the Athenians gave the metic Teukros 1,000 drachmas; to the slave Andromachus, the first to speak up, they presented 10,000—a very considerable sum (Andocides *On the Mysteries* 28). The citizens of Athens did all they could to safeguard their ancestral *nomoi*. They even gave sizable rewards to those of low status.

THE MANY SIDES OF ALCIBIADES

The testimony of citizens and noncitizens alike implicated Alcibiades in acts of religious impiety, and these accusations severely limited his ability to perform on the Athenian political stage for several years to come. As the religious crisis continued to unfold in Athens and the fast ship raced from the Piraeus, Nicias, Lamachus, and Alcibiades were nearing Sicily with the armada. After landing in the south of Italy, where they hoped to establish a base of operations, they met with unexpected resistance. The three generals regrouped to discuss possible next steps and strategies. Nicias wished to help settle affairs between the cities at conflict (Segesta and Selinus) and then go home, Lamachus proposed immediately attacking Syracuse (the city most coveted by Athens and currently allied with Selinus), and Alcibiades wanted to attack Syracuse only after forging alliances with neighboring cities. With Lamachus's support, Alcibiades' plan won out (Thucydides 6.47–50). When the fast ship found the Athenian naval commanders later in the summer of 415, they were off the east coast of Sicily, trying (unsuccessfully) to build alliances against Syracuse. Alcibiades was officially recalled to Athens to stand trial. While accompanying Alcibiades and his ship back to Athens, the convoy stopped in the southern Italian city of Thurii. There Alcibiades escaped and fled in the night. When he next resurfaced he was in the heart of the Greek Peloponnese, where he presented himself to the Spartans (Thucydides 6.61, 88). Alcibiades turned traitor.

The Athenians were aghast. The enemies of Alcibiades who had been warning others about his treacherous nature and secret wishes for an oligarchy believed they now had real proof. These enemies led the charge in the Athenian Assembly, and Alcibiades was found guilty in absentia of profaning the Mysteries of Demeter (Thucydides 6.61). The punishment levied was the harshest possible. Alcibiades was condemned to death, and a reward was placed on his head. His family property was confiscated, and his name, along with the names of others found guilty of *asebeia,* was inscribed on a special plaque erected on the Acropolis (Fornara 147). Alcibiades became an official enemy of the *polis* and of the city's gods. The Athenian *dēmos* even passed an additional decree that called upon the priests and priestesses of the Eleusinian cult of Demeter to publicly curse his name along with the names of all others found guilty of profaning Demeter and her rites celebrated at Eleusis (Plutarch *Alcibiades* 22; cf. Thucydides 8.53, 61).

Officially banned from Athens, Alcibiades worked closely for the next few years with the Spartan leadership, advising them and slowly earning their trust. He encouraged the Spartans to send an officer to serve as commander alongside the Syracusans, and this commander was instrumental in helping to put together a strategy that brought defeat to Athens in Sicily. Most significantly for Athens, Alcibiades advised the Spartans to establish a permanent military presence in rural Attica by building a fort in the outlying deme of Decelea (Thucydides 6.91–93, 7.18). In effect this changed how the Spartans waged war against Athens. In the early years of the war, Spartan incursions into Attic territory had been only seasonal events: in the early summer when the grain was high the Spartans marched north across the Isthmus of Corinth and into Attica, where they laid waste to the crops before retreating back to their home base in the Peloponnese. Most of these invasions were temporary and short-lived—lasting anywhere from two to six weeks. But with a permanent fort in northern Attica the Spartans could menace year-round. Alcibiades knew the Athenians' weaknesses well, and completing the fort at Decelea in the spring of 413 had tremendous long-term consequences. The Spartan presence in this region disrupted commerce between Euboea and Athens. For the remainder of the war Athens was forced to spend resources in Decelea, sending out cavalry to skirmish with the Spartans throughout the year. The construction of the fort at Decelea marks a turning point in the course of the war.

Following their betrayal by Alcibiades in 415, ill fortune dogged the Athenians. After the two remaining generals, Nicias and Lamachus, had almost reduced Syracuse during a siege in 414, there was a severe crisis in leadership among the Athenians. Lamachus was killed during this siege, and Nicias fell seriously ill. Athenian forces faltered. The renowned piety of Nicias then became a stumbling block: a lunar eclipse that occurred just as they were about to withdraw from Syracuse made the Athenian soldiers and marines uneasy (Thucydides 7.50). Greek scientists and intellectuals largely understood the phenomena of lunar and solar eclipses, but the strange darkness cast by an eclipse was considered ominous by the pious. On this occasion, shortly after the Spartan commander Gylippus arrived to help the Syracusans, Nicias chose to follow the advice of a seer. Even though the Athenians still had time to sail away before another Syracusan attack, Nicias had the soldiers and sailors encamp nearby; they did not move for nearly a month following the eclipse.

A month later the Athenian navy found itself blockaded and defeated at Syracuse. When the men refused to go back on board their ships and instead tried to escape overland, they ran short of supplies and were eventually captured. Without ships or any hope of help Nicias felt that the only thing they could do was surrender to the Spartan commander Gylippus. The Athenian soldiers who had survived the betrayal of Alcibiades, the naval battles, and the shortages of food and other supplies in the confused land retreat were then thrown into an abandoned quarry outside Syracuse. The Syracusans—acting over the objection of Gylippus—executed Nicias and the other Athenian commander by publicly slitting their throats (Thucydides 7.86). Thucydides reports that for two months, more than 7,000 men starved, suffered, and died in their own filth in the quarry before some non-Athenian survivors were sold into slavery. The Athenians and their allies were deliberately left behind in the quarry to rot. And so the Sicilian Expedition ended in complete failure for the Athenians (Thucydides 7.87).

In the fall of 413, just as the Athenians were coming to grips with the Spartan occupation of a fort in Decelea, they received the news that the great Sicilian expedition had ended in total disaster. At first the Athenians refused to believe that so great an undertaking could meet with such destruction. But as more reports arrived the truth became undeniable, and citizens grew angry at the oracle readers and seers who had prophesied the conquest of Sicily when the armada set sail from the Piraeus two years earlier (Thucydides 8.1). Frustration with religious officials did not distract the Athenians, however, and they made plans to build more ships to protect their empire.

Meanwhile Alcibiades the traitor took civic misconduct to new heights. He was not satisfied with victory in Sicily and an established presence in Attica. He could see the Athenians' empire declining, and he encouraged the Spartans to devise plans that would take further advantage of Athenian weaknesses. The Spartans developed a new navy and established diplomatic ties with Persia. Cities in the Athenian *archē* that wished to revolt petitioned the Spartans for military and financial assistance. As more Greek *poleis* in Asia Minor called upon the Spartans for aid, representatives from the neighboring Greek cities under Persian rule accompanied the diplomatic missions to Sparta. The Persians, too, promised aid to Sparta. Both Tissaphernes, who governed the Persian provinces on the coast of Ionia, and Pharnabazus, the satrap who administered the area around the Hellespont, sought alliances with Sparta. Alcibiades had by now earned the trust of the Spartan leadership, and he persuaded the Spartans to support a revolt and accept an alliance with Tissaphernes (Thucydides 8.17–19; cf. 8.37). The substantial Persian resources—money, men, and ships—could give Sparta the edge it needed to defeat the Athenians. In return for Persian support, the Spartans promised to hand over to the Persian Empire at the end of the war all Greek cities in Ionia that Persia had lost in conflicts with Greek *poleis* several generations earlier in the 470s and 460s, thereby allowing the Great King of Persia to collect his tribute.

Persia's entrance into the conflict between Athens and Sparta marks another significant shift in the course of the war, and indicates a new direction for Alcibiades as he maneuvered within the limitations that the Athenians' curse had placed upon him. Spartan support for the ongoing revolts in eastern cities of the Athenian empire also sets the stage for the final phase of the conflict between Athens and Sparta: from this time on, most of the action would occur in the eastern Aegean along the Ionian coast of Asia Minor. In the naval war that followed, Sparta kept pressure on Athens while maintaining its alliance with Persia, and Athens maintained its navy while working to keep allies in the empire. To fund the war in Ionia the Athenian *dēmos* voted to draw on reserve funds in the treasury on the Acropolis that Pericles had set aside at the beginning of the war as a precaution, including sacred funds intended for gods (Thucydides 8.15; cf. 2.24). Meanwhile the Athenian navy was actively supporting a revolt against the ruling oligarchic faction on the island of Samos off the coast of Ionia. The Samians gladly accepted Athenian ships and men, and soon Samos became a permanent base of operations for the Athenian navy as it fought with Sparta in the eastern Aegean.

Alcibiades' tendency to flout religious and social customs followed him into the eastern Aegean, where he served as an adviser and naval commander for the Spartans. Apparently the Spartans became aware of his questionable private behavior, and the Spartan general Agis reportedly grew to hate him. Plutarch (*Alcibiades* 23) records that Alcibiades had carried on an illicit affair with Agis's wife (who bore him a child), and Thucydides simply states that the Spartans wanted him dead. In fear for his life among the Spartans and unable to return to Athens because of the curses and death sentence against him, Alcibiades turned to the only potential friends he had left: Tissaphernes and the Persians. The man who had betrayed the Athenians and gone over to the Spartan side in 415 now betrayed the Spartans, too (Thucydides 8.45).

Once established in the court of Tissaphernes, Alcibiades assumed an advisory role, and took his first steps toward rapprochement with the Athenians who had found him guilty of *asebeia.* He counseled Tissaphernes to play Athens and Sparta off one another while stringing along the Spartans with (mostly empty) promises of ships and abundant money. Perhaps Alcibiades subtly undermined Sparta and articulated to Tissaphernes the advantages of an eventual alliance with Athens. Such would appear to be the case, because he quickly made contact with aristocratic friends among the Athenians stationed on nearby Samos. Alcibiades expressed his desire to return to Athens, but since he had been found guilty of religious charges he first needed political allies to arrange a pardon for him. He brokered a deal with some Athenian leaders on Samos. If they would clear his name in Athens he would do two things for them in return: he would help them establish an oligarchy in Athens, and he would bring Persia and Persian money over to the Athenian side. With Persian assistance Athens could defeat Sparta, and with Alcibiades' help the aristocracy could be the ones to lead the Athenians to victory. The only thing standing in Alcibiades' way was his civic impiety and guilt in profaning the Mysteries of Demeter.

Alcibiades' friendship with Tissaphernes and the Great King held out the possibility of great wealth for the *dēmos,* and Alcibiades and his supporters on Samos relied on the greed of soldiers and sailors to win them over. But any potential Persian financial support would come at a high price: relinquishing democratic rule in Athens. Although the rank-and-file soldiers agreed, Alcibiades' plan did not bring about his immediate restoration. At least one general, named Phrynicus, could see the raw ambition behind

Alcibiades' plan. There followed a series of secret messages, betrayals, and reprisals as the Athenian and Spartan leaders and Tissaphernes all jockeyed for position. Back in Athens circumstances were ripe for revolution. When an Athenian officer named Pisander arrived in Athens with a delegation to report on the situation on Samos, Alcibiades' offers to establish an alliance with Persia and a "different" form of democracy in Athens met with resistance. Some were opposed to the change in government, and those who were still angered by Alcibiades' past lawlessness and impiety were especially outraged. The priests of Demeter took a hard position in the Assembly and they called upon the gods in their efforts to block Alcibiades' return (Thucydides 8.53).

In the end Demeter's priests lost that debate: Pisander persuaded the *dēmos* that Alcibiades was the only man who could save Athens and the empire, and he traveled back to Samos with the news. But when he and Alcibiades sat down to negotiate with Tissaphernes, Alcibiades inexplicably changed course: as he negotiated between Tissaphernes and Pisander he made the Persian demands on Athens so great that the talks had to fail. When Pisander and the Athenians realized they could not rely on Alcibiades, they abandoned the talks and pursued an oligarchic revolution without him. Even the Athenian naval leaders on Samos gave up on Alcibiades when they saw he could not deliver on his promises (Thucydides 8.56).

After the talks between Alcibiades, Pisander, and Tissaphernes failed, a coup unfolded in Athens even without Alcibiades leading it (Thucydides 8.63–70). Pisander's first reports had stirred up aristocratic *hetaireiai* in Athens, and some elites quietly prepared to overthrow the democracy. By the time Pisander returned to Athens in 411, several democratic leaders had been mysteriously murdered. While the *ekklēsia* and *boulē* did continue to meet, a group of aristocrats (eventually called the Four Hundred) was systematically placing itself in power. On the advice of the Four Hundred the Athenian *dēmos* voted to suspend the old constitution and ruled that citizens would no longer receive pay for public service. Their provisions for a less selective body called the Five Thousand were a sham, at least initially, since the Four Hundred never convened it.

The duty of the *dēmos* to maintain political relationships by practicing civic cult remained in place. At first the Four Hundred were careful about their use of ancestral religious customs and symbols. They initially chose to assume civic authority not in the heart of the city but a little outside the city walls in a sanctuary of Poseidon, a fitting place, since this god, whose authority extended over the sea—and hence a naval empire—had a tradition of conflict with Athena on the Acropolis. Later, when the Four Hundred moved into the council chamber in the Agora they used traditional religious rites to normalize their seizure of power. Thucydides reports that they spoke all the ancestral prayers and made all the customary sacrifices that accompanied taking office (Thucydides 8.67). But for all the appearance of normality at the cultic level, the administration they put into place was far from normal, and expressing political dissent became dangerous. A handful of citizens who exhibited democratic tendencies were killed, a few mysteriously disappeared, and many were imprisoned or banished.

Alcibiades had not yet given up his hopes of overturning the curse and returning to Athens, and he maintained his connections with the soldiers and sailors on Samos who had helped ignite the revolution in the first place. The sailors soon resisted the new oligarchy in Athens, especially after hearing reports of how harshly the Four Hundred were ruling. Once the sailors realized their latent power, they determined to restore democracy in Athens and return the city to the rule of the ancestral laws that had been undone. After deposing their generals and electing new ones with more democratic inclinations, the army looked for a spokesman who could best represent their cause. They turned to Alcibiades. They voted to pardon him of all charges, even the religious ones; they brought him back from exile and immediately made him general. Alcibiades—adviser for the *dēmos,* the Spartans, the Persians, and the Athenian aristocracy—was back to being a favorite of the people (Thucydides 8.76–82).

Although the sailors pardoned Alcibiades on Samos, the guilty verdict and the curses still hung over his head in Athens, where the reign of the Four Hundred continued and grew even more ruthless. One of their objectives appears to have been peace; they repeatedly sent envoys to the Spartans, but none of their attempts met with success. As the Four Hundred received reports from Samos they began disagreeing among themselves on key issues: on how to defend the city and its port, how to respond to Alcibiades, and whether to make peace with Sparta. Even the status of the Four Hundred itself came into question. While some in power wished to maintain an extreme oligarchy, men who claimed to be more moderate among the Four Hundred wanted to empower the Five Thousand in earnest.

Infighting among the Four Hundred reached a peak when they started to kill each other and to pervert established social and ritual customs. Regardless of the type of regime, oligarchic or democratic, Athenian citizens defined themselves by their relationships to their sacrificial communities among the living, and by their obligations to their dead ancestors. Maintaining a burial monument by performing tomb cult at the proper times was a responsibility upheld by every male citizen. It served such an important function that men without adult sons would adopt in order to ensure the continuity of rites performed at ancestral tombs. Tomb cult, like the civic rituals discussed in chapter 2, was an area where democracy and religion were thoroughly implicated in one another. The absence of tomb cult could have devastating effects on both the individual and the community.

Such effects were felt by one of the principal leaders of the Four Hundred, Phrynicus, who was assassinated in the Agora after returning from a failed peace mission to Sparta. His assassin slipped away. But then Phrynicus was put on trial and found guilty of treason *after* his death. Critias, a demagogue with considerable rhetorical expertise, led the motion to exhume his body (Lycurgus 112–15). Although exhuming a grave and revoking the privileges of citizenship from a corpse sounds grisly if not bizarre to us, in the context of fifth-century Athens the punishment carried real meaning. Because they lost all possibility for tomb cult on Attic soil, Phrynicus and his entire family had their family cult rites and many political rights stripped away: Phrynicus's descendants were forbidden from taking part in political and cultic activities that involved him and his ancestral burial monument. The ability to memorialize the dead through ancestral rites could become highly politicized in this society, especially during wartime. Pericles' funeral oration at the start of the war demonstrated the power that these civic rites held for the living, and the fate of fallen warriors in a battle a few years later would come to haunt the Athenians in more ways than one.

Critias's role in this episode is noteworthy both for his past and his personal connections: he was related to Andocides, he was known to be a close associate of Alcibiades, and he had been imprisoned after being named by Diocleides in the mutilation of the herms in 415. He was released after Andocides gave his testimony. Although the mutilation of the herms and the profanation of the Mysteries had happened four years earlier, the bitterness surrounding the accusations of religious impiety made in the summer of 415 continued to have an impact on Athenian political life. Critias would later take a leading role in the second oligarchic government of 404, where he would stand out as an extremist.

As the situation grew increasingly dire in Athens, counterrevolution and civil war erupted. The navy on Samos had effectively mutinied, and some armed hoplites in Athens and the Piraeus supported the moderates and the

Five Thousand. As in the earlier rise of the Four Hundred, the significance of religious sanctuaries in Athenian political life again became evident. The hoplites who supported the moderates met in an alternative assembly, and when they did so they convened in a sanctuary of Dionysus in the Piraeus. They used the theater space in a sacred precinct as a meeting place to discuss their response to the Four Hundred back in Athens, just as those oligarchs had met in the temple of Poseidon at Colonus (Thucydides 8.93). Dionysus was a god whose rites encouraged the *dēmos* to question the ruling power structures (see chapter 6), and when the moderate democrats met in this god's urban sanctuary at Athens' harbor they continued that tradition of internal political criticism.

Alcibiades' maneuvering among Athenian forces stationed on Samos soon paid off: the democratic faction in Athens got the upper hand. A Spartan naval incursion into Euboea helped bring about the end of the Four Hundred, whose hurried response failed to keep the large island just north of Attica in the empire. With the Four Hundred in disarray, the Athenian *dēmos* took again to assembling at the Pnyx. Only a few months after they had seized power the Four Hundred were deposed, and democracy was partially restored with the government of the Five Thousand, who were by definition armed hoplites capable of supplying their own weapons. Before long the assembled citizens voted to officially rescind the exile of Alcibiades. They sent messengers to Samos to urge him to accept the new government, and the man who helped instigate an oligarchic coup in 412 became a supporter of the new regime of 411/0. Soon thereafter democracy was fully restored (Thucydides 8.97–98).

But Alcibiades did not yet return home to Athens to resolve the issues surrounding his impious behavior. As general of the fleet in Samos he turned his attention north to the Hellespont. Late in 411 he won an important victory at Cyzicus over the Spartans, who continued to benefit from their alliance with the Persians. Alcibiades remained in this region as general of the Athenian fleet until 407. When he did arrive back in Athens early in the summer of 407, Alcibiades defended himself before the Assembly against what he claimed were unjust charges associated with profaning the Mysteries of Demeter (Xenophon *Hellenica* 1.4). Although he still had some political enemies, Alcibiades now had many more supporters, who voted to clear him of all charges of impiety. The inscriptions on the Acropolis recording his crimes against Demeter were thrown into the sea (Diodorus 13.69), and his confiscated property was restored (Plutarch *Alcibiades* 33). The Athenian *dēmos* placed all its hope in him, and they passed a decree ordering the city's priests of Demeter to revoke their earlier curses. It is impossible to know the priests' personal opinions about this order, but it was their official pardon that fully restored Alcibiades to Athenian public life as a civic leader in the tradition of Pericles. Many considered Alcibiades the only man capable of returning Athens to its earlier glory, and they voted to make him supreme commander of the Athenian forces.

Once cleared of the charges associated with profaning the Mysteries, Alcibiades' first public act underscored the close ties between Athenian political life and civic worship at ancestral festivals. It was now autumn, the month of Boedromion and time to celebrate the Mysteries of Demeter. Because of the Spartan fort in Decelea the Athenians had suspended the customary march through the countryside of Attica, and instead initiates approached Eleusis by sea every fall. That year Alcibiades reinstated the march of the initiates, and he was the one who led the procession from Athens to Eleusis (Xenophon *Hellenica* 1.4; Plutarch *Alcibiades* 34). With the army and ephebes in tow, Alcibiades accompanied the civic priests and priestesses of Demeter and the sacred cult objects in the baskets and carts. The civic rites of Demeter were unusually grand that year. Alcibiades, a man found guilty of profaning Demeter's mystic rites, sentenced to death and publicly cursed by Demeter's priests, and later publicly pardoned by these same civic priests, gloriously demonstrated his outward civic piety to the Athenian *dēmos* and their ancestral *nomoi*.

ANCESTRAL PRACTICES AND THE END OF AN EMPIRE

The war in the Aegean continued, even as Alcibiades led the celebration of the Mysteries in Athens and Eleusis. Ionia in 406 was the scene of the next pivotal confrontation between Sparta and Athens. Any renewed confidence the Athenians felt after the return of Alcibiades was immediately dashed: at Notium Lysander led the Spartans to victory against the Athenian fleet. Alcibiades had left command of the fleet to his lieutenant and was not present at this battle. Athenian disappointment with their general was proportionate to the heady welcome he had received just a year earlier. They deposed Alcibiades and voted in ten entirely new generals. One of these new generals was Pericles the son of Pericles and Aspasia. The younger Pericles must earlier have been specially granted full citizen status, since his mother was a foreigner and the terms of the Periclean citizenship laws of 451 stipulated that an Athenian could be a citizen only if both parents were Athenian citizens. Meanwhile Alcibiades retreated to a private fort he owned on the Hellespont and withdrew from active duty.

Lysander commanded a Spartan naval force that now had the full support of the Persian prince Cyrus, who had recently taken control of the Persian fleet from Tissaphernes. The next naval engagement between Athens and Sparta resulted in victory for the Athenians. Further north of Notium near Mytilene lay the Arginusae islands, a chain that stretched between the mainland and the island of Lesbos. The battle there was fought in tight quarters and both sides lost many men and ships, but the tactics of the Athenian fleet brought defeat to the Spartans and their allies. The Athenians captured seventy Spartan ships. As the Spartans fled to neighboring Chios some of the Athenians pursued them, and others patrolled the waters to pick up the dead and wounded from disabled and wrecked ships. A sudden storm that blew up cut short their efforts (Xenophon *Hellenica* 1.6).

Despite the victory, news of the failure to recover all the survivors and dead bodies after the naval victory at Arginusae drew an immediate and negative response back in Athens, and the generals were called home. Of those who commanded at Arginusae, two simply fled rather than face the Athenian *dēmos*. When the remaining six generals appeared before the Assembly to give an account of the battle and the sudden violence of the storm that followed, they found themselves, in effect, put on trial. Many issues came into play here—accountability, decision making, custom, and the rule of law. Theramenes, who had served at Arginusae as a naval officer, led those who insisted that the blame for failing to rescue survivors and gather the dead should fall on the generals and not the ship commanders like himself. But Xenophon also reports that bribes changed hands, and that the Athenian people were deliberately deceived (*Hellenica* 1.7). The irregular "trial" held before the Assembly was plagued with procedural problems; emotions were running extremely high, and at one point members of the prytany, the executive committee presiding over the Assembly meeting, were so intimidated that they permitted the people to undermine their own established laws. Only one member of that committee stood up and refused to act contrary to ancestral laws of the *polis*. Through an odd quirk of fate, we happen to know the identity of that lone dissenting prytany member: Socrates. In an irrational and deluded rush to justice, the Assembly then tried the generals not as individuals, as required by law, but as an entire group. All six were found guilty and executed by the state—including Pericles' son (Xenophon *Hellenica* 1.7).

Arginusae turned out to be the bitterest of victories. The intense and conflicted atmosphere of the generals' trial in Athens created a social and political storm that was ultimately far more destructive than the storm at sea that thwarted the rescue mission. Many issues that came into play here, but they evidently included civic piety, impiety, and tomb cult. The same concern for the proper observance of ancestral burial customs that was apparent in the curious post mortem condemnation of Phrynicus in 410 became politicized again in the trial of the generals in 406. Survivors from ships that had been crippled in naval engagements were normally rescued following a battle, and it was likewise customary to collect the dead and give them a solemn state burial. While the type of ancestral tomb cult practiced by families in Attica could not be exactly followed at a mass grave overseas, nonetheless a publicly marked grave did allow survivors to respect traditional funerary rites for fallen warriors. When the sudden storm blew up, commanders were faced with a tough decision: when did the safety and well-being of the surviving men on sound ships take precedence over the rights of the men who died at sea or the wounded whose ships were wrecked? What is the responsibility of the living in regard to the men who died serving the *polis?*

The relationship between the individual and political/religious groups was on every Athenian's mind at this time. In the midst of the trial of the generals Athenians were celebrating an annual three-day civic festival called the Apatouria, ancient Ionian rites held in the fall among the venerable religious groups of citizens called phratries. Each phratry held its own celebration. During the festival phratry members met to sacrifice together and to welcome new members into the group—ceremonies were designated to welcome babies, ephebes, and wives. The Apatouria was a time when extended families and networks of friends gathered together to feast, socialize, and worship the gods. But this year some families who had recently lost men at Arginusae were in mourning, and the Apatouria became a stage for political maneuvering. Theramenes reportedly instructed some of his friends attending the festivals to pretend they were in mourning; they came to the Assembly dressed in mourning clothes and with their hair ritually shorn, and they raised the emotional intensity among everyone gathered at the Pnyx (Xenophon *Hellenica* 1.7).

The issues as defined by the speakers and citizens in the Assembly that day focused on burial rites for citizens, above all the civic funerary rites for men who died serving the *dēmos* and the naval empire. Yet at a deeper level the trial of the generals was also motivated by some citizens' desire to exert their influence over the *dēmos* as the military conflict with Sparta and Persia grew more desperate. The need for patient consideration and thoughtful decision making gave way to political infighting. Contrary to all custom and law, the six generals on trial were denied the right to defend themselves as individuals when it was moved that they be tried as a group. The prytany presiding over the Assembly that day initially resisted the motion to abrogate the standard trial procedures for individual citizens. But the frantic energy of the *dēmos* persuaded all but one of the sitting prytany members to change their minds. Only by deciding to change traditional judicial procedures could the democratic Assembly vote to execute all six generals. The will of the people stood fast, even when the *dēmos* contradicted itself and its own acknowledged customs. Some in the Assembly, like Theramenes, contended that the generals' act of disregarding civic burial rites for fallen soldiers deserved a guilty verdict, but that claim may have been only a pretext for simple self-interest. By evoking the authority of ancestral funerary rites Theramenes saved his own skin.

The final and decisive naval engagement of the war happened not much later, to the east in the critical waterway of the Hellespont. Given the loss of eight experienced and victorious Athenian generals after Arginusae (six executed and two in exile), the Athenian navy was demoralized, and it was also running low on funds. When the Spartan naval commander Lysander attacked undefended Athenian ships beached on the shore near Aegospotami in the Hellespont he virtually wiped out the fleet—only 9 of 180 ships escaped. Lysander then ruthlessly executed the several thousand Athenian sailors taken prisoner (Xenophon *Hellenica* 2.1). The loss of so many ships and men compromised the security of Athens and its harbors, and after gathering reinforcements in the Aegean Lysander sailed for the coast of Attica and blockaded the Piraeus. In the meantime Spartan land forces under the commander Pausanias marched on Athens and laid siege to the city. The Athenians held out for a few months. With the grain trade interrupted after the loss at Aegospotami and facing starvation during the stormy winter, they finally capitulated in the spring of 404. Tradition has it that the Spartans tore down the Long Walls between Athens and Piraeus to the sound of flutes playing and with festive dancing (Xenophon *Hellenica* 2.2).

Some of Athens' enemies were now urging the Spartans to mete out to the Athenians the same sort of harsh justice that Athens had dealt to upstart allies in their *archē:* kill or enslave the citizens, demolish the defeated city, and transform Athena's land into pastureland sacred to Apollo. But the Spartans looked beyond any impulse for vengeance. They recalled the losses Athens had suffered in the Persian Wars two generations earlier when the Athenians united with the Spartans, abandoned Athens, and allowed the Persian army to destroy their city twice. Instead of razing Athens the Spartans generously permitted the city to remain standing—minus its defensive walls. Sparta's terms for peace further required Athens to relinquish the naval empire that had for many decades shaped Athenian domestic and foreign policy. Finally, Spartan terms required the Athenians to recall political exiles and reinstate their ancestral constitution and *nomoi*— all the customs that ordered political life and directed the civic rites that were sacred to the gods.

The victorious Spartan Lysander had never been overly fond of democracies, and to help the Athenians implement their ancestral laws he suspended the democratic institutions that Athens was famous far. Lysander organized an interim oligarchic government of thirty commissioners who were charged with reinstating the ancestral constitution, the *patrios politeia*. The oligarchic faction within the Athenian populace had long expressed aristocratic tendencies that favored Sparta. These tendencies were apparent in everything from pro-Spartan policies during the war itself to fashion statements. Young aristocratic men wore their hair long in an old-fashioned style that was associated with Spartan warrior culture, and they dressed more austerely. Pro-Spartan, oligarchic tendencies had endured after the restoration of the democracy in 410, and some aristocrats continued to meet together in their private associations called *hetaireiai*.

When the oligarchs came into power with the help of Lysander in 404, they ruled reasonably at first. The Thirty won the support of the *dēmos* with a handful of sensible judicial reforms, and the Spartans fully supported their oligarchic regime. But this committee proved to be far harsher than the Four Hundred who had ruled in 411–410 and their rule soon grew tyrannical. Among the members of the Thirty were men from the family of Plato: Critias, the uncle of Plato's mother, and Charmides, Critias's adopted son and Plato's cousin. Critias was reputed to be among the most harsh of the Thirty. Theramenes, a moderate oligarch who had abandoned the Four Hundred when their methods became overbearing in 410, was also appointed to this commission, and again his voice was among the more temperate.

Initially the Thirty empowered their political allies, establishing ten sympathetic administrators in the Piraeus and appointing eleven commissioners in charge of prisons. The Thirty then went to work removing their opponents from office or disfranchising them. Only those whom they approved had full citizen rights. Prisons were soon filled with citizen prisoners who opposed the Thirty's policies. As their rule grew more ruthless, the Thirty maintained authority by employing 300 attendants armed with whips who patrolled the public areas. In short order, more than 1,500 Athenian citizens had been assassinated and countless others unlawfully detained. Metics suffered too; even though they were not among the *dēmos* some metics had accumulated considerable property and the Thirty were keen to imprison or secretly kill them so they could confiscate their wealth (Aristotle *Athenian Constitution* 35).

Critias and the more extreme among the Thirty met with opposition from the committee's moderate members, as well as from courageous citizens. When Theramenes stuck to his moderate position and protested that the Thirty's methods were becoming too extreme, Critias had his name struck from the roll of select aristocratic citizens who enjoyed the full protection of the law. Theramenes was publicly executed at once (Aristotle *Athenian Constitution* 37). Another famous instance of resistance to the Thirty's terror involved a rich metic named Leon of Salamis and the Thirty's practice of covert political assassination. Plato and Xenophon describe in detail how the Thirty killed so many Athenians so quickly: they called in small groups of citizens who were not among the Thirty's leadership and commanded them to go out and assassinate certain other citizens or risk being killed themselves. In this way, the Thirty implicated as many as possible in their oligarchic violence. On one occasion they summoned five men and commanded them to kill Leon of Salamis. One of the five citizens flatly refused to participate in the hit squad, and this citizen was Socrates (Plato *Apology* 32d; cf. Xenophon *Memorabilia* 1.2.32).

In response to the Thirty's reign of terror, citizens and metics with democratic sympathies fled Athens and organized themselves under Thrasybulus on the border of Attica and Boeotia. When the democrats in exile had sufficient forces they sailed into the Piraeus and engaged the Thirty's army. A civil war in Athens raged in the summer of 403, and Critias died in a battle waged alongside the remnants of the Long Walls near the harbor. The Spartan governor Lysander supported the Thirty's rule, but their authoritarian control became so brutal that the two Spartan commanders Lysander and Pausanias could not agree on a course of action. In the end Pausanias undermined Lysander by marching to Athens with Spartan forces and ultimately compelling the two sides to reconcile. A full amnesty was proclaimed for everyone on both sides—everyone except for the Thirty and their immediate subordinates. By autumn democracy was fully restored. And so the fifth century, which began with the destruction of Athens in a foreign war, ended with the fall of Athens at the hands of former allies and a civil war among Athenians.

The ultimate fate of Alcibiades was also decided at this time, and it was just as grim as what was happening in Athens. Before the Athenians capitulated to Lysander, Alcibiades turned traitor one last time. His offer of help and advice at Aegospotami was rejected in 405 (Xenophon *Hellenica* 2.1), and shortly thereafter he sought refuge under the Persian satrap Pharnabazus, who provided him with a haven in Phrygia. In the end Alcibiades was assassinated in 404, perhaps by orders of Lysander and the Persians. According to Plutarch, agents ambushed his house and set fire to it. They then stabbed him as he ran out of the burning building (Plutarch *Alcibiades* 39). He could never return to Athens again.

When Xenophon in his *Hellenica* (1.4) recalled the fateful return of Alcibiades to Athens in the summer of 407, he related the claim of some Athenians that even then they recognized a bad omen. Plutarch too preserves a similar account (*Alcibiades* 34). On the day that Alcibiades decided to sail into the Piraeus the Athenians were celebrating the Plynteria, an annual festival of Athena held in the early summer. Athenian women, maidens, and ephebes took an ancient seated statue of the goddess from the Acropolis, stripped it of its usual robes and adornments, veiled it, and processed down to the sea at Phaleron, where maidens washed the wooden cult image in the sea. It was thought to be an unlucky day; many temples were closed and public business was suspended. Because the image was covered when it arrived at the sea where Alcibiades was disembarking, some thought that Athens' patron goddess was not willing to welcome him home. Alcibiades returned anyway. These accounts of Alcibiades' return and Athena's rejection were composed well after the fall of Athens and the death of Alcibiades, and they bear witness to the ways in which Athenians came to later understand how their city's ancient rituals anticipated Alcibiades' fate.

SIX

Dionysus

Civic Rituals of Wine, Theater, and Transformation

ALL THINGS ARE IN FLUX. Plato famously attributed this aphorism to the Ionian philosopher Heraclitus (*Cratylus* 402a). Alcibiades' twists and turns, from Athens to Sparta to Persia to Athens, certainly illustrated the flux of power and personality, and Athenians who during one decade suffered two coups, two counterrevolutions, and a general amnesty could speak directly to the often painful process of political transformation. But long before Alcibiades, Heraclitus, or Plato there was Dionysus, the god with the great power to transform. Grapes yielded wine, the youth matured to adulthood, the domestic wife could become wild with Dionysian madness, and the masks of drama revealed truth. Whereas life led to death in the natural order of things, death itself yielded to renewed life with the regenerative energy of Dionysus.

Dionysus today beckons as one of the most recognizable of the Olympian gods. His close association with wine leads many modern readers to identify him as the god of intoxication, but the Greeks generally drank their wine diluted with water—only barbarians drank it neat—and in fifth-century art and literature Dionysus is seldom depicted actually drinking wine or intoxicated. Viewing Dionysus mainly as a drunken god limits our potential for understanding Athenian religious life. Although Romans several centuries later would identify the Greek Dionysus with a drunken Italian god named Liber, for fifth-century Athenians Dionysus represented not so much the powerful effects of wine as the actual wine itself and the process that rendered grapes into wine. Dionysus inspired not simple intoxication but rather transformation at the natural, the individual, and the collective levels.

Like Demeter, the Greek god called Dionysus began as a deity with particular connections to agriculture and fertility, and only later developed additional cultural resonances for men and women who lived in market towns and small cities. By the fifth century the civic face of Dionysus in Athens looked in two directions: toward the rural countryside and toward the city with the Agora and its political institutions. The state festivals that Athenians celebrated reflected both aspects of Dionysus's identity. As the god of the grapevine, Dionysus was the agricultural deity whose beneficial powers extended over an important product in the economy of Attica. According to ancestral tradition he watched over the cultivation of the grapevine and the wine made from grapes. Nurturing the vines required careful attention across generations, and invoking the protective presence of this god at the right times of the year kept grapevines under his protection. But Dionysus also became a god who brought new forms of culture to people dwelling in the city, and Dionysian dramatic festivals were generally celebrated in or very near the Agora in the fifth century. Just as the worship of Demeter changed over time, so the festivals of Dionysus were also adjusted to reflect the interests of a unified and autonomous *polis,* and later the Athenian empire.

Familiar images that depict Dionysus with wine cups and masks only partially reflect the state of extant evidence. Inscriptional and archaeological sources augment our knowledge of the god of the vine and madness, and illustrate for us further complexities of religious life in the polytheistic *polis* of classical Athens. Athenian civic calendars document how Dionysus shared festivals with Apollo as well as with Hermes and Athena. Public festivals celebrated in the demes and in the center of Athens featured dramatic performances; these tragic festivals offered perhaps the most visible way to take part in and experience the power of Dionysus, but other civic holidays for this god were celebrated in the private homes of Athenians, among extended families and groups of intimate friends. Unlike the civic worship of Athena that generally took place on the prominent height of the Acropolis, not all fifth-century civic traditions that honored Dionysus at home or in the countryside required grand building programs. Theaters during the lifetimes of Pericles and Socrates were temporary wooden structures disassembled when the festivals were over, and Dionysus's sanctuary on the south slope of the Acropolis contained a simple and modest temple. Historians find it difficult if not impossible to fully document all the Dionysian festivals, but sources do consistently confirm that the festival system in Athens encompassed the entire political community in the city and countryside to create a whole, coherent system.

The details of Dionysus's exploits preserved in archaic and classical poetry hint further at the flexibility of the Greek religious mentality. Dionysus was a god of life as embodied in the grapevine, a god of the dead, and a god of the potential to overcome death. Dionysus was celebrated for simply having arrived long ago among the Athenians. His initial arrival happened by sea in one account, and by land in another. He could appear in animal or human form—as a beardless youth, a bearded mature man, or a young woman. In one tragedy produced on the Athenian stage in the late fifth century, true Dionysian madness is reserved not for the god but for those mortals who do not have the sense to worship Dionysus at his civic festivals and thus to experience his presence alongside other residents of the *polis*.

The walled imperial Athens of Pericles' and Socrates' lifetimes grew into a densely populated urban center, many of whose citizens were probably more concerned with current events, the administration of the *polis*, and the status of the *archē* than with the condition of vineyards and the outlook for the year's grape harvest. The civic festivals of Dionysus actively reminded all Athenian residents of their close historic ties to traditional life in the Attic countryside. Of the five major Dionysian festivals celebrated in the fifth century, two drew attention to viticulture and the production of wine, while three placed emphasis on wine and its place in dramatic performance and competition. Some of the themes that emerged from Dionysian worship also resurfaced in different forms in the god's more secretive *mystēria* and *orgia*. Athenian traditions surrounding Dionysus provide another glimpse into how civic worship extended throughout the *polis* and helped transform political life in the classical city. The varieties of expression found in Dionysus's civic rites reveal a good deal about the continuities of Athenian social and political life, continuities that transcended the traumatic political changes that wracked Athens as the empire came to an end.

ANTHESTERIA: DIONYSUS AND HERMES

The rhythm of Dionysian worship in the civic calendar of Athens focused on the winter months, from the time in the late autumn when harvested grapes were pressed into new wine to the spring when the new wine was first opened and tasted. Within these six months were situated at least five publicly financed festivals for the god: the Oschophoria, the Rural Dionysia, the Lenaea, the Anthesteria, and the City Dionysia. Four of these festivals lasted three or more days; this totals more than two weeks of public Dionysian celebration during the cool winter when the demands of the agricultural economy were less compelling. Like the civic festivals discussed in earlier chapters, public rituals for Dionysus required dedications: offerings of grain, libations of wine, and animal sacrifices with the festive communal meals that followed *thysia*. State festivals offered the residents of Athens a respite from work, whether they labored in the markets and industries of the city and its harbor, or on the farms in the outlying rural demes and villages.

In the spring of the year the Anthesteria celebrated the civilizing power of Dionysus experienced in the transformation of the harvested grape into wine, the essential beverage of Greek ritual practice and human social interaction. Grapes can grow even in the wild, but it takes human culture to create wine. New wine that had been stored in the fall was for the first time opened in the spring at a three-day festival that ran from the 11th to the 13th of Anthesterion, approximately late February or early March. The Anthesteria was one of the oldest of Athenian festivals, widely observed among *poleis* that claimed an Ionian heritage, and so probably dated back to at least the ninth century. Though each day of the Anthesteria had its own particular mood and festivities, all three days alike brought to mind the god who helped civilize humans with the gift of the vine and the knowledge of how to turn the grape into wine. Anthesterion, the month of *anthea* or flowers, was a time for new life and new beginnings, both for *polis* communities as a whole and for the individual residents. The new wine symbolized the annual renewal, and rituals celebrated during the festival showed how the wine of Dionysus had the ability to invigorate the civic community when residents were allowed to reexperience the city from a different perspective. At the same time that residents experienced new beginnings, the spirits of the dead also returned for the Anthesteria. The god of transformation required Athenians to dissolve their normal social order and change the way they typically experienced their communities.

Each day of the Anthesteria had its own name—Pithoigia, Choes, and Chytroi—and these names concretely recalled the god of the grape by referring to customs of storing and serving wine. Storing new wine when it was first pressed required skills beyond those of a farmer in the countryside, namely the skills of the potters who produced the vessels needed to store and transport the liquid and then serve and consume it. Ceramic skills were another mark of men who live in a civilized community, and Athenian craftsmen excelled in the production and decoration of pottery, especially after the sixth century. The English word "ceramic" comes from the neighborhood in Athens where skilled potters plied their craft: the Kerameikos (also spelled Ceramicus). The Anthesteria festival celebrated Dionysus by evoking the skills that enabled an ancient Mediterranean society to capture the power of the grapevine: each of the three days was named for a different type of vessel used for wine.

The first day, Pithoigia, celebrated the opening of large storage jars called *pithoi*. New wine had been stored and sealed in *pithoi* after the initial wine pressing in the fall, and vessels were ceremoniously brought to Athens, where civic priests opened the jars and dedicated the wine to Dionysus. When first opened the new wine dedicated at the Anthesteria constituted an *aparchē*—a first fruits offering to the god. This initial opening took place in the sanctuary of Dionysus in the Marshes, a sanctuary that has yet to be identified. The Pithoigia filled an important function for the *polis* during this time of year, since it required the citizen farmers of Attica to gather as a community at a common location in the city. Plenty of priests and civic officials must have been present to receive offerings on behalf of the god, as well as to direct traffic.

Local farmers brought their great *pithoi* to the sanctuary individually, but it was as a civic community that the jars were opened. Wine was an essential ingredient used in prayers directed to all the gods of the Olympian pantheon; when a worshipper invoked any god or goddess, he or she poured a small stream of wine onto the ground—the *spondē* or libation—to accompany the words addressed to the deity. Wine was equally important to the whole community since wine, diluted to greater or lesser degrees with water, was the principal beverage in the daily diet of every Athenian, regardless of age, gender, or civic status. All those who had a place in the *polis,* human and divine alike, had a stake in the new wine being presented to the god and officially recognized by the ritual institutions of the *polis.*

Once the *pithoi* of wine were opened on the first day and civic priests had received Dionysus's share, the civic community could then get on with the social activity of consuming wine together. This was one of the main activities of the Anthesteria's second day called the Choes—the day of jugs. A *chous,* the singular of the plural *choes,* generally held about three-quarters of a gallon of liquid. On the Choes new wine was poured from the large *pithoi* storage jars into these more manageable ceramic serving pieces. Thousands of *choes* of various sizes have been excavated in Athens over the years, and we know from later sources that a special ceramic market was held in Athens in preparation for this festival. *Oinochoai*, literally "wine jugs," is another word for these particular vessels that are so well represented in museum collections today. A variety of domestic and mythical scenes decorated the jugs, and one of the more charming characteristics of these *choes* is that somewhere on the vessel the artist often depicted a *chous*—either in the hands of a worshipper or in the background of the scene.

On either the first or second day of the festival, Athenians also celebrated Dionysus by organizing a great procession through the city that commemorated the god's initial arrival in Athens in the distant past. Images of this *pompē* are preserved on a number of vases; in these striking scenes the god is shown coming into the city on a wagon fashioned to look like a ship. Dionysus was always depicted in Athenian art and literature as being from somewhere else—from Thebes, or Thrace, or even Lydia; he was a foreigner, and a potentially disruptive one, too. At the Athenian Anthesteria, Dionysus entered the city after a journey over the sea. Since Dionysus was never imagined as being a native of Attica, it was the job of the Athenians to welcome him into their civic community. While Dionysus was always identified as a foreigner in Athenian myth and cult, careful scholarship in the twentieth century showed that the deity Dionysus did originally arise in Greece in the second millennium BCE. Some scholars have therefore concluded that the energy of Dionysus was so potent that Greeks and Athenians hesitated to claim him as one of their own. It was psychologically more comfortable for residents to consider him an alien and allow him a place in the *polis* only when everyone had gathered together as a larger community to welcome him.

The community at large observed the Choes by gathering both as a civic group in the Agora and afterward in individual homes. In public and private celebrations alike, the customs of wine drinking were turned on their head. Normally citizen men drank together among their peers at a meal called a symposium in a citizen's home, or they shared a meal in the Tholos, the Prytaneion, or one of the other common dining rooms found in the Agora. Formal dining in this culture did not involve chairs set around a common table; rather, sofas were lined up along the walls of a dining room, with small trays of food set before each diner. Reclining on couches in a dining room, citizens were typically served from a common mixing bowl of wine (krater) supplied by the host. The host was also responsible for diluting the wine with water in whatever proportion he thought best. At smaller domestic symposia and in the larger public dining facilities, male citizens segregated themselves from women and slaves, drinking their wine among political peers while enjoying lively conversation and argument.

Contrary to the normal customs, at the Choes Athenians watched a traditional drinking ritual in which prominent public figures competed against each other. A trumpet call signaled the start of this unusual race and the priest of Dionysus oversaw that the proper *nomoi* were followed. Each person participating in the drinking contest brought his own wine already mixed in his *chous* as well as his own wine cup; he sat upright at his own table, and drank the new wine in complete and solemn silence. The first person to finish his jug of wine was declared the winner, and sources list a variety of items as prizes: perhaps a goatskin full of wine, or a cake specially baked for the occasion. Similar drinking rituals were probably celebrated elsewhere in Athens and in the outlying village districts.

On the second day of the Anthesteria the typical Dionysian shift in normal behaviors played a part not only in the heart of the *polis* but also at home in the *oikos,* or individual household. This domestic side to the festival of the Anthesteria is noteworthy since most civic cults were not celebrated in the home. But on the day of Choes the festival used household rituals to reposition the power of male citizens: worshipping Dionysus meant new roles for slaves as well as children in the *oikos.* The inclusion of slaves in domestic festivities again inverted normal customs for drinking and dining. This day was one of the few in the Athenian calendar when slaves were allowed to drink and dine alongside their masters—the other possible occasion was at the Rural Dionysia later in the winter. Normally domestic slaves labored to complete the countless menial tasks required to run a household, such as cooking meals and serving citizen men in the dining room, but on this day slaves could enjoy the license that the worship of Dionysus offered and become the social and ritual equals of their masters. Dionysus the god of transformation functioned as a social leveler.

The inclusion of children in the Choes marked not so much an inversion of social roles as a shift in boundaries that marked a social transition. Physical evidence fills in what is missing from the literary and historical record. While archaeological excavations in Athens have unearthed thousands of full-sized *choes,* hundreds of miniature *choes* have also been found. These smaller versions of the wine jug belonged to the children of Athenian citizens—boys mostly but girls too sometimes, judging from the images of children painted on the vessels. The toy jugs apparently marked a social coming-of-age for small children who had made the transition out of infancy and dependence on milk and into the larger community of Athenians who drank wine. To celebrate the occasion family members gave children miniature jugs—a smaller-scale toy replica of the three-quarter-gallon jug that their parents used. What may be most curious from our point of view is the age of the children in this rite of passage that led the child into the company of wine drinkers in Athens: the children on the miniature jugs are barely more than toddlers, and certainly no older than 4 or 5. The little *choes* jugs depict children at play, amusing themselves with dice, tops, and hoops. As they did on adult-sized jugs, artists painted in the scene's background an image of the small *chous* that was a part of every Athenian child's life, as can be seen in figure 11.

One Athenian inscription listed the celebration of the Choes alongside birth, the Ephebia (an adolescent coming-of-age celebration), and marriage. These four important rituals marked the development of an Athenian citizen as he reached full adulthood and assumed a political identity among his peers. Burial customs also underscored the ritual importance of the Choes for Athenians: some toy jugs have been found in the graves of small children. Archaeologists speculate that *choes* were buried in the graves of infants who died before they could reach their first celebration of the Anthesteria, much as older Athenian girls who died before marriage were buried with *loutrophoroi,* the particular water vessel that was part of a bride's preparation for marriage. Burial customs in both cases ensured that those who died before their time could still enjoy the rituals, and the ritual vessels, in the afterlife.

According to the Greek custom of reckoning time from sunset one day to sunset the next, the final day of the festival called Chytroi began on the evening of the Choes with an unusual ritual celebrated in the Agora. The traditional custom on this final night of the Anthesteria cemented the welcoming of Dionysus into the city with the public celebration of a sacred marriage, or *hieros gamos.* The Athenian *basilinna,* the wife of the *archōn basileus,* took center stage on this evening as she symbolically wedded the god in a temple located near the public dining rooms of the Prytaneion in the Agora. While the mythological tradition recounted other sacred marriages among the Olympian gods, above all that of Zeus and Hera, and while the union of Hades and Kore was perhaps acknowledged at the Eleusinian Mysteries, this ritual at the Anthesteria is the only instance we know of in which a mortal was symbolically united with a god in Athens. How it was done remains uncertain: did the *basilinna* go to a place sacred to Dionysus to couple with her husband, or with a priest of Dionysus?

Figure 11. An example of a child's first wine *chous* from the celebration of the Athenian Anthesteria. Red-figure Athenian *chous* (wine jug), ca. 420 BCE. Boston Museum of Fine Arts. Henry Lillie Pierce Fund, 01.8087.

Did her husband the *archōn basileus* actually become a priest of Dionysus for this one evening? We do not know the details, but at the wedding of Dionysus and the *basilinna* Athenians not only welcomed the stranger Dionysus into their midst, they ritually made him a member of their civic family. This solemn sexual union represented the joining of the Athenian political community with the vegetation god whose power made their lives sweeter, more harmonious, and more productive.

One last ritual from the Anthesteria also included a segment of the population normally absent from Athenian civic life, namely the spirits of the dead. Athenians sought contact with the long-ago inhabitants of Attica by inviting them to a public meal on this day, Chytroi. It was named for the type of simple vessel that was used either for cooking or for storing water in the kitchen—water that could be mixed with the wine of Dionysus. Families at home cooked a dish of mixed seeds and grains and dedicated it to Hermes Chthonios, the manifestation of Hermes that tied him to the earth (*chthonos*) and to the departed souls that he accompanied below the earth. Dionysus thus shared the Anthesteria with another Olympian god: Hermes, the god in constant contact with both the upper and lower worlds. Honoring Hermes on this day brought the departed dead a bit closer and allowed Dionysus to oversee yet another kind of transformation. At the same time, however, the Athenians didn't want ghosts too near. They canceled any official business that would require them to swear oaths, and they closed off all civic sanctuaries and temples so that no spirits would pollute the public holy spaces. At home, Athenian householders also marked their doors with an apotropaic sign, and started the day by chewing on a special leaf that protected them from the dead.

The transformative power of Dionysus linked the city back to the vineyard and civilized all the residents of Athens regardless of where they lived. Citizens drank with slaves and children, and a mortal queen married the god. The dead momentarily crossed the boundary that normally separated them from the living. The ancient rites of the Anthesteria brought the entire community together, and everybody celebrated the god of the vineyard who was also the quintessential god in the city.

OSCHOPHORIA AND PYANOPSIA: DIONYSUS, THESEUS, AND APOLLO

Dionysus may have started out as a vegetation deity who nourished the grapevines of Hellas and Attica, but in Athens the god also came to signal the transformative power of political unification. Much as Athenians celebrated the Anthesteria wine festival in the spring, in the fall of the year when the grapes were being harvested in the countryside Athenians honored the god of the vine at an urban festival called the Oschophoria. *Ōschoi* are clusters of grapes, and at the Oschophoria youths brought a token sample of the grape harvest and presented it to the god of the vine. Two ephebes from an aristocratic and wealthy Athenian family were chosen to be *ōschophoroi,* "the bearers of the grapes." These young male citizens just entering into adulthood presented the gift to Dionysus on behalf of the entire *polis* community in a first fruits offering (*aparchē*) dedicated before the year's first wine was pressed in the rural villages. Visual evidence from vases and sculptural friezes suggests that grapes were brought while still on the vines—young men carried branches heavy with the fruit, led a merry parade throughout the city, and dedicated the branches at one of Dionysus's temples.

Dionysus shared the harvest season with his divine half-brother Apollo, who was worshipped with similar rituals at his own festival called the Pyanopsia. Inscriptional sources are not completely clear as to whether the festivals were held the very same or nearly the same day. Either way, the Athenians honored Dionysus and Apollo more or less simultaneously not because they were culturally opposed to each other but because the two gods shared important functions in polytheistic Greece. Tradition held that these sons of Zeus had more in common than the same father: they also shared the sanctuary at Delphi. Although it is often forgotten today, the famous oracle in the mountains of Phocis was sacred to Dionysus as well as Apollo. One account attests that the *omphalos* was the tomb of Dionysus, a reference to the mythical death and rebirth of the vegetation god. For four months every year, starting in the late fall, Dionysus had jurisdiction over the seat of prophecy at Delphi. Apollo returned in the spring, and exercised authority until the following autumn.

As the annual transition from Apollo to Dionysus was being made at Delphi, the Athenians celebrated the Pyanopsia and the Oschophoria near the beginning of Pyanopsion, a month named after the Apollo festival. Those leading the procession at the Pyanopsia appear in Athenian art to be boys just barely entering adolescence. Pyanopsia itself means "bean boiling," a reference to a stew that was prepared and eaten on this day. The stew was composed of a variety of available produce, beans, and grains— but no meat. Because the Pyanopsia was another of a handful of festivals celebrated by *poleis* that claimed Ionian ancestry, scholars suspect that it is among the more ancient of Athenian festivals, reaching back to at least the ninth century and the Ionian migrations from the mainland into the Aegean Sea. In perhaps the sixth century, Athenian rituals of the Pyanopsia became linked with the island of Delos and stories about the Athenian hero Theseus. Traditional oral accounts held that when Theseus landed at Delos after slaying the Minotaur on Crete, he made a vow to Apollo that he would dedicate a special offering to the god if he arrived home to Athens safely. When he finally landed on the shores of Attica, Theseus and his companions took what was left over from their provisions on the ship, concocted a stew of beans, grains, and vegetables, and dedicated it to Apollo before sharing it among themselves. These ritual connections between Athens and Delos took on an added dimension following the Persian Wars when Delos served as the seat of the Delian League.

As chapter 2 showed, the political community typically defined itself through the rituals of *thysia* and the distribution of meat among citizens. Even though ancestral *nomoi* precluded rites of civic sacrifice at the Pyanopsia, other traditions associated with the festival still point to the Athenian political community and its mythical origins in the heroic past. The tale recounting how Theseus dedicated his leftover food to Apollo may reflect the rising popularity of the Theseus cycle of myths that emerged in Athens during the last quarter of the sixth and early fifth centuries. Modern studies of changing iconography in Attic vase painting have shown that interest in Theseus suddenly intensified during the rule of the Pisistratids and Cleisthenes. The hero had long been credited with many feats: myths famously related Theseus's defeat of the monstrous Minotaur in the labyrinth of Minos on Crete. But equally impressive to Athenians in the early fifth century were accounts of how Theseus was the first Athenian leader to unite all of Attica into a single political community—what the Athenians referred to as the "synoecism" of Attica. A second surge of interest in Theseus occurred shortly after the Persian Wars, when the Athenian leader Cimon, following the instructions of an oracle, reportedly brought home to Athens the bones of Theseus and placed them in a new shrine. It seems likely that during these decades under Cleisthenes and Cimon traditional stories about Theseus's adventures were adapted and attached to older Ionian festivals in the Attic calendar, including this festival for Apollo. Unified Athens gained power and prestige during the late sixth and early fifth centuries, and Theseus became an iconic figure who symbolized its new prominence. At traditional annual celebrations, Athenians continued to observe a common and ancient Ionian festival while they simultaneously called attention to a native heroic figure who long ago solidified their own larger political community in Attica.

Another important feature of the Pyanopsia was the bearing of a sacred olive bough, the *eiresiōnē*, to Apollo. Wool was woven through the branches and food items—figs, other fruits, breads, and pastries—were tied on. The boys carried the decorated branches throughout the city and sang songs, stopping at houses every so often to beg for gifts. The boughs, symbols of fruitfulness and abundance, were seen as a blessing, and Athenians hung them above the doors to their homes. When the procession ended the youths presented at least one *eiresiōnē* in the temple of Apollo. Literary sources, especially comedy, record that the festive activities of the youths at the Pyanopsia held a special appeal for the residents of fifth-century Athens.

Although Apollo is not often considered a deity overly concerned with the fertility of the land, practices on this festival day clearly suggest that in Attica he came to have associations with the agricultural rhythms of the year. The beans and grains that made up Theseus's stew were the very same products that would soon be sown as winter crops. At the Pyanopsia Athenians looked both forward and backward as they worshipped Apollo: looking back at the abundance of the current harvest symbolized with the vegetables and the *eiresiōnē,* and looking forward toward the fertility of the crops to be sown—the grains in the Pyanopsion stew. By dedicating portions of produce, beans, and grains to Apollo, they affirmed their continuing relationship with a god who had once helped the young hero credited in myth with the unification of Attica and foundation of their *polis* community.

Similar energies also motivated the Oschophoria, the Dionysian festival that took place at about the same time in Athens. Two ephebes headed the Oschophoria celebrations and, just like the younger boys at Apollo's Pyanopsia, carried branches. The young *ōschophoroi* came from a group called the Salaminioi, an ancient Athenian family that traced their common descent through the male line and fulfilled specific ritual obligations. The two young men leading the procession through the streets of Athens were followed by a chorus of youths, singing traditional songs to Dionysus that were said to blend together both joy and sadness. A group of young women were included in the party. The procession started in the heart of the city at a sanctuary of Dionysus and then went south, stopping some distance outside the city in the sanctuary of Athena Skiras in the deme of Phaleron. Within this precinct of Athena stood a smaller shrine for Dionysus, the Oschophorion, where the remainder of the festival was held.

While some earlier scholars classified the Oschophoria as a festival primarily honoring the goddess Athena and not Dionysus, a closer analysis of the Oschophoria reveals significant Dionysian elements. Named after the *ōschophoroi,* the aristocratic young men who led the procession and carried the *ōschoi* to the shrine in Phaleron, the Oschophoria celebrated wine and fertility at multiple levels. *Ōschoi* was an uncommon word, but it probably referred to bunches of grapes as they hung on the vine. The procession with the branches of *ōschoi* mirrored the procession with the *eiresiōnē* at Apollo's Pyanopsia: in both cases young males carried branches laden with fruit and produce—branches with grapes for Dionysus, branches with other fruits for Apollo. These boys and youths, who represented the future of the community, dedicated the branches as an *aparchē* and thank offerings to the gods at precisely the time of year when the annual produce was being harvested. Visual evidence for the Oschophoria from vases and friezes supports this understanding. We see depictions of young men alongside Dionysus carrying the branches with bunches of round, ripe grapes hanging from them.

Dionysus was a god who encouraged his worshippers to take on a new identity, and Dionysian role reversal was celebrated at the Oschophoria in ways not evident at Apollo's Pyanopsia. The ephebes bringing the *ōschoi* to Dionysus did not lead the procession dressed as youths; rather their public appearance deliberately mimicked that of adolescent Athenian girls. The Oschophoria ritual called for the two chosen ephebes to be transvestites. Cross-dressed in what appears to be an Ionic chiton, an obsolete fashion for men in the fifth century though still sometimes worn by women, the two ephebes approached Dionysus with the grapes that would create a new vintage of wine. They came to Dionysus as boyish young women—or as girlish young men. Such striking androgyny and gender reversal were a hallmark of Dionysian worship.

The leadership of the two *ōschophoroi* recalled the myth of Theseus and the synoecism of Attica. Ancient sources explain the ritual transvestism at the Oschophoria through the same myth of Theseus celebrated at the Pyanopsia. When Theseus was sent to Crete to battle the Minotaur in the labyrinth of Minos, he was one member of a cohort of fourteen young Athenians—seven ephebes and seven maidens. But one version of the myth included a curious detail: Theseus substituted two fresh-faced youths for two of the maidens. He dressed them in women's clothing, and hoped that the advantage of two additional young men would help him overcome the Minotaur. In the end, victory over the monster was accomplished not through physical might but through cunning and the power of erotic love felt by the Cretan princess Ariadne for Theseus. Still, the Athenians preserved the memory of Theseus's ruse by annually choosing two ephebes from an ancient family and reenacting this particularly Dionysian aspect of his adventure.

Other worshippers of Dionysus took on new social roles at the Oschophoria: in addition to these two symbolic maidens who led the procession carrying grape vines to Phaleron, a group of real females, adolescent daughters of noblemen, processed behind the cross-dressed *ōschophoroi* and chorus of youths. These women carried food for them all. An oral tradition maintained that they represented the Athenian maidens who accompanied Theseus to Crete. These *deipnophoroi,* or "supper carriers," were not simply female servants waiting on the young men and priests of Dionysus; they became the ritual equals of the ephebes. Once the maidens with the dinner, the chorus, and the ephebes carrying the vines arrived in Phaleron, sacrifices were made at the altar of Dionysus. On this occasion the young women shared in the feast as social equals alongside the young men—contrary to the normal customs of *thysia* and segregated ritual dining. In this moment of ritual inversion, the maidens and the ephebes drew attention to Dionysus's ability to promote fertility and transformation in the community. The young people, all on the verge of adulthood, clearly held the promise of future generations of citizens, and at the same time they paid honor to the heroic deeds of Theseus and his companions—deeds the Athenians believed had culminated in the unification of Attica. Following the festival meal the young men continued to commemorate the adventures of Theseus by competing in athletic events: ephebes competed in hotly contested footraces organized by tribe. In this ritual play, young men on the verge of adulthood prepared for the competitive field of Athenian politics they would soon be entering.

But the Oschophoria's embrace of fruit, fertility, and the future extended beyond the feast and the games. Perhaps the most curious and cryptic of details about this festival has to do with its name. Ancient literary sources are inconsistent in their spelling of *ōschoi* and Oschophoria. The ancient Greek alphabet contained two different representations of the vowel "o": a short o, omicron, and a long ō, omega. Spelled with omega, *ōschoi* mean "bunches of grapes," and the Oschophoria was the festival when ephebes brought harvested grapes to the sanctuary in Phaleron and dedicated them to the god. But spelled with an initial omicron, Oschophoria refers to carrying not a bunch of grapes but scrota, from *oschē,* a term found in ancient medical texts.

The visual likeness between a cluster of ripe grapes and the male testes is clear. Even if scholarship has not yet confirmed that Greeks themselves made a direct and conscious link between the grapes the youths carried and a word for the male genitals, at the very least a Greek pun is at work here. The difference between the two spoken words is a fraction of a second. In the celebration of a festival, with the music, noise, and organized chaos that accompanies a procession, how could you be sure whether the "o" you were hearing was long or short? Possibly both meanings registered, the grapes sacred to the god (long ō) and the latent fertility of ephebes on the cusp of becoming adult citizen men (short o). Each form could easily symbolize the other.

In the end, the Oschophoria was a wild and joyous Dionysian festival, and a popular one too. Young men dressed as girls carried branches bearing symbols of male fertility while other youths sang seasonal folk songs, with young women accompanying them and in the end sharing in the god's feast as equals. In ritual all celebrated and enacted the traditional narratives of civic identity. While some normal social customs were ignored (women normally ate separately from men), other roles were inverted (men disguised themselves as women). New grapes were grapes, the gift of the god to humans, and at the same time they were the symbols of human fecundity. In both senses the grapes indicated the abundance of life, and it was this abundance that was celebrated publicly in the late autumn in honor of the god Dionysus.

The rituals of the Pyanopsia and Oschophoria reveal deep connections between the gods Apollo and Dionysus. Recent scholarship is coming to see the god Apollo in new ways: not only was he the god of rationality, prophecy, and healing, he was also a deity who protected the civic community in the assembly and watched over young men as they made the transition from childhood and adolescence to full citizen adulthood. Likewise the worship of Dionysus honored the life force of the grapevine in the rural vineyards, and also the vibrant social energy that wine brought to civic gatherings. Both festivals worked to bring citizens together in harmony, and the civic community needed both gods. Some scholars see traces of ancient male initiation rites in the two fall festivals of Dionysus and Apollo. Boys and ephebes gradually made the transition to adult citizenship in the context of the larger body of citizens. When the Oschophoria festival culminated in athletic contests at Phaleron, the young men who competed in their tribes honored a deity and a hero whose shared concern for the political future of the community spanned the boundary of the generations.

As Dionysus shared the harvest season with Apollo, so too he shared it with Athena and to a certain extent even with Demeter, goddess of grain; the sanctuary of Athena Skiras in Phaleron where the Oschophoria was celebrated was also the site for the celebration of Demeter's Skira in June. Life in an urban community relied on the rural areas where crops were harvested and new wine pressed; but equally important for the *polis* was the socialization of young people of both sexes. The civic rites of autumn that honored multiple gods and included boys, maidens, and ephebes linked the social world of the *polis* with the natural world that supported life in the *polis.* Attaching traditional tales of Theseus to older Ionian festivals of Dionysus and Apollo allowed the residents of Athena's city to commemorate the synoecism of Attica at the same time that they reaffirmed their social and military ties to allied Ionian *poleis* in the Delian League. When the Athenians created a naval empire following the Persian Wars, they relied more than ever on the idea of shared Ionian interests and customs. In these two festivals we can see how polytheism in classical Athens was no simple matter; the functions of different gods complemented each other to maintain stability and continuity in the *polis.* Civic festivals implicitly acknowledged the interdependence of the Olympian gods in their support of human communal activity. Political life in the city relied on the structures and stories of ancestral polytheistic practice, and over time civic rites reflected changes in the *polis* itself.

While rooted in the ancient rhythms of viticulture and winemaking, the autumn Oschophoria and the Anthesteria in the spring also served the needs of residents in the urban center of Athens. Like all Dionysian celebrations, these two civic festivals allowed worshippers to break free from some of the normal social barriers that kept citizens and residents highly stratified and segregated within the *polis:* on these days women, slaves, and children could join with male citizens in the worship of the god of wine. Dionysus also was a god who helped young men find their political identity in the community of adult citizens. The civic rites of this god were both ancient and innovative, responding to the needs of the *polis* community as they changed. This same ability to adapt will play a role in the other Dionysian festivals in Athens, the dramatic festivals.

DIONYSUS AND THE DRAMATIC FESTIVALS

Once the grape harvest was celebrated in the fall, grapes pressed, and the new wine sealed in storage jars, the Athenian ritual calendar focused on entertainment, relaxation, and creative expression found in the worship of Dionysus. Dionysus was the god of theater, and theater had deeply religious roots. Athenians worshipped Dionysus with theatrical performances three times a year: the Rural Dionysia and the Lenaea were celebrated during the dead of winter, and the season of dramatic festivals culminated with the City Dionysia in the spring. The three festivals were evenly spaced over four consecutive months, and at all three festivals worshippers directly experienced Dionysian transformation through the rituals of dramatic production. Like Athena's Panathenaea in the summer, these festivals and sacrifices for Dionysus were publicly financed and organized. The same Athenians who celebrated solemn civic rites for a virginal goddess of victory under the summer sun then engaged in public drinking and voiced ritual obscenities at official, state-financed religious holidays.

The dramatic rituals that honored Dionysus went beyond simple role-playing to enable worshippers to examine themselves and their community. Fifth-century theater could directly comment on what it meant to be a citizen of a democracy at war. Under Pericles the annual dramatic festivals of Dionysus became religious occasions that celebrated the Athenian empire itself. At the same time the worship of Dionysus celebrated political dissent, and allowed for critiques of political leaders. The dramatic festivals of the Athenians underwent a rich and complex development in the decades following the Persian Wars. The discussion that follows presents an overview of these three Dionysian holidays, analyzing them as though they were static and unchanging. This is far from the truth: the political realities of the Athenian empire, the ongoing war with Sparta, and factional fighting among Athenians themselves all had an impact on how citizens, residents, and visitors in Attica encountered the god of the vine and theater in the *polis*. The worship of Dionysus changed as Athens itself changed.

Rural Dionysia

The Rural Dionysia comprised numerous local festivals throughout Attica held over the course of many days in the midwinter month of Posideon, approximately December. These festivals did not focus on the seat of power and urban life in Athens, but rather reflected the deep agricultural roots of the *polis* in the rural districts of Attica. In demes and villages townspeople celebrated Dionysus with processions, old-fashioned fun and games, and deeply traditional symbols. At its most minimal, the Rural Dionysia featured a procession and ribald, abusive (but nevertheless ancestral) songs. The central symbol of the god in the festive *pompē* was an oversize phallus made of wood and leather. On Attic vases that depict the procession, young men are dwarfed by the phallus pole they support together on their shoulders. The procession ended with sacrifice and a communal feast. After the *pompē* and sacrificial feast, men played traditional games and sang the customary phallic songs of humor and abuse. Scholiasts and late antique commentators who discussed the games played at the Rural Dionysia made special mention of jumping and balancing games—hopping up and down on one leg, and trying to stay balanced atop a greased goatskin that was filled with wine. Doubtless the goatskin of wine did not stay full for long.

A comic version of the procession and song is preserved in the *Acharnians,* a play written by the Athenian comic poet Aristophanes in 425. In this comedy the hero's daughter serving as basket bearer, or *kanephoros,* led the *pompē;* the slave who processed behind her carried the phallus on a pole, while the hero Dicaeopolis sang a song of abuse that harshly criticized the current politicians in the city (*Acharnians* 241–83). Scholars are not sure what to conclude from Dicaeopolis's inclusion of his slave Xanthias in this comic depiction of the Rural Dionysia. Does the presence of the slave reflect the idiosyncratic nature of Dicaeopolis's private celebration, or were slaves included at home on this occasion as they were at the Anthesteria? Is it a comic touch, or is this another Dionysian festival that overturned normal social boundaries? We need more evidence. Plutarch's first-century description of a traditional Dionysian festival included the vine and a jar of wine in the procession alongside the goat and the phallus, and he noted that this was a day when slaves and masters dined together—but this later evidence cannot confirm what happened in classical Athens (Plutarch *Moralia* 527d).

There is evidence for traditions of rudimentary dramatic performances at some, but probably not all, celebrations of the Rural Dionysia in Attica. Inscriptional records of fifth-century decrees detail the rites, sacrifices, and proceedings at local festivals, and sometimes these details include dramatic productions. In at least three outlying rural demes, archaeologists have unearthed remains of small stone theaters that can be dated to the classical period. Such theaters may have been built for the Rural Dionysia; the oblong theater in Thoricus is the best preserved of these. Literary evidence also provides insight into the festivals and theaters outside the center of Athens. When Thucydides narrated the struggle in 411 between the oligarchs and the democrats, he noted in passing how the democratic hoplites laid down their arms before entering the theater of Dionysus in the Piraeus. They used the large sacred precinct as a meeting place to discuss their response to the Four Hundred back in Athens (Thucydides 8.93). While the hoplites' meeting had little to do with the worship of Dionysus, it does demonstrate that the physical space occupied by Dionysus in the *polis* facilitated civic life in Athens.

Since the Rural Dionysia were celebrated on a rolling basis throughout the demes of Attica, it seems reasonable to speculate that traveling companies of actors made the rounds during this month of local festivals, along with citizens who took special pleasure in watching drama. An anecdote from Plato's *Republic* provides us with perhaps the clearest picture of how Athenians celebrated the Rural Dionysia in the late fifth century. The dialogue describes how men "eager to see new things" traveled from village to village at this time of year to attend as many Dionysian festivals as they could (Plato *Republic* 5.475d). Given that work obligations were not terribly demanding during the winter months, it is easy to imagine men taking a break and crisscrossing the countryside of Attica for a few weeks. Observing this festival entailed visiting relatives and friends and sharing in free meals among the demes, all the while imbibing wine in the worship of the god. The social nature of the Rural Dionysia promoted communication between Athens and the rural districts of Attica, thereby helping to maintain a common civic identity. Worshipping Dionysus meant participating in the shared activities of the entire *polis*.

The Lenaea

The festival of Dionysus known as the Lenaea was also celebrated in the dead of winter, but in the month called Gamelion, roughly January. The month of Gamelion honored marriage (*gamos*), above all the divine union of Hera and Zeus, which was celebrated at a festival called the Gamelia. Marriage in the human community was also the focus of ritual attention at this time of year: in ancient Athens, Gamelion was the most popular month for weddings.

Like the Anthesteria and the Pyanopsia, the Lenaea was one of the festivals common to all Ionian *poleis;* in most other Ionian calendars this midwinter month was actually called not Gamelion but Lenaion, after the Dionysian festival. On the 12th of Gamelion, in Athens the Lenaea was celebrated at an urban sanctuary called the Lenaion, probably located somewhere near the Agora. The *archōn basileus* headed a procession that ended in the Lenaion, and high officials from the civic cult of Eleusinian Demeter also took leading roles in the *pompē* and the sacrifices. Later in the fifth century the procession included wagons and carts; as participants rode past onlookers they were said to have shouted the sort of abusive jokes and insults that were popular at the Rural Dionysia. The procession ended with sacrifices for Dionysus and a great civic feast.

Current scholarly consensus concerning the name of the festival connects the Lenaea with *lēnai,* another term for maenads, the women who traditionally worshipped Dionysus with ecstatic rites in the mountains of Thebes. Some Athenian women traveled to take part in these biennial rites; perhaps citizen women danced for Dionysus in Athens, but no evidence for such dances remains. It is in fact a challenge for scholars to connect this ecstatic form of Dionysian worship with the other civic rite we have evidence for at the Lenaea—the dramatic performances. Starting perhaps in the 440s during the height of Pericles' influence, dramatic competitions were included in this midwinter festival. *Polis* officials organized and managed the competitions. Most of the plays produced at the Lenaea seem to have been comedies; in fact many of Aristophanes' extant comedies were produced for the Lenaea. Some tragedies were produced as well, though it appears to have been a less prestigious forum for that type of drama.

With few foreigners able to travel the Aegean during stormy winter months, audiences for plays produced at the Lenaea were composed largely of resident Athenians. This meant that comic poets like Aristophanes could write topical insider jokes that abused Athenian public figures and criticized Athenian policy, much the same way that late-night comedians and spoofs of newscasts comment on the American political scene today. The ridicule of fellow citizens, especially men holding positions of authority, reversed the normal social order. Aristophanes' relentless abuse of Cleon in the *Knights,* which won first prize at the Lenaea in 424, typifies the reversal, with its portrayals of slaves and common workers who replace those in positions of political power. Its invective was similar to the ritual abuse evident in the traditional songs sung at the Rural Dionysia, and in the jokes from the wagons in the Lenaea procession. When Athenians wrote and staged comedies for the Lenaea they exercised the same Dionysian spirit of abusive ridicule, parody, exaggeration, and criticism. At times the criticism must have been harsh: an Athenian decree passed in 440 tried to limit the abusive speech and ridicule common in comedies produced at any dramatic festival, but the decree apparently proved unpopular and was repealed three years later (Fornara 111).

Plato gives us an interesting window into the worship of Dionysus at the Lenaea in his famous dialogue called the *Symposium.* Plato probably wrote the dialogue in the 380s, well after the execution of Socrates, but the dramatic date for the *Symposium* is set very specifically during the Lenaea of 416 BCE, just a few months before the mutilation of the herms and desecration of the Mysteries discussed in chapter 5. In fact some of the men present at the drinking party depicted in this dialogue would be implicated in one or both of these affairs during the trials that gripped Athenians in the following summer and fall. Alcibiades plays a central role in the second half of the dialogue.

The occasion for this semi-fictional dinner and drinking party in 416 was the very first victory at a civic competition for the tragic poet Agathon (*Symposium* 173a). Although Agathon's plays exist today only in fragments, in antiquity he was ranked among the top tier of Athenian tragic poets—right behind the canonical Aeschylus, Sophocles, and Euripides. In the *Symposium* Plato pointedly reminds the reader of Agathon's youth—he was competing for the first time in a festival that had lower stakes than the City Dionysia. This symposium was the celebratory dinner party hosted by the victorious Agathon on the evening following the Lenaea; he gathered with a few close friends in his home in Athens, where they drank together and exchanged speeches in honor of Eros, the god of Love. The afternoon of public sacrifice was over; the meat had been distributed to deme members, the plays completed. Now Plato reveals how Athenian citizens in a private home continue their worship of Dionysus and gather around a big krater, or mixing bowl of wine. Groups of revelers come and go all night, Alcibiades arrives drunk and unannounced, and eventually most of the men fall asleep on their couches. When the sun rises the next morning over Agathon's house in Athens, the dialogue reports that Socrates is one of only three men left awake. He is still talking. He is not at all drunk; rather he, the tragic poet Agathon, and the comic poet Aristophanes are debating the merits of comedy and tragedy. Socrates concludes that the true writer of tragedy is simultaneously a writer of comedy (*Symposium* 223c).

The Lenaea offered citizens of Athens an opportunity to come together during the quiet winter months and enjoy a civic feast followed by publicly funded entertainment. Tragedy and especially comedy supplied the frame for communal reflection, criticism of public officials, and the free exchange of ideas. As Plato shows, the experience of Dionysus did not stop when the last play ended. Even during a time of war, a group of friends and political equals gathered on a cold winter night to drink and enjoy each other's company at a symposium. When Alcibiades burst into Agathon's party that night in 416, he gave a vivid description of Socrates as a soldier fighting on behalf of the Athenian empire at Delion and Potidaea. The Lenaea, like many civic rites in Athens, encouraged citizens to take a honest look at themselves, even as the normal social order was inverted and the wine flowed freely.

The City Dionysia

Winter was the season of Dionysus: the Oschophoria, the Rural Dionysia, and the Lenaea (October, December, and January) were followed by the

Anthesteria (late February). The five winter celebrations of the gods of wine and theater culminated in the biggest Dionysus festival of all: the City Dionysia, held in the following month of Elaphebolion—roughly March, as winter ended and spring began. The festival of the Elaphebolia gave its name to this month of Elaphebolion, but by Pericles' time the sacrifices at the Elaphebolia in honor of Artemis slayer-of-the-deer (*elaphēbolos*) had become somewhat obscure. The City Dionysia started a few days after the Artemis festival, and then ran for nearly a week. This festival of Dionysus completely dominated the month. During the fifth century the City Dionysia was celebrated on a grand civic scale in the center of Athens; it emerged as one of most important Athenian festivals of the entire year, second only to the Panathenaea in midsummer. Like that festival of Athena, the civic rites of the City Dionysia placed the *polis* of Athens itself front and center in a festival of cultural pride and self-presentation. Springtime marked the return of travel throughout the Aegean, and the city was full of visitors.

The precise order of all the rites observed at the City Dionysia remains uncertain, but scholars have put together a general picture. The festival ran for five or six days, at least three of which were given over to performance and dramatic competition. The Athenians—like all Greeks—loved to compete, especially against members of other tribes. As one Cleisthenic tribe competed against another in athletics at civic festivals like the Panathenaea and the Oschophoria, so they competed by tribe at the City Dionysia—but at this festival, the competitions took place on the stage. Poet vied against poet, actor against actor, chorus against chorus, and producer against producer.

Preparations for the competition were begun long before the actual performances were staged, and these preparations depended on the men who trained the choruses and produced the plays. Of all the varieties of *leitourgia* or public service that wealthy Athenians could fulfill for the *polis*, being a *chorēgos* or a producer of plays (literally, "leader of a chorus") brought perhaps the most fame and glory. The annual City Dionysia offered abundant opportunities for wealthy citizens to display their largesse to their fellow citizens. Archons were responsible for recruiting *chorēgoi* during the fifth century; it took almost thirty producers to put on the City Dionysia. Twenty of the appointments were made according to the ten tribes created by Cleisthenes. Every tribe prepared two choruses for the festival, one chorus of fifty men and one of fifty boys, and each chorus performed a traditional cult song called a dithyramb. Every dithyrambic chorus had its own *chorēgos,* each of whom was charged with recruiting the choral members from his tribe, training them, and providing them with any costumes required.

The most prestigious dramatic offices were reserved for the wealthiest men who put on the tragedies and comedies. Each *chorēgos* was assigned a poet to work with; poets had been chosen earlier in the year after auditioning before the archons. Comic poets each wrote one play, while tragic poets wrote four: three tragedies plus one play called a satyr play. Like the citizens who produced the dithyrambs, the *chorēgoi* recruited, trained, and provided costumes for their actors and choruses. Archons also designated a pool of citizen judges who would judge the dramatic performances at the festival. To reduce the potential for bribery, hundreds of names were placed in jars ahead of time, and when the festival began only ten names were pulled out. These citizen judges performed their civic duty by watching the plays and voting for the best poet and actor. A simple majority was needed to win. Civic officials kept careful accounts of the winners, organizing them according to the name of the eponymous archon. Names of the victorious *chorēgoi,* tribes, poets, and actors were inscribed on stone tablets and placed in public; our earliest list of victors goes back to 473 BCE, but clearly the Athenians had been recording the winners' names long before this.

Once the choruses were trained, a public meeting prepared the Athenians for the coming competitions. A *proagōn* or preliminary ceremony was held in Athens just before the opening day of the City Dionysia; at this meeting all the men involved—the producers, poets, actors, and chorus members—appeared out of costume and presented themselves as fellow citizens before the Athenian public. A torchlight procession introduced the god into the city. An ancient wooden image of Dionysus was brought in from the suburban neighborhood called the Academy northwest of the city; this preliminary festivity commemorated the god's initial arrival in Athens from Boeotia. The procession ended at Dionysus's sanctuary and temple just south of the Acropolis. The festival proper began the next day with an official *pompē* that was one of the most grand and colorful processions of the Athenian year. Ephebes led bulls for *thysia,* while a procession of metics in bright red cloaks carried trays with nonbloody offerings. Citizens bore leather bottles of wine, great phalluses, and long sticks of bread slung over their shoulders, and an aristocratic young woman carried the basket with the sacrificial knife. The goal of the *pompē* was the civic altar in the sanctuary of Dionysus, where *polis* officials sacrificed the bulls and hosted a great feast at public expense for all those attending. We don't know how large the feast was in Pericles' or Socrates' time, but one fourth-century inscription states that 240 bulls were sacrificed for the City Dionysia that year—enough meat to feed thousands of people. Wine flowed freely, and the evening following the procession was known for its torchlight revelry throughout the city, a ritual known as a *kōmos*. Whereas a *pompē* was a formal procession that ended with *thysia* at the altar, the *kōmos* was a diffuse and informal party that spread itself throughout the city.

Dawn on the following morning saw the start of the dramatic competitions. For the next few days, residents returned to the south slope of the Acropolis and the sanctuary of Dionysus. Athenian citizens, metics, and foreigners all attended the performances. The presence of women at the dramatic festivals is still debated among scholars; comments in Aristophanes' comedies imply that at least some women attended, especially women of the upper classes. In the fifth century there was no permanent stone theater for the audience—the Athenian statesman Lycurgus built that structure a century later. Instead the city constructed temporary wooden benches called *ikria* on the hillside overlooking Dionysus's altar and the *orchēstra*, a smooth flat surface around the altar where the actors and choruses performed. The best seats in the front rows were reserved for visiting dignitaries and high civic officials; behind the benches on the hillside others lounged on the ground. Audience members brought their own pillows, cushions, and rugs to make themselves comfortable through the performances. Tragedies were staged in the morning, and comedies in the afternoon. We are not sure when the dithyrambic choruses competed—perhaps interspersed between the other events. Theatergoers brought wine and snacks along with them as well, and spent the day drinking wine and munching on dried fruit, nuts, and other finger food. Athenians were said to be an active audience that applauded when pleased, and hissed, hooted, or beat on their wooden seats when they saw or heard something they didn't like. Tickets to the performances cost about a day's wage (2 obols); this price effectively excluded some of the poorer working residents. In response, the Athenian *ekklēsia*—probably in the early fourth century—instituted the theoric fund, which disbursed state money to citizens who otherwise could not afford to attend the festival.

The worship of Dionysus was widespread throughout all of Greece, and evidence for the earliest forms of drama is not unique to Attica. Early examples of both comedy and tragedy have been found in communities in the Peloponnese. Scholars and theorists have long discussed the origins of drama, and research into the development of theater has occupied some of the very best scholars. Even Aristotle in the fourth century BCE found theater to be a compelling topic for his scientific investigations. His *Poetics* remains one of our most important sources for the study of all ancient literary forms, including tragedy and comedy. The current scholarly consensus for the origins of theater follows Aristotle but also supplements the *Poetics* with other evidence, including archaeological remains, inscriptions, vase paintings, and literary evidence from other ancient authors.

It is clear that drama emerged from ancient Dionysian rites that were similar to rituals celebrated at the rural Dionysia and the Lenaea, but certainly older than those two festivals as the Athenians observed them in the fifth century. One feature of Dionysian worship called the revel, or *kōmos,* emerged from rural festivities that celebrated the gift of grapevine and wine. Early comedy is thought to be connected with this mode of worship. But Dionysus also had strong associations with areas beyond the villages found in cultivated areas: he was at home in the untamed wilderness, and he could at times inspire behaviors that were considered not fully civilized. Rituals of parody, exaggeration, and verbal abuse were an integral part of traditional Dionysian festivities, and some men who participated in the ritual abuse dressed up as satyrs, mythical wild-man figures who were part human, part animal—either horse or goat. Satyrs were known for aggressive public behaviors, and for their unquenchable appetites for wine and sex; they arguably represented a type of ancient masculinity outside the *polis*—or at least what Greeks thought mythical masculinity looked like before the civilizing power of the *polis.* Still, the classical *polis* made room for these symbolic wild men in its civic rituals: men dressed as satyrs accompanied Dionysus in the ship-cart at the procession of the Athenian Anthesteria, and men dressed as satyrs entertained the public at Dionysian festivals with traditional performances called satyr dramas. Examples of early satyr dramas are lost (indeed they were probably never recorded), but some elements of these ancient plays were preserved in what was to become Greek tragedy and comedy.

In addition to the satyr drama, the poetic form called the dithyramb played a significant role in the development of fifth-century drama. The dithyramb was a form of cult song sacred to Dionysus with Dionysian content, and the earliest dithyrambs were probably composed even before Greek became a written language. It is thought that a group of citizens gathered in a sanctuary of Dionysus and sang a dithyramb celebrating the god; perhaps one of them took on a leading role and sang a solo part, or even acted out the song in a rudimentary way with gestures and dance steps accompanied by music. It was during the first part of the fifth century that what we today recognize as tragic drama emerged from dithyrambic cult poetry and took on its now familiar form. The singer with the solo part soon became an actor who engaged in an ongoing conversation with the chorus, while the chorus listened to the actor's speeches and responded to the actor's emotions as the play's tragic situation emerged. Around the time of the Persian Wars the tragic poet Aeschylus increased the number of actors from one to two, and not much later Sophocles increased it again from two to three. Sophocles also introduced the use of scene painting to give the unfolding drama a more vivid sense of place. The role of the chorus slowly evolved, too, as plots became more complex and the performances of the actors became more dynamic.

Euripides, the youngest of the three canonical Greek tragedians, began his career as a tragic poet in the 450s, by which time the traditional satyr drama and the dithyrambic chorus had fully evolved and combined to create Attic drama. As the program for dramas produced at the City Dionysia became more fixed, comic poets each contributed one play, while tragic poets submitted a satyr play in addition to three tragedies. Civic officials evidently started to require the satyr play once tragic plots and characters moved away from those found in the more traditional Dionysian ritual dramas. The fifth-century Athenians themselves observed that drama was a ritual associated with publicly financed civic festivals such as the City Dionysia, the Lenaea, and the Rural Dionysia. But at the same time some, including Aristotle, held that drama "had nothing to do with Dionysus," a possible reference to trends that were moving it further away from the recognizable customs found in older forms of Dionysus worship.

Scores of poets wrote hundreds of plays for the tragic festivals during the fifth century. Today we are left with only thirty-three complete tragedies by the three major tragedians: Aeschylus (seven), Sophocles (seven), and Euripides (nineteen). Of the comedies written at this time we possess only eleven complete plays by Aristophanes. All the plays by other poets have been lost over the ages or exist only in fragments and quotations in later writers. We do know the names of some poets (e.g., Agathon and Phrynicus) as well as the titles of some plays. Tragic poets in Athens during the time of Pericles and Socrates held a place of honor and respect. There is even an ancient tradition reporting that the philosopher Plato began his career as a young man wanting to be tragic poet; he shifted his attention to writing philosophical dialogues only after his teacher and friend Socrates was executed by the Athenian state.

Early on poets wrote tragedies about current events as well as mythological tales and characters, but the historical plays sometimes hit too close to home. In the 490s, during the thick of the Greeks' conflict with Persia, the tragic poet Phrynicus wrote of the sack of Miletus, the Ionian city and Athenian ally that had instigated the Ionian Revolt in 499 and persuaded the Greeks to come their aid against the Persian Empire. Miletus was besieged and destroyed by the advancing Persian army in 494, and Phrynicus's dramatization of the city's tragic fall was staged at a Dionysian festival not long afterward. Herodotus reports that seeing the destruction portrayed on the stage so upset the Athenians that they levied a large fine on the poet for "reminding them of their troubles" (Herodotus 6.21). Poets continued to engage with contemporary subjects: Phrynicus wrote at least one other play with a historical subject, and other poets followed him. We are fortunate to possess one complete tragedy that handles current events: the *Persians* of Aeschylus, produced shortly after the end of the Persian Wars. Aeschylus set this play in Persia itself. The king Xerxes comes home to the capital of Susa after the naval defeat at Salamis in 480. The outcome of the battle is portrayed entirely from the Persian point of view: there is not a single Greek—not even a general or naval officer— named in the tragedy. The *chorēgos* for this daring portrayal of a defeated enemy was the young aristocrat Pericles, who in 472 was just starting his career in public service to Athens.

Sometime after this production of the *Persians,* Athenian poets made a deliberate move away from historical subject matter, focusing instead on mythical events from the heroic past. Characters such as Odysseus, Agamemnon, and Achilles from the Trojan War were certainly favorites, as were mythological personalities from neighboring Thebes—Oedipus, Antigone, Tiresias, and Pentheus. The conventions of myth-based tragic drama enabled Athenians to peer inside the experience of peoples who had little political power in the workings of a Greek *polis.* Foreigners, slaves, the very old and the young, and above all women were placed in critical circumstances where their abilities to act and react were severely limited. Poets explored how characters with such circumscribed choices negotiated with the men who held power. All the characters in dramatic productions— even those with no power in the *polis*—were played by citizen male actors who were masked and robed in costume; the dramatic characters were then viewed by thousands of onlookers who experienced this Dionysian role-playing produced on the stage at the civic festival.

Although most characters from Athenian tragedy were heroic figures from the long-ago past, the themes and issues they addressed on the stage often touched upon current topics of public debate in Athens: issues surrounding justice, punishment, and the role of the courts (Aeschylus's *Oresteia*); the rightful exercise of knowledge and authority by men in positions of power and the response to those who exercise their authority wrongfully (Sophocles' Theban plays *Oedipus* and *Antigone*); and the treatment of powerless people and the abuse or murder of defeated captives (some of Euripides' later plays). At the same time, comedy was uniformly set in the present. Here the commentary on current politics was absolutely explicit, but the situations of comedy were full of fantasy and impossibility: for example, citizen wives calling a sex strike and negotiating a peace treaty for the war with Sparta (*Lysistrata*), women taking over the *ekklēsia* (*Ecclesiazusae*), a god and a slave journeying to the underworld to talk to tragic poets now dead (*Frogs*). Even a philosopher named Socrates was a major character in Aristophanes' *Clouds,* as will be discussed in chapter 7.

In the modern world the Greeks are perhaps best remembered for depicting the gods on stage interacting with mortals in dramatized retellings of traditional myths. The gods could appear in the prologue of a play to introduce characters and set up the action, and they could also resolve the action in the final scenes, as Athena does at the end of Aeschylus's *Oresteia* trilogy. It was the tragic poet Euripides who perfected the *deus ex machina,* a sort of crane that suspended the actor portraying a god or hero over the stage. The *deus ex machina* would typically arrive on the scene once the tragic plot had unfolded and the dead body (or bodies) had been brought forward on a wheeled, turning platform called the *ekkyklēma.* Dramatized murder and suicide in Athenian drama always happened behind the scenes but within easy earshot of the audience. The god or hero *ex machina* could look down on the scene and pronounce the final judgment about the rightful relationship between gods and humans.

The Olympian deities on the dramatic stage in Athens were capable of great cruelty in their dealings with mortals. They did not look kindly upon any impious human behavior; they demanded worship, and they would undertake punishment and revenge with little hesitation. The myths retold on the stage were not sacred narratives that reflected Athenians' beliefs about how the gods interacted with humans. The relentless demands and cold detachment displayed by the gods onstage also stand in contrast to the propitiating prayers of real Athenian men and women who relied on ancestral customs to secure the protection of their ancestors' gods. Civic rites generally ensured the stability of the community, but within the protected confines of the *polis*-funded dramatic festivals, Athenians could explore what happened when mythic characters walked away from ancestral practices and rejected one of the gods.

One of the most memorable depictions of the god Dionysus on the stage was presented in Euripides' *Bacchae,* produced in Athens at the City Dionysia in 406, shortly before Athens fell to Sparta. Euripides raised provocative questions about human impiety and the nature of the gods with this play. Pentheus, a youthful royal prince in neighboring Thebes, utterly rejects the worship of the newly arrived god called Dionysus, and he even denies the god's divinity. Pentheus claims that Dionysus is a foreigner, a fraud, and an effeminate fool set on luring the wives of upstanding citizens away from their homes. The women seek Dionysus in the mountains, where they allegedly engage in sexual acts with the mysterious foreigner who claims to be a god. Pentheus is dismayed to see that Dionysus's rites have even infected old, respected citizen men. But Dionysus demands that he be worshipped, even if that worship overturns social norms. What is a young citizen to do when faced with this choice? What kind of ancestral custom would require the reversal of all traditionally held values?

While Pentheus's mother leads the Theban women up the mountain to celebrate Dionysus's rites, the god takes on a disguise and approaches Pentheus, promising to reveal to him the women's licentious behavior. After dressing Pentheus in women's clothing, Dionysus leads the young man to see the women of Thebes, many of whom have lost their senses. Pentheus experiences the extreme madness that Dionysus can inspire, and he dies at the hands of his own mother when she mistakes him for a wild animal. Only then is Dionysus satisfied that his worship has been properly recognized by the Thebans. A play like the *Bacchae* provides us today with a view of Dionysian consciousness at its most vivid. The civic ritual of the dramatic festivals brought Athenians together as a group in order to shift their awareness by exploring different identities and implausible possibilities. Poets and actors embodied the transformative power of Dionysus; at the same time, the thousands of citizens and noncitizens in the theater experienced the god of wine as the patron of Athenian civic rites in the theater. The indifferent nature of divinity and the hard divine justice that Euripides depicts in this play may reflect the Athenians' mentality as they found themselves at the end of a long and devastating war with Sparta. Yet

Euripides chose to bring issues surrounding gender, power, and the gods into the Athenians' awareness at civic rites in honor of Dionysus. By watching a play about one man's arrogance and impiety toward Dionysus, the Athenians were themselves worshipping that same god. Such was the paradoxical logic of Dionysus. He was a god that could not be denied.

POLITICS, EMPIRE, AND THE DRAMATIC FESTIVALS

Festivals of Dionysus were celebrated in *poleis* throughout Greece, and not just in Athens; for centuries these annual rituals preserved ancestral customs that brought a rural god of agricultural fertility into the communal life of an urban *polis*. But however traditional Dionysian rites may have been, they nevertheless did change over time: at certain moments particular rulers or regimes could expand a civic festival or even institute a new one. The historian Thucydides provides us with evidence for this sort of innovation when he refers to the Anthesteria in the early spring by an alternative name, the Older Dionysia (Thucydides 2.15). The "newer" Dionysia, which remained unnamed but was implicitly acknowledged and familiar to Thucydides' original audience, was the City Dionysia held later in the spring. Although literary and inscriptional evidence is scarce, some classical scholars today follow Thucydides and suggest that the City Dionysia was indeed a new festival, modeled in the sixth century on other popular Dionysian celebrations. The City Dionysia may have been instituted during the reign of Pisistratus, and the political reforms of Cleisthenes brought further changes to the festival, evident in the dithyrambic competitions that required two *chorēgoi* from each of the ten Cleisthenic tribes to train and put forward tribal choruses of men and boys each year.

The season for sailing in the Aegean got under way in the spring as the winter storms ceased, and this change in the Athenian festival calendar took advantage of the change in weather. Celebrating the new City Dionysia in the spring month of Elaphebolion, rather than in the depth of the winter when dramatic festivals of Dionysus normally fell, allowed visitors from beyond Attica to attend the civic holiday. During the Peloponnesian War foreign embassies and diplomats were compelled to travel to Athens to attend the City Dionysia, where they renewed alliances with the Athenians. When Thucydides outlined the terms of the peace negotiated between Athens and Sparta in 421, the terms stipulated that both parties were to renew the treaty annually with the pouring of libations at public festivals: Athenians were to attend a Spartan festival sacred to Apollo called the Hyacinthia, while Spartans would pour *spondai* with the Athenians at the City Dionysia every spring in Athens.

During the latter half of the fifth century, celebrations of the other Dionysian festivals in Attica changed in response to this new festival of Dionysus. As the choral and dramatic productions at the City Dionysia developed under the influence of the great tragic poets, other festivals reflected the innovations. Competitive dramatic performances were added to the Athenian Lenaea around 440, when smaller rural towns were also beginning to emulate the popularity of the urban theatrical performances by adopting elements from the City Dionysia for the celebrations of the Rural Dionysia. The ancient rural festivals in Attica took on a new importance during the mid-fifth century as residents of the rural demes began building theaters in their outlying villages. Performance and public entertainment had always been an essential aspect of the Rural Dionysia, but the advent of theaters might suggest that performances were somehow becoming more formalized. Previously organizers of the deme festivals must have built temporary theaters and stages, but setting aside space and resources for permanent stone structures, however small, demonstrated the commitment of the demes to the god whose worshippers traveled throughout Attica every year. Indeed, our earliest archaeological evidence for permanent stone theaters comes from Attic demes like Thoricus, and not from Athens itself; the monumental theater of Dionysus that still stands on the south slope of Acropolis dates to the fourth century. During the time of Pericles and Socrates Athenians were still sitting on *ikria,* the temporary wooden seats rising in tiers up the lower slope of the Acropolis, or else lying on blankets on the ground above the wooden seats.

Whereas the wintertime Lenaea and the Rural Dionysia were frequented almost entirely by citizens and residents of Attica, the Athenians came to consider the City Dionysia a festival where they could present themselves and their *polis* to foreign visitors. New customs and ceremonies were added as the Athenian empire grew and the war continued, and at discrete points in the civic festival Athenian citizens used the occasion of Dionysian ritual to articulate their commonly held civic and imperial values. Just as Spartan diplomats annually renewed the peace with Athens by pouring *spondai* at the City Dionysia (for a few years, at least, after 421), so the democratically elected *stratēgoi* who waged war also made libations in the sanctuary of Dionysus at the start of the festival (Thucydides 5.23). These directly elected generals were honored with this civic rite, and others who contributed significantly to the well-being of the *polis* community were also recognized. Not all of these honorees were Athenian citizens—some were foreigners or metics. In the fourth century (and possibly also the fifth), city benefactors received honorary crowns and garlands on stage in the sanctuary of Dionysus.

As the war with Sparta dragged on and Athenian men continued dying, more and more children lost their fathers. When Athenians gathered together in the theater at the City Dionysia, they set aside time to honor the fatherless sons who were coming of age and making the transition from ephebe to adult citizen. The procession of ephebes entered the theater in full armor, ready to pick up where their fathers had left off in service to the *polis* and its empire. Other Dionysian festivals—like the Oschophoria, which celebrated the peaceful gifts of Dionysus—focused on young men at this critical time of life; during wartime the City Dionysia allowed citizens to welcome the orphaned ephebes on the stage. The public transition of the young men was witnessed by the citizen body, who stood in place of fathers who had fallen in battle.

The City Dionysia during the fifth century had to constantly respond to changing circumstances as the Athenians' pursuit of empire kept them in conflict with Sparta. During periods of intense fighting in the Peloponnesian War, Athenians reduced the total number of plays staged for the festival, perhaps as a cost-cutting measure; in wartime plays were staged for three consecutive days, but in peacetime four. But regardless of the number of days given over to performance, one thing did remain the same: the civic rituals of the City Dionysia reminded Athens' subject-allies of their subordinate status in the larger Athenian *archē*. Members of the Delian League were required to attend the annual springtime festival and participate in the procession of Dionysus, which came to a halt in the god's sanctuary south of the Acropolis. In a visible display of imperial power Athens reserved places in the procession for subject-allies. Some cities were required to carry a phallus honoring Dionysus in the *pompē*. But all subject-allies sent diplomats to march in the procession in which Athenians exhibited the empire's tribute. In this way the greatest honor was reserved for the Athenian *archē*, which used this religious festival to receive the annual *phoros* or tribute from its subject-allies. One source states that the tribute was displayed in the theater for all to see (Isocrates *de Pace* 82). Some of these funds from the allies in the Delian League were dedicated to Athena, and some tribute eventually rested in Athena's treasury on the Acropolis. The first day of the civic festival saw Dionysus cooperating with Athena. The glory and power of Athens, visible in the display of tribute, itself became an annual performance in the sanctuary and theater of Dionysus.

Theater, both comedy and tragedy, may well be one of the most important cultural gifts that Greece bestowed upon the West. Dionysus was a god who demanded shifts in awareness, and his capacity to coax worshippers out of their habitual modes of thought and behavior arguably liberated the Athenians by allowing them to express potentially dangerous ideas that they normally repressed. Drama was a good framework for thinking: tragedy and comedy both provided the Athenians with a ritual structure and a language they could use to safely explore contemporary social and political issues. The civic rites of theater enabled the Athenians to criticize themselves and their government, and voice dissent. The one attempt we know of to limit that dissent was unpopular and short-lived. At the same time, Athenians also used the City Dionysia to celebrate their empire and glory in their rule over subject-allies. The god Dionysus, with his many and sometimes contradictory faces, was uniquely equipped to express this paradox in fifth-century Athenian public life.

TOWARD THE DIONYSIAN MYSTERIES

Writing in the 1960s, the cultural anthropologist Victor Turner observed how ritual behaviors that temporarily invert normal relationships in the end serve only to reinforce established social structures. The same could be said of civic festivals for Dionysus. The adolescent boys and young men who dressed as women at Dionysian festivals—both dramatic festivals such as the Lenaea and Dionysia and the wine festival of the Oschophoria—would in time become voting citizens in the Athenian Assembly and members of the *dēmos*. Those ritualized moments of gender-bending and inverted identity in the state calendar reminded all in Athens that through transformation and transcendence Dionysus could empower not just worshippers but the whole *polis* itself.

In art and myth Dionysus also had a close association with Hades, the god of the underworld, who also had the power to transform human experience. This tradition was reflected in a dramatic role played by the character Dionysus in the *Frogs*, a comedy by Aristophanes produced at the Lenaea in 405. In this play a slave named Xanthias accompanies Dionysus to the underworld. Dionysus is still trying to understand the Arginusae disaster, and he is looking for some good tragic poets to write new plays for the Athenian stage. In the house of Hades they meet up with both Euripides, who had only recently died, and Aeschylus. The two debate the merits of their tragic styles. In the end Dionysus decides to bring Aeschylus back to Athens so he can save the city. A play like the *Frogs,* with its irreverent humor (often at the god's expense) and frank assessment of the political situation, shows how anyone who took part in a dramatic production or simply attended the theater participated in the civic rites of this god.

The transformative power found in Dionysian festivals of wine and drama was also experienced in the god's famed ability to possess his worshippers. The mysteries and *orgia* of Dionysus celebrated the ecstasy of the god and the new life that accompanied death. Unfortunately, physical and literary evidence for this aspect of Dionysian worship in Athens is largely lacking for the fifth century. Some scholars look to the maenads depicted on stage in Euripides' *Bacchae,* but their behavior may actually have been the inspiration for some cult activities known to have existed in the fourth century and later. The Derveni papyrus, a mid-fourth-century fragmentary text with philosophical commentary, offers scholars tantalizing clues about Dionysian mysteries. Found half-charred in a grave in Macedonia in 1962, the papyrus was published in full only in 2006. The poem quoted in the papyrus is concerned with the origins of the gods, and the attached commentary reveals insights about those initiated in Dionysus's mysteries. These rites may perhaps be related to late fifth-century practices in Athens, and the ideas appear to be those popularized by traveling scholars like Anaxagoras; even today, scholars are studying these connections.

However the Dionysian mysteries were celebrated in the time of Pericles and Socrates, they did not require the sort of monumental infrastructure that Demeter's Eleusinian Mysteries acquired in the fifth century. Dionysus's *orgia* were experienced at home. A detailed outline of initiation rites from fourth-century Athens is preserved in the corpus of speeches belonging to Demosthenes. Demosthenes sneeringly described a nighttime Dionysian ritual celebrated by a mixed group of men and women. The young son Aeschines assisted his mother in the *orgia* and read from a sacred book; initiates dressed in fawn-skins sat in the dark around a krater of wine. After a frightening priestess lurched out of the dark, the initiates rose up screaming and announced, "I escaped the evil, I found the better." By day the boy then led a small procession through the public streets of the city; now the initiates wore garlands, and the boy brandished a snake (Demosthenes *On the Crown* 18.258–61). Demosthenes clearly was a hostile witness to such Dionysian rites in Athens, and no evidence for such initiations exists for the Periclean city, but small-scale celebrations of the god were probably common.

One type of Dionysian celebration was represented on vases commonly produced throughout the fifth century. The vases depict women in various postures of ecstatic dance. Maenads play music and dance around the altar as they worship the god in total abandon. Often Dionysus himself is present on the vases in the form of a pillar or column that is draped or clothed in a rudimentary way, and topped with the bearded mask of the god. Large containers of wine stand at the ready. Vases made in the mid-fifth century depict women who are more composed; they stand at tables ladling wine from a larger container into a smaller cup, as in figure 12. The column with the mask representing Dionysus remains constant as he oversees the worship of the Athenian women. It is thought that these images depict rites from the Lenaea or possibly the Anthesteria; inarguably, they show women worshipping the god in their own way. Another type of vase similarly shows how intimate groups of men sometimes worshipped Dionysus. These so-called Anacreontic vases depict men in women's dress—wearing long, effeminate tunics and earrings, dressing their hair like a woman's, and sometimes carrying a lady's parasol. The men dance while a flute girl plays music. Such ritual transvestism seen elsewhere in the worship of Dionysus recalls the god's ability to cross the gender boundary, as he combined both male and female physical characteristics in the *Bacchae*.

Archaic and classical vase paintings depicting the god of wine and his inspired worshippers are still recognizable to many modern viewers. Pictures of the bearded god and his ecstatic female followers encircled by ivy vines and clusters of grapes suggest that Dionysus's worshippers experienced a sense of freedom and license. Museums throughout the world are full of pots and vases that document the cultural reality of drinking in ancient Greece, and tourists throughout the Mediterranean visit amphitheaters, some of the best preserved and most visible of ancient Greek architectural ruins. Today the Hellenistic theater at Epidaurus in the Peloponnese is again hosting productions of classical drama on warm summer evenings.

For Socrates in Plato's *Symposium,* the custom of worshipping Dionysus through drama enabled Athenians to experience the full and sometimes contradictory complexities of human life: Socrates argued that comedy and tragedy were so closely bound up together that a true poet could not master one without the other. In the *Bacchae* Euripides imagined the ecstatic worship of Dionysus as practiced in myth among the

Figure 12. Women worshipping Dionysus, serving wine, and dancing in front of the god's image. Red-figure stamnos by the Dinos Painter, ca. 420 BCE. Naples, 2419.

maenads and women of Thebes long ago; this transformative experience was then embodied by male actors on the stage in Dionysus's sanctuary in Athens. The public watching in the audience reached a deeper knowledge of the god through the actors. While drama did not bring on the same degree of ecstasy experienced by the Theban maenads in the mythic past, it still had the power to transport the audience and transcend the limits of the present.

In the late nineteenth century the German philosopher Friedrich Nietzsche popularized the idea of drawing a sharp distinction between the gods Apollo and Dionysus. This proposed opposition lives on in the modern imagination, which contrasts cool Apollonian rationality with energetic

Dionysian madness. Nietzsche's famous differentiation compels us with its clarity, but this now common understanding of the two gods effaces the similarities between them. Apollo's gift for prophecy was, like the sun, a gift that enlightened, and he brought healing to mortals through his son Asclepius. The madness of Dionysus, known to the Greeks as *mania,* possessed a similar power to reveal. Dionysus brought the dark corners of the human experience into the open and the light of day. Dionysus drew mortals out of themselves, whether they came under the influence of wine or were witnessing a dramatic role on stage played from behind a mask. The civic rites of Dionysus healed the city.

In the end, Dionysus exists simultaneously beyond the edges of accepted society and at the center of shared activities in the *polis.* He is an outside insider, a gentle scourge, an innocent young man dressed like a girl accused of seducing citizens' wives. Dionysus nurtures civic cohesion by demanding that his worshippers break the normal rules of society—if only for a short while. Like the topsy-turvy Christian Carnival that ends the season of Lent, festivals of Dionysus are often raucous affairs that overturn conventional patterns of civilized decorum. As long as the Dionysian energy and joie de vivre prevail, residents in the *polis* are encouraged to celebrate life in their city with a different sort of awareness. Dionysus is the god who incites shifts in consciousness.

SEVEN

Socrates

Impiety Trials in the Restored Democracy

ATHENIANS VOTED. THEY VOTED AS judges in the law courts, and at Dionysian festivals. They voted in their demes, and in the Assembly on the Pnyx. In a law court a jury voted to convict Socrates. This final chapter will return to episodes presented in earlier chapters to reflect one last time on the historical evidence, its cultural context, and most importantly its connection to the trial of Socrates. Four pivotal moments had repercussions that reached beyond the restoration of the democracy in 403: the events leading up to the trials of 415, the two coups of 411 and 404, and the trial of the generals after Arginusae in 406. Athenians' interpretations of the role played by law and religious custom, *nomoi*, in each earlier instance helped the *dēmos* reach a critical decision concerning Socrates' guilt in 399.

Long traditions of free speech and artistic expression allowed Athenians to voice—and sometimes reject—new ideas. Just as ritual drama could contain contradictory truths that enabled Athenians to witness the harsh and mild side by side, so the public drama of political life following the fall of Athens presented the best and the worst that the city's citizens had to offer. Dramatic poets brought their audiences a sharp awareness of the human compulsion to power, and the final restoration of democracy in 403 added another level of awareness for the *dēmos*. Collectively they survived the tyranny of the Thirty, and then turned to the past to try to understand how such a group of men could have come to power. For the next few years, themes that had been performed on the stage in ritualized drama were played out again in the shared life of the city. During this time Athenians could not stop returning in their public debates to the episodes of 415, 411, 406 and 404. They understood themselves and their recent past in a different light after they restored the democracy in 403 and put their ancestral laws back into place. This reinterpretation of traditional cultic *nomoi* itself provided another way for citizens to reflect on the past and debate what they wanted for the future of their *polis*.

In the four years leading up to Socrates' trial, Athenians were returning to the business of running the *polis* and worshipping the gods according to their ancestral customs. With the Thirty deposed and democracy restored, Athenians again debated what they called the *patrios politeia,* their ancestral constitution. Disagreements soon arose about the content of their actual laws and customs. Some *nomoi* had been abolished during the reign of the Thirty, and before that some had perhaps never been written down in full. In part, disagreements that arose reflected long-standing differences between average citizens and wealthy aristocrats, and in public debates each side called upon its memory of *ta patria* to support its own interests and point of view. In the absence of any universally held understanding of the past, it proved challenging to move forward. In the end Athenians settled on a new concept for *nomos,* one that placed the sovereignty of written law over the sometimes fractious outcomes that had been produced by popular votes in the assembly during the last decades of the war. It was the complex process of restoring the democracy after 403 and setting religious and civic customs back in place that brought Athenians to their new understanding of law and *nomos.*

New practices confirming the sovereignty of law were implemented, and while this was happening three significant trials took place, each of which addressed *asebeia* and the place of public piety in Athenian communal life. These were the trials of Andocides, of Nicomachus, and, in 399, of Socrates. In times of social tension Athenians were inclined to respond to political crises by evoking ritual norms and cultic behaviors. In the affairs of the Herms and the Mysteries in 415, reports of secret impious acts had raised fears that aristocratic *hetaireiai* were fomenting an oligarchic revolution, and the trial and execution of the Arginusae generals in 406 reminded Athenians of the centrality of ancestors and funerals in the communal life of the *polis*. The trials of Andocides, Nicomachus, and Socrates suggest that after the restoration of the democracy Athenians still considered political and cultic issues completely interwoven. To work out tough issues as a community, the *dēmos* relied on civic rites.

The trial of Socrates, today the best known of the three, exemplified Athenian legal procedures that involved cult practices in the restored democracy after 403. Socrates' accusers officially presented their claims of *asebeia* before the *archōn basileus,* who had oversight over cases involving religious matters and homicide. After reviewing the evidence against Socrates, this magistrate determined that the case required a trial. In a matter of a few weeks Socrates was brought before a jury of Athenian citizens, found guilty, and sentenced to death. The means of execution was a potion poisoned with hemlock. Although the Athenians had witnessed emotional public trials for *asebeia* in the past, they perhaps could not have predicted the final outcomes of this particular trial in 399. Even after Socrates' death, public debate continued as speakers and writers replayed the trial by publishing examples of prosecution and defense speeches that were, or could have been, delivered in the courtroom that day. Plato's *Apology* became the most famous of the published defense speeches for Socrates, but other men wrote on both sides of the issues that surrounded the indictment, trial, and execution of Socrates.

According to one biographer of the ancient philosophers working in the third century CE, the Athenians experienced a change of heart soon after Socrates' execution: they regretted that they had convicted the philosopher and put him to death. Diogenes Laertius reports that the Athenians passed a motion to honor Socrates by commissioning a bronze statue of him to be set up in the Pompeion, a new public building going up in the Kerameikos district (Diogenes Laertius 2.43). The Pompeion was intended to serve as a gathering place for civic religious processions, *pompai,* that marched through the city. Diogenes also reports that some men who had prosecuted Socrates were subsequently put on trial themselves and banished, with one accuser given a death sentence for taking the leading role in Socrates' prosecution. Diogenes had access to documents and materials now lost, but these materials were not always accurate. The tradition that he recorded may or may not be true, but even if it is not wholly reliable Diogenes' biography of Socrates does give us a glimpse into what historians in the ancient world believed the impetuous Athenians were capable of at this moment in their history. This biographical tradition documents how religion and politics continued to interact with each other in Athenian society. At times the interaction had results that were quite unforeseen.

The charges of *asebeia* leveled against Socrates were grounded in the larger historical and cultural contexts that surrounded the Peloponnesian War and the fall of Athens. The surrender of Athens in 404 did not bring an end to all civic and social strife within the city. On the contrary, a continuing Spartan military presence only heightened factional tensions. With the support of Sparta the temporary committee of citizens leading the transitional government launched a coup d'état. Although they were charged with simply restoring the *patrioi nomoi,* these thirty Athenians turned Athens upside down (Xenophon *Hellenica* 2.3). Among the first acts of the Thirty was the suspension of the *polis*'s most ancient laws: the laws of Solon and Ephialtes on public view at the Areopagus were removed (Aristotle *Athenian Constitution* 35). Following this action, other laws that allowed for disagreement and public debate were annulled. Little discretionary power was left to the Assembly, the Council, or the juries in the law courts. It became impossible to amend the Thirty's authority by passing new decrees.

Even the physical spaces of Athens changed under the rule of the Thirty. The Pnyx, the outdoor area where the Assembly met to debate and vote on issues, was physically reconfigured by the Thirty. Since the late sixth and early fifth centuries the Athenian *dēmos* had met on a hillside just west of the Agora and Acropolis. The gentle grade of the hill near the ridge provided a natural theater: the speaker's platform stood on the downward slope and the *dēmos* ranged on the hillside above. From that position Athenians could look northeast over the Agora, or southeast across to the recently completed Propylaea on the Acropolis above; to the south they could see the Aegean Sea. Aristophanes' comedies joke about how distractible the *dēmos* was when attending the Assembly on the Pnyx—they were mesmerized by the sight of their public monuments and the sea that gave power to the naval empire (Aristophanes *Acharnians* 27–33 and *Wasps* 31–42). But tradition has it that under the Thirty the Pnyx was remodeled; a long retaining wall was built along the northeast edge, the side of the hill was carved away and regraded, and the orientation of the *dēmos* and the speaker's platform reversed (see figure 2). Subsequently, Athenian assemblymen could no longer enjoy the inspiring views of their city and its navy; instead they looked upon an inland plain, the source of wealth for the aristocrats of Attica (Plutarch *Themistocles* 19).

Meanwhile a Spartan garrison occupied the most sacred spot in Athens, the Acropolis, and the Thirty governed from the Tholos: the building that formerly housed the committee that ran the Council was now the source of terror and threats of terror. Citizens mysteriously disappeared in the night, and by day 300 men armed with whips patrolled the public streets. Critias became the regime's most feared leader. What had started as a temporary government brought on open civil war between an oligarchic faction in Athens headed by the Thirty and democrats who in time organized a resistance and made their base in the port city of the Piraeus. Eventually the Spartan general Pausanias stepped in to put down the democratic faction, and only then did he forcibly depose the bloody regime of the Thirty.

As soon as Athenians had restored the democracy a second time, they started work on normalizing the routine operation of the democratic constitution that had been suspended during the Thirty's reign. They were determined to renew the *polis,* and the best way to accomplish this was by reinvigorating the constitution, or *patrios politeia,* and returning to the customs of their ancestors. The *dēmos* elected a new interim governing council of twenty that had an equal number of democrats and oligarchs; each of the ten Cleisthenic tribes probably elected two men. Working from within their traditional structure of demes and tribes, the Athenians strove to reestablish the traditional foundations of their *polis.* Even stripped of the empire they still had plenty of issues to debate, and plenty of decisions to discuss together.

The interim committee of twenty arranged elections for magistrates who would oversee the reinstatement of the Assembly, the Council, and the *prytaneis.* At the same time the temporary committee also needed to revive another underpinning that was essential to maintain civic life in Athens: the law courts, and thus the rule of law. During the last quarter of the fifth century the Assembly and the law courts had turned into public forums where civil strife and social tensions played themselves out. Individuals frequently exercised their right to publicly accuse others of crimes against the state through a procedure called the *eisangelia.* The *eisangelia* was probably employed in 415 when Pythonicus stood up at a meeting and accused Alcibiades and others of profaning the Mysteries, and again when the Assembly condemned Alcibiades to death in absentia and instructed the priest of Demeter to curse him. This procedure enabled private citizens to lodge damaging information against others at a meeting of the Council or Assembly by bringing forward information about alleged misconduct, subversion, or treason. If the *dēmos* wished to pursue the matter, the case was referred to law courts; the most egregious cases were tried before the entire Assembly. It was even possible under this earlier system to accuse someone of serious crimes that were not specified in any written decree or law but were generally assumed to be part of the unwritten code of ancestral *nomoi*. This is how many cases of impiety, *asebeia,* were apparently handled prior to 403. *Asebeia* was nowhere defined as a legal term—it was just an aspect of Athenian law that the *dēmos* assumed everyone understood, and the final judgment for such cases was left in the hands of citizens.

The restoration of the Athenian constitution included some procedural changes in the judicial system. The *eisangelia* procedure was apparently modified, and some attempt was made to define sacred laws more precisely; as a result, piety and impiety were no longer interpreted according to the oral transmission of *nomos*. Another of the essential foundations for the restoration was an act that modern scholars call the Amnesty of 403. The precise terms of the amnesty are not known today; what is clear is that this reconciliation agreement set guidelines for the trials of those citizens who had been intimately involved in the two coups during the last decade of the war. The reign of the Thirty received especially close scrutiny. The interim leadership drew up ground rules, and agreed that only citizens with taxable property would be eligible to sit on the trials for the Thirty. An oligarchic property qualification for jurors diverged from the standard practices of the democratic law courts, which not only had lacked any wealth requirement but even went so far as to offer daily pay for jurors. But only social and economic peers would be qualified to sit in judgment of the leaders of the short-lived but heavy-handed oligarchies of 411 and 404.

Significantly, the amnesty agreement also limited the scope of the prosecutions: only the top leadership of the oligarchic governments could be tried in court. Although thousands had supported the cause of the oligarchic revolutions of 411 and 404, or been somehow associated with oligarchic factions and *hetaireiai,* the amnesty stipulated that ordinary citizens could not be indicted for crimes against the state that had occurred prior to the restoration of the democracy in 403. Homicide was the single exception to this guideline. Only the Thirty themselves could be put on trial, plus a handful of their underlings: a committee of officials known as the Eleven who ran the political prisons and supervised torture, and the Thirty's subordinates in the Piraeus. Once any ringleaders who had survived the civil war were tried and sentenced, no one else could be charged with committing crimes against the state during the period of political uncertainty and instability that followed the fall of Athens. This amnesty was no abstract proclamation; it reached down even to the everyday routines of ordinary Athenian citizens. Xenophon reports that in accordance with the Amnesty of 403, an additional oath was required of all jurors when they took their daily oath of office at the start of the day in the law courts: "We will remember past offences no more" (Xenophon *Hellenica* 2.4).

The Amnesty of 403 sought to address several important needs of the rehabilitated democracy. First of all, it explicitly stated that past offenses should remain in the past. This helped create an environment for healing the city's wounds. The Thirty's reign of betrayal and murder had been traumatic and the danger was great that factional strife would continue. By bringing to trial only surviving members of the oligarchic leadership, Athenians were able to maintain some degree of public accountability for civic wrongdoing without branding everyone involved—especially those with little authority who got caught up in any atrocities. Establishing a wealth requirement for the citizens sitting on these juries demonstrated an effort to limit the severity of the punishments: poorer citizens who had supported the democrats and suffered greatly in the civil war could not use the court proceedings to exact revenge, though they could be called to give evidence against the Thirty.

Equally important, the amnesty also freed up the courts to handle the more mundane tasks of governing the *polis* in the way that ancestral civic customs had traditionally governed the city of Athens. For several generations citizens had been chosen by lot from all classes to serve on the law courts, and they were given the task of sitting in judgment over their peers. Jurors were considered experts in judging their peers' adherence to *nomoi*— the ancestral laws and religious customs that governed cases involving theft, inheritance and citizenship disputes, impiety, subversion, misconduct in office, and corruption of elected and appointed officials. Athenian law allowed for the prosecution of two types of cases: private cases of personal injury and public cases of wrong committed against the state. The latter category could be prosecuted by any citizen. Most murder and homicide cases were handled separately by the Areopagus. The law courts and citizen juries were never intended, nor were they equipped, to handle cases of high treason, political assassination, and insurrection on such a grand scale as would be needed following the final restoration of the democracy. During the few short months of the Thirty's reign more than 1,500 citizens had been assassinated, and thousands of others fled the city after they had been wronged or unlawfully disfranchised. The Amnesty of 403 provided Athenians with an acceptable mechanism for trying the most egregious offenders of the coup.

The amnesty may have had a calming effect for a few years, and life in Athens appears to have returned to something resembling what it had been before. But while the amnesty could legislate and limit the *dēmos*'s response to punishable behaviors in the recent past, it could not legislate citizens' private thoughts and memories. For some citizens hard bitterness and an urge to fix blame rankled behind their façade of forgiveness. The impulse to punish former political foes could not be entirely removed by any official decree, act, or law. Although the Amnesty of 403 did successfully block one main avenue for the prosecution of public crimes against the state, other means still remained open. The prosecution of crimes against the Athenian state committed before 403 was forbidden, but apparently little was said about cases of private injury. Individuals seeking to redress prior injuries found this loophole, and soon Athenians again were indicting fellow citizens for ritual offenses, as they had done in 415. Charges of *asebeia* became a way of pursuing political enemies. The three cases of Andocides, Nicomachus, and Socrates were part of this pattern.

THE TRIAL OF ANDOCIDES: 'ASEBEIA' AND DEMETER

The impulse to punish political enemies by obtaining indictments for infractions of religious law is illustrated by the case of the wealthy nobleman Andocides, who was prosecuted for *asebeia* by fellow Athenians shortly before Socrates' own trial for impiety. The accusers cited Andocides' alleged recent impious actions (probably dated to the fall of 401), and they also referred back to acts committed in the summer of 415, when Andocides had been imprisoned during the affairs of the Mysteries and the Herms. In fact much of our information about the profanation of the Mysteries and the mutilation of the Herms in 415 comes from the defense speech Andocides gave in 399. Just as he had managed to do in 415, Andocides again successfully defended himself in 399—in this case, against a group of at least four prosecutors who were seeking the death penalty against him.

In a highly unusual coincidence, two written accounts that were composed for this case have survived: a speech for the prosecution and the speech for the defense. These documents provide scholars with the rare glimpse inside the minds of typical Athenian citizens during the time shortly following the restoration of democracy. In fifth-century Athens there were no trained lawyers. Individual private citizens represented themselves in court, both as defendants and prosecutors. While citizens did compose their own speeches, they could also hire professional speechwriters to frame the oral arguments they would give in public before the jury. The speech delivered by the prosecution in the trial of Andocides is an example of this latter sort. It is preserved today among the speeches of a successful speechwriter named Lysias, who was well known for composing persuasive speeches that effectively captured the attention of the Athenian citizen jurors. When scholars study the speeches of Lysias, including this one, they can reconstruct the kinds of assumptions held by the average citizen. Lysias was a metic, and he was well-attuned to attitudes common among the citizen population. He was also a master at using this familiarity to his full advantage.

Andocides, about 40 years old at the time of this *asebeia* trial in 399, composed his own defense speech. Though it lacks some of the rhetorical flair and sophistication of the speech preserved in the corpus of Lysias, it too reveals how an elite Athenian citizen judged it best to present himself to his fellow citizens, many of whom did not share his wealth and high social standing. In his defense, known as *On the Mysteries,* Andocides names four of his most active and vocal prosecutors: Agyrrhios, Epichares, Kephisios, and Meletus. Callias son of Hipponicus, an aristocrat with particular interests in religious matters who also had ties to the oligarchs, may well have been the moving force behind the indictment. Callias was apparently embroiled in a quarrel with Andocides over the estate of a mutual kinsman, and he was also a civic religious official with priestly responsibilities as *dadouchos* at the Eleusinian Mysteries. Andocides delivered *On the Mysteries* in his own defense. Nothing from either speech indicates which of the four named men delivered the prosecution speech that is preserved in Lysias. Some scholars feel that all four men spoke at the trial, with Kephisios acting as main prosecutor; the speech preserved in the Lysianic corpus may well have been delivered by the man named Meletus.

It is clear from both speeches that while the accusers were charging Andocides with an act of impiety performed in the immediate past—namely, taking part in the Eleusinian Mysteries and in other Athenian civic rites sacred to Demeter around the year 401—they also had in mind earlier instances of Andocides' admitted acts of impiety. Andocides' troubles with proper civic behavior and the norms of Athenian public piety had first surfaced back in 415 at the height of Athenian imperial power, when he was perhaps about 25 years old. As discussed in chapter 4, Andocides, who belonged to a leading and wealthy Athenian family, had been imprisoned when Diocleides accused him and others of meeting in private and profaning public shrines and civic rites. The *dēmos* suspected that the same aristocratic *hetaireiai* responsible for mutilating the Herms and profaning the Eleusinian Mysteries were organizing an oligarchic conspiracy.

Meletus and the other prosecutors mentioned these more remote examples of *asebeia* at every possible opportunity in the speech they gave against Andocides in 399. The accusers appealed to the Athenians' still-raw emotions about the course of the war and the fall of the city and empire. Athenians also continued to suffer the grief and regret associated with the earlier losses of the Sicilian expedition. In the minds of the Athenians in 399, the two crises that took place in the early summer of 415—the mutilation of the Herms and the desecration of the Mysteries—were bound up with the betrayals of Alcibiades and the subsequent loss of the Athenian navy at Syracuse. Such blatant disrespect for the laws and customs of the ancestors in 415 had been widely interpreted at that time as an ill omen for the upcoming expedition to Sicily. It was Alcibiades' treason that helped bring on the devastating defeat in Sicily in 413, not to mention the escalation of the war on Attic soil at Decelea after 413. Some Athenians felt that open acts of impiety exhibited by bands of aristocratic young men in 415 overstepped the norms of *ta patria;* some reportedly even believed that the military losses were the direct result of the gods punishing Athens for allowing such impious behaviors in the *polis.*

The prosecution speech delivered in 399 took advantage of such shared memories, and the jury members were forced to recall that these two religious and social crises from 415 had also sparked the major impiety trials that took place during the Peloponnesian War. In the initial wave of trials conducted in the summer of 415, acts associated with religious and civic impiety were for the first time openly connected with oligarchic treason against the state. Extensive investigations were launched, wrongdoers identified, and those judged guilty punished. Andocides had gained notoriety in the trials of 415 as a prime witness for the state's investigation. On the basis of earlier information provided by Diocleides, Andocides had been arrested and imprisoned for sacrilegious behavior: mutilating the Herms. In return for immunity Andocides then testified as an eyewitness to the impious activities that took place shortly before the launch of the naval expedition. Andocides was willing—and able—to name names. Although Diocleides had claimed that more than 300 men took part in the mutilation of the Herms, Andocides testified that Diocleides was really a paid informer giving false witness and maintained that a smaller number were involved. He identified some in the *hetaireia* by name and even included himself among them, although he was careful to say that he was absent on the particular night in question and to explain why: he had recently been thrown from a horse and was home recovering from an injured collarbone. Moreover, in the defense speech given fifteen years after the fact Andocides offered a credible account of the alleged profanation of the Mysteries of Demeter that also had taken place in the spring of 415. The Athenians had readily believed his account in 415, and they had granted him immunity in exchange for the names provided in his testimony. Andocides in 399 had every reason to hope that the jury would believe him a second time.

After his testimony in 415 Andocides was found guilty of impiety, but he was not exiled because he had been granted immunity. Nor were his citizen rights taken away. But those Andocides had named did not fare so well. They were found guilty of impiety and ordered into exile; many had their property confiscated by the state. Diocleides was executed. Although Andocides was not officially exiled in 415, he did become the target of a significant amount of political ill-will. Shortly after he testified a decree was passed in the Assembly aimed specifically at him: it forbade those who had openly confessed to acts of civic impiety from entering any of sanctuaries or temples in the *polis*—even the Athenian Agora. Since the Agora—with its altars, public monuments, state institutions, and shady stoas—was the civic, cultic, and financial center of the city, this decree successfully brought forward by Isotimides effectively blocked Andocides from every aspect of public life in Athens. In response to this form of civic and ritual exclusion, Andocides, a young man of wealth, connection, and promise, willingly chose to go into exile. He became a prosperous merchant and trader, traveled all over the Aegean, and reported in his defense speech in 399 that he had undertaken business activities in Sicily and Italy that supported the Athenian navy. Doubtless the continuing hostilities between the Athenian empire and the alliance headed by Sparta afforded him many business opportunities.

In 399 Andocides claimed that he had always remained loyal to Athens, even while in exile. Shortly before the first oligarchic revolution in 411 he showed his goodwill to the democratic leaders of the *polis* by reportedly selling the Athenian navy a shipment of oars at cost. Andocides then tried to return to Athens, but by the time he actually arrived in the city the oligarchy of the Four Hundred had seized power and the democratic leaders had fled. Among those new leaders of the oligarchs in 411 were men whom he had named in the investigation of 415. Those in power imprisoned and tortured him for a second time and then released him. Andocides returned to his self-imposed exile.

More than ten years later all of this ostensibly lay in the past, and according to the amnesty agreement of 403 Andocides was not liable for crimes against the state committed prior to the reign of the Thirty in 404. Indeed, Andocides considered the second restoration of the democracy and the amnesty another opportunity to return home to Athens. But his political foes persisted, and they found a way to prosecute him even in a time of forgiveness and reconciliation. In the impiety case brought forward in 399, Andocides was charged with violating the decree of Isotimides. The prosecution argued that Andocides had broken this law twice since his return from self-imposed exile: first by attending the Mysteries of Demeter held in Eleusis in the fall of 401 and a second time when he reportedly entered the Eleusinion, the sanctuary sacred to Demeter on the north slope of the Acropolis, where he placed a suppliant's olive branch at the altar of the goddess.

It is significant that Meletus and the accusers at Andocides' trial in 399 repeatedly reminded the jury of the crimes from 415. Both the earlier profanation of the Mysteries and the mutilation of the Herms were cited as evidence for Andocides' admitted membership in a *hetaireia* that committed acts of impiety. At the trial in 399 Andocides did not deny having participated in some acts of civic impiety in 415, associating himself with those who had mutilated the Herms; but he went to great lengths to distance himself from those who had profaned the Mysteries. Furthermore, once he returned from exile around 403 he began spending his hard-earned wealth on the city of Athens. For the next three years he consistently demonstrated a willingness to perform liturgies for the *dēmos,* such as underwriting the Attic festival of the Hephaestia and serving as the Athenian representative in panhellenic embassies to the Olympian and Isthmian athletic festivals.

Though the complete truthfulness of Andocides' first account given in 415 cannot be ascertained, the repetition of his testimony in 399 reflects what a jury of Athenians after the restoration of the democracy believed aristocratic citizens had been capable of before the coups of 411 and 404. In 415 some citizens had feared that the democracy was in danger; they suspected that aristocrats like Andocides were fomenting a revolution and using private religious associations as venues for organizing themselves. In the memories of the citizens in 399, opportunities in the past for oligarchs to meet and plan insurrection became equated with "impious" cultic worship. By 399 Athens had indeed suffered two oligarchic coups, and some citizens may have felt (after the fact) that their earlier suspicions had been justified. Yet

Andocides, who never denied his aristocratic connections or even his guilt, was able to align himself with the democratic side in the revolutions of 411 and 404. This position, so cleverly captured in his speech, reveals the Athenians' concern for their own actions, especially during the rule of the Thirty. Citizens who had been absent from Athens during the Thirty's reign could use their absence as proof of their democratic leanings. This strategy would also come into play in the other two trials of 399.

THE TRIAL OF NICOMACHUS: 'ASEBEIA' AND PUBLIC 'NOMOI'

Soon after the trial of Andocides there was another important trial in Athens that centered on a particular citizen and the correct public worship of the ancestral gods. This was the trial of Nicomachus. Of the three impiety cases known from 400/399, the one involving Nicomachus remains the most unclear. Still, the basics of the case against Nicomachus are reasonably secure. Nicomachus was an ordinary citizen who was employed by the state. He spent a long time—possibly as many as ten years—researching, organizing, and republishing the laws of Athens. Although this work was begun after the first oligarchic revolution was suppressed in 410, it wasn't completed until after the second restoration of the democracy in 403. Shortly thereafter, Nicomachus was brought to trial on charges that he was a lawbreaker, *paranomos,* who had deliberately and repeatedly perverted the laws of the ancestors.

Back in 410 the *dēmos* had determined that reinstating the ancestral customs and constitution was the right thing to do once the Four Hundred were removed from power. Since tensions still remained between the oligarchs and the democrats about the particulars of the *patrios politeia,* it was agreed that a committee of citizens called the *anagrapheis,* those who "write up," would go through available written records and codify the laws. Nicomachus was one of those assigned the responsibility of overseeing the research and the transcription of laws onto stone tables that would be publicly displayed in civic buildings in the Agora. The earliest laws, including the homicide laws of Draco, were quickly republished, but it took the codification committee a longer time to review and organize the laws and decrees passed in the time of Solon and afterward. Sometime between 410 and 405 the Athenians showed their continuing support for the codification project by approving the creation of a new and central public archive located in the Agora.

The work of the *anagrapheis* was interrupted by the second oligarchic revolution in 404; with the resumption of the democracy in 403 another committee of law experts was formed, this time known as the *nomothetai*, the men who "place laws." Nicomachus was apparently one of their number, too. As he was finishing the work of the *nomothetai*, he was indicted for using his office to secretly change and manipulate the ancestral *nomoi*. The speech Nicomachus gave in his own defense has not survived, but the prosecution speech, like the prosecution speech for Andocides' trial, is preserved in the corpus of Lysias. The precise charge is not stated in Lysias, but the accusers do repeatedly argue that Nicomachus was not preserving the worship of the city's gods in the way that *ta patria* demanded. The prosecutors argued that Nicomachus was not publishing the *nomoi* correctly, especially the *nomoi* concerning civic sacrifice and the public worship of the gods.

In a world without books, newspapers, or the printing press, making written information available for public access involved different technologies than it does today. For fifth- and fourth-century Athenians and their ancestors, "publishing" meant posting information in a public place, often by inscribing the words on stone or wood. Since the Renaissance, inscriptions have been incorporated into buildings and monuments in the West as decorative architectural elements. Inscriptions in block capital letters evoke Greco-Roman antiquity in a stylized and highly recognizable way. Inscriptions on neoclassical American structures generally provide basic information; for instance, the lettering over an entrance to a public building may distinguish the county courthouse from a U.S. post office. But as simple descriptive titles, these modern-day inscriptions do not serve a significant function for citizens as they pursue their civic responsibilities.

For classical Athenians, inscribed boards, stones, and plaques were ubiquitous in public places, and they served a purpose absolutely essential to Athenian democracy. Since bound books had not yet come into use, much of the Athenian law code was inscribed onto stone tablets known as *stēlai* and then erected in public, often in or near the Agora. Wooden planks and plastered walls and other vertical surfaces were also used for publishing civic documents and laws. The words of decrees and laws were inscribed or painted in uniform block letters, without any punctuation or even spaces between the words. Official inscriptions often used abbreviations for commonly used phrases, and many Athenian laws began with an abbreviated evocation of the city's gods. Since some Athenians were not literate enough to read the complex inscriptions, those citizens who were unable to read relied on their family and friends to read the published laws and decrees out loud for them.

Inscribing law codes for public display was a nearly universal custom among all the Greek *poleis,* regardless of the form of their constitutions. The inscribed law code from the *polis* of Gortyn on the island of Crete is another important and early example that is today much studied by scholars. Indeed, other peoples in the eastern Mediterranean basin and West Asia also published their law codes on hard surfaces and placed them in public. Examples of this common practice are evident in the Egyptian hieroglyphs inscribed on stone pillars or painted on walls, the ancient Mesopotamian law code of Hammurabi inscribed on stone, and the stone tablet of laws said to have been presented to the Israelites by Moses at Sinai.

The Athenians prided themselves in their democratic constitution and its customs of equal participation for all citizens. Public access to the laws in their published form was a high priority. The base of the monument for the eponymous heroes in the Agora (constructed in the fourth century) served as a public forum for publishing information relating to the demes, and it has been suggested that the vertical surfaces on the sides and the back of herms also served as notice boards. Decrees and acts passed by the Assembly were published on wooden planks and stone *stēlai,* and laws and regulations related to public temples and sacred shrines were published on stone blocks and placed at the entrance to the holy areas. Inscribed boundary stones marked the limits or *temenoi* of public sacred areas; archaeologists have unearthed boundary stones for many Athenian public spaces, including the Agora and the Pnyx. *Nomoi* regulating cultic behavior stipulated who was and was not permitted to enter a sanctuary, and under what conditions entrance was permitted. Stone *stēlai* also listed the types of sacrifices and votive gifts allowed and not allowed. Official calendars of *polis* and deme festivals and sacrifices were published on these stone blocks and displayed, and public proclamations of acknowledgment and thanks were inscribed and dedicated to the gods in their sanctuaries, as inscriptions and other inscribed objects at panhellenic sanctuaries such as Delphi, Eleusis, and Olympia bear witness.

The most ancient laws of Athens, those of Draco and Solon, were inscribed on wooden pillars and stone blocks and placed on display in the Royal Stoa in the Agora. These wooden pillars, called *axones,* appear to have been inscribed on all sides and mounted on a vertical axis so that they could be rotated as they were read. There is also evidence for a late fifth-century method of publishing laws provisionally and temporarily by inscribing or painting the text on wooden boards, which would be displayed in public before a copy of the document was stored, possibly on papyrus in the public archives. It is indeed highly likely that laws were stored on papyrus, but papyrus, like wood, does not last in the Mediterranean climate and only a few examples have survived to be excavated by modern archaeologists. Finally, not all laws were written. There is evidence from the fifth century for "unwritten laws," *agraptoi nomoi*. As a part of the body of inherited ancestral custom, these unpublished laws were so basic that the Athenian *dēmos* assumed they were universally known and upheld.

Clearly this profusion of public legal records, stone *stēlai,* and painted wooden boards constituted thousands of inscriptions and documents, and eventually created a serious storage problem. Volumes of books can take up considerable shelf space in modern libraries, but imagine how much more space wooden boards and stone tablets required. While some of the more current laws, decrees, and proclamations would be on display in the open for all to see and read, a backlog of older inscriptions needed to be transcribed to a different material and stored in a public place where citizens could still have access to them. In the waning days of its empire in the fifth century, while still a democracy, Athens created a central archive for the storage of public records in an older, sacred public building. This archive called the Metroön was, like most public buildings in Athens, located in the Agora, in the old Council house immediately next to the new Council house (built sometime between 410 and 405). The Metroön combined civic, legal, and cultic functions; it served as a shrine to the Mother of the gods at the same time that it stored the records of the Athenian *dēmos*— the official *nomoi* as published on papyrus, wood, and stone *stēlai.*

Some *stēlai* were stored and the texts from other stone blocks were copied onto papyrus, but the remaining stones were not permanently lost or destroyed. Fortunately, large cut limestone blocks had another important function in Athens for many centuries: they were used for building materials. The Athenians simply recycled obsolete inscriptions by literally making them the building blocks of the city. The inscribed surfaces of *stēlai* could be turned away from view or smoothed away, if need be. Recycled *stēlai* were sometimes used in the construction of public and private buildings; the city's fortifications from all periods and the Long Walls connecting Athens and the Piraeus also contained recycled stone *stēlai* that had once displayed official *polis* records. In fact, much of what is known today about Athenian law is the result of archaeological excavations of Athenian buildings and defensive walls, whose building stones and foundations were discovered to be actually *stēlai* recording decrees and laws of the Athenian *dēmos*.

This ancient publishing industry was part of the backbone of the Athenian democracy, and it must have employed a fair number of skilled craftsmen and unskilled laborers. Workers toiled to quarry and transport the stone; they prepared the blocks and carved the stone *stēlai* for publication; they transcribed texts; and finally they catalogued and stored the laws in the public archives. One tradition records that Socrates was a stoneworker in Athens. As noted above, Nicomachus, the man accused of distorting the laws in 399, was employed in the state-supported publishing industry.

Like Andocides' trial on *asebeia* charges, Nicomachus's trial had a background that stretched ten years into the past. Nicomachus's first appointment as one of the *anagrapheis* dated to 410. During the decade when Nicomachus and the other magistrates were busy researching and publishing Athenian *nomoi*, Athens fell to Sparta, suffered a second oligarchic coup, and enjoyed a second restoration of the democracy. During the reign of the Thirty, Nicomachus apparently joined other Athenian democrats in fleeing the city to avoid torture and assassination. When the restored democracy appointed a second committee, now called the *nomothetai*, Nicomachus returned from exile; he and the other *nomothetai* fulfilled their responsibility by returning to the state archives in the Metroön. They finished researching, organizing, and transcribing all the relevant laws. After they completed this task, wooden boards were perhaps placed on display in the Athenian Agora for review before being inscribed on stone. As the provisional texts of the laws were approved by the people, the *nomothetai* supervised the transcription of the final drafts, and the official texts were displayed in public or filed in the Metroön.

Once they began reading and reviewing the newly drafted laws, some Athenian citizens became disgruntled. The laws as published did not always accord with their memories of what the sacred laws had been before the first oligarchic coup of 411. A group of these dissatisfied individuals banded together and accused Nicomachus of manipulating and perverting the ancestral laws. From an Athenian's point of view, to deliberately change a law amounted to a type of impiety: *asebeia*. The accusers claimed that rather than simply republishing the laws as they had always existed, Nicomachus had done some significant editing of the *nomoi* without the approval of the *dēmos*. These Athenians charged Nicomachus with selectively transcribing the original decrees, leaving out some laws entirely and inserting others that the Assembly had never passed. In one instance the accusers alleged that Nicomachus had made changes to the *polis* calendar, adding some festivals to the official calendar of civic sacrifices. Increasing the occasions for *thysia* would place a greater financial burden on the *polis* and the wealthiest aristocrats, who by tradition were expected to perform liturgies and help finance state-sponsored festivals for the gods.

The prosecution argued that Nicomachus's actions resulted in injury to the state and to the *dēmos* as a whole. They claimed that Nicomachus consistently avoided the customary annual audit procedures in place, that he remained in his magistracy long after the initial appointed term, and that he willfully and secretly altered the very laws he was supposed to be preserving. An additional assertion was that he was the illegitimate offspring of an Athenian woman and a male slave; if true, Nicomachus would not even have been a citizen, and therefore would have been unqualified to interpret the ancestral laws of the Athenian people.

As the *nomothetai* finished restoring the ancestral laws and religious customs, the Athenians themselves were reflecting on the mutual relationship between the *polis* and expressions of public piety. They apparently felt that private actions of individuals had the potential to do great harm to the state, a belief reflected in the writings of the metic Lysias. The arguments that Lysias constructed for the trial of Nicomachus were based on an assumption that ancestral Athenian *nomoi* linked the individual citizen and the political community. Nicomachus, some felt, had behaved impiously while serving as one of the *nomothetai*. Recognizing the full scope of Nicomachus's responsibilities to the *dēmos* can also illumine some of the underlying issues in the case of Andocides. Nicomachus and the other *nomothetai* were researching and transcribing the ancestral sacred laws concerning the public worship of the gods—*ta patria*—for the benefit of the *dēmos* in the restored Athenian democracy. Likewise Andocides made an effort to observe ancestral *nomoi* concerning the worship of Athena and Demeter after he returned from exile and started reintegrating himself into Athenian civic and cultic life.

The allegations of impiety raised by the accusers in both cases rest in part on the understanding that observing *nomoi* enabled Athenians to maintain the ancestral traditions of worshipping the gods, traditions that supported the *polis* and its institutions. By charging Nicomachus with altering ancestral customs, *ta patria* and *patrioi nomoi,* his opponents were claiming that he privately conspired with an anti-democratic faction to selectively edit some laws and elsewhere add laws and customs where none had existed before. They alleged that Nicomachus was acting in a subversive and dangerous manner that was harmful to the whole *dēmos*. Similarly, Andocides had allegedly harmed the people through private religious behaviors that some of his fellow citizens interpreted as impious. Yet both defendants evidently demonstrated that they had been absent from Athens during the reign of the oligarchs, which proved to the jury their loyalty to the democracy. This was a strategy that Socrates could not employ in his trial.

THE TRIAL OF SOCRATES: 'ASEBEIA' AND INQUIRY

For centuries the trial and execution of Socrates have been considered among antiquity's most infamous examples of injustice. Socrates was indicted and brought before a jury of his peers on a charge of impiety, just as Andocides and Nicomachus were accused of breaking laws and subverting customs that lay at the heart of Athenian civic religion. When seen in the context of these two other contemporary cases, Socrates' trial becomes a piece of a larger puzzle; it can be viewed as one event in the larger pattern of civic life immediately following the fall of Athens and the restoration of democracy. Although the war with Sparta was over, the empire dissolved, and democracy restored, the Athenian *dēmos* continued to examine and reinterpret its recent collective experiences. The Athenians' ongoing commitment to weave together civic rites and democracy, evident in the trials of Andocides and Nicomachus, played out again with Socrates.

Ancient sources unanimously report that Socrates was charged with three counts of *asebeia*. The charges of corrupting the youth and introducing new gods in Athens remain the most familiar today. The third count of the impiety charge leveled against Socrates, *mē theous nomizein*, is difficult to translate and understand from a twenty-first-century perspective. There are several accepted ways of rendering this phrase into English, including "not believing in the gods," "not recognizing (or honoring, acknowledging) the gods recognized (honored, acknowledged) by the city." The most common translation, "not believing in the gods," to the modern ear sounds like full-blown atheism, and some scholars in the nineteenth and twentieth centuries saw in Socrates a precursor to the rational humanists of the European Enlightenment. But personal faith had little if any role in ancient Mediterranean religious systems prior to Christianity, and Socrates was no atheist—at least not in our modern sense of the word. After the war Athens rededicated itself to its ancestral customs, and Socrates was no stranger to *ta patria,* according to the reports of his contemporaries.

The main obstacle to understanding and interpreting this phrase hinges on how to translate the verb *nomizein.* While it may be translated as "think, consider" or "believe," *nomizein* at its core is connected to the concept of *nomos,* the Greek noun that covers the English words "law, legal decree," and "custom, tradition." The direct association with religious customs and ritual conventions allows *nomizein* to be rendered "practice, customarily use; observe custom." Since *nomizein* can mean adhering to the ancestral practices of worshipping the gods, the positive formulation *theous nomizein* would describe the proper, publicly sanctioned practices that maintained the traditional worship of ancestral deities that supported the *polis.* Perhaps a better way for readers today to understand the third charge of impiety hinges on the shades of meaning that connect *nomos/nomizein* to ancestral law and religious custom, so *mē theous nomizein* can be translated "not observing the city's laws and customs concerning the gods"—"not doing the customary things for the gods."

Ta patria, patrios politeia, nomoi, ancestral customs and laws—all were upheld by the Athenian *dēmos* in the fifth and fourth centuries, and at the same time these laws supported the *polis* and ensured the well-being of its citizen residents. As evidenced in the trials of Nicomachus and Andocides, the Athenians were acutely sensitive to the demands of piety and the *polis* in the years immediately following the restoration of democracy in 403. Athenian democracy was built on a foundation of reciprocal relationships between law, civic life, and ancestral religious practices in the public sphere. The trial of Socrates is part of this pattern, and viewing his trial in the light of the other two trials can reveal the Athenians' priorities at this time.

Our knowledge of Socrates, including the tradition of his trial and execution, comes primarily from three contemporary sources: Aristophanes, Plato, and Xenophon. Aristophanes was a comic playwright who some twenty years before the trial authored the *Clouds,* a comedy renowned for its parody of a philosopher named Socrates. Plato, the most famous of Socrates' followers, composed accounts of Socrates conversing with friends and acquaintances—these are the dialogues of Plato. In a similar vein Xenophon, an aristocratic career military man who was a friend of Socrates, wrote a few Socratic dialogues and essays that have no pretensions to philosophy, containing instead more personal anecdotes and historical background.

Plato probably wrote his *Apology* of Socrates in the mid- or late 390s, possibly a few years after the actual defense in court, and Xenophon apparently wrote his own *Apology* about the same time. The title can sometimes mislead English-speaking readers; the Greek word *apologia* does not mean that Socrates appeared before the jury to "apologize" for harms done in the past and acknowledge accountability for his actions. Rather, an *apologia* is simply a defense speech delivered in court. Literary records from antiquity record the names of additional early fourth-century authors who wrote about this trial, but these accounts have not survived. Some of the works were reportedly full of praise for Socrates, but it is also clear that Socrates continued to have detractors after his death. These detractors published highly critical pamphlets and speeches about the philosopher and the potential dangers of his teachings. Polycrates' *Kategoria,* or *Accusation,* was among the more famous of these speeches critical of Socrates. One twentieth-century scholar called the *Kategoria* the "literary sensation" of its day; Polycrates' speech apparently reinforced a commonly held belief that Socrates was haughty, anti-democratic, and a slick rhetorician. It is even possible that this harsh *Accusation* prompted the flurry of *Apology* writers—maybe even Plato himself. Unfortunately Polycrates' speech is lost, and the best that scholars can do is tentatively outline a reconstruction of the argument based on common features in the two defense speeches that have survived. What exactly Athenians were discussing in the aftermath of Socrates' trial and execution can never be known, but for a certain time Athenian intellectuals did have a keen interest in writing about Socrates, his teachings, and his trial.

Socrates himself wrote nothing during his lifetime, and in important ways the accounts of Plato and Xenophon are at odds with each other. Taken together these facts have led to the so-called Socratic problem. Who was Socrates, really, and what did he teach? Xenophon's *Memorabilia,* a collection of anecdotes about Socrates—his life, his teachings, and his trial—offers significant background for scholars trying to reconstruct the prosecution's frame of reference when addressing the jury in Socrates' case. But Socrates does not express the same penetrating philosophical insights in Xenophon that he does in Plato. Most of Plato's twenty-eight philosophical dialogues have survived intact, and Socrates is the central character in all but one of these dialogues. Yet even in that dialogue, the *Laws,* written at the end of a career that stretched over several decades, Socrates' presence is still palpable. The main speaker is called the Athenian Stranger, and the arguments and conversational style of this stranger bear a marked resemblance to Socrates' arguments and style of discourse found elsewhere in Plato. Did Plato throughout his lengthy career faithfully represent the ideas of the historical Socrates, or did the character of

Socrates over time become a mouthpiece for Plato's own evolving views? Modern scholars are far from agreement, and classicists and philosophers still debate the consistency and accuracy of Plato's portrayal of Socrates. But even if Plato's fictionalized dialogues do not always accurately record Socrates' own ideas, a real historical figure named Socrates did spend a good deal of his life talking with fellow Athenians in the public spaces of the city, and he was executed by the state for religious offences in 399.

Four Platonic dialogues record the trial and execution of Socrates: the *Euthyphro*, the *Apology*, the *Crito*, and the *Phaedo*. The *Apology* reads as though it were a transcript of the actual defense speech Socrates gave in the courtroom. The *Crito* and the *Phaedo* are both dialogues named after Athenian men who, together with a few intimate friends, conversed with Socrates during his last days, when he was in prison awaiting execution. The Athenian state was at that time observing the Delia, an annual religious festival for the hero Theseus. By custom all public executions were stayed until the festival's completion. *Polis* officials were expecting the return of the ship with the Athenian embassy from Delos so that they could arrange the final sacred procession to the Acropolis; a full month of unforeseen weather delays and adverse winds forced the postponement of Socrates' execution until the embassy's return (*Crito* 43d, *Phaedo* 58b; Xenophon *Memorabilia* 4.8.2). Even while awaiting death Socrates continued to talk with Crito and other friends. Together they inquired into the concept of the laws in Athens, and what it meant to abide by the laws in a democratic state. The *Phaedo* depicts the execution itself, and it includes the moving final scene of Socrates' courage and dignity when drinking the fatal cup of hemlock.

Plato set another Socratic dialogue, the *Euthyphro*, around the time of Socrates' trial. The *Euthyphro* depicts the meeting between Socrates and an acquaintance, a fellow citizen named Euthyphro, at the Royal Stoa in the Agora. Euthyphro and Socrates were both to appear before the *archōn basileus*, the magistrate who had jurisdiction in the Athenian judicial system over cases involving serious religious infractions, including impiety and murder. Euthyphro was going to the *archōn basileus* to charge his own father with murder, while Socrates was going to take part in a pretrial hearing to determine whether the indictment for *asebeia* actually merited a full public trial. When Euthyphro told Socrates the details of the impiety case against his father, who had killed a laborer, Socrates was prompted to engage Euthyphro in a long discussion about the very nature of piety and impiety. The *Euthyphro* thus presents Socrates in public at the very start of a legal process engaging in critical inquiry about the worship of the gods. Questions about pious and impious actions clearly were on Socrates' mind when he was on his way to talk with the archon about his own indictment—or at least this is what Plato wished his readers to believe about his teacher. We do not know what Socrates and the *archōn basileus* said to each other that day. But we do know the magistrate decided that Socrates' impiety case should be brought before a jury of 500 Athenians.

As was true of the trials of Andocides and Nicomachus, the particulars of the *asebeia* charge against Socrates implicitly referred to events from earlier decades, events that continued to stir the Athenians' passions even after the war had ended. In Socrates' defense speech, as reported by Plato, the older man distanced himself from political life in Athens. But a close reading of available sources shows that Socrates had been visible in some arenas of Athenian public life for many years. In fact some of Socrates' students, friends, and acquaintances were the very men who shaped Athenian policy throughout the war, and Socrates himself was deeply engaged in the intellectual currents of the day. Although Plato's Socrates did not boast about his role in politics and public life, he did acknowledge a predilection for ceaselessly inquiring into civic virtues that were valued in fifth-century Athens. Together with his discussions of power, knowledge, and rhetoric in the *polis,* Socrates also spoke openly about how he honored the gods, attended state festivals, and participated in Athenian civic religion.

Plato's *Apology* shows Socrates making every effort to remove himself from the Greek intelligentsia. Indeed, Socrates opens the *Apology* with a refutation of the accusers' allegations that he was a clever speaker who investigated the latest scientific theories. For an Athenian juror these claims may not have rung completely true. Socrates was publicly known to be someone who had long enjoyed discussing new ideas, and in Athenian popular culture he was associated with the foreign teacher Anaxagoras and others like him. In Aristophanes' *Clouds* the character named Socrates was a philosopher who ran a school that taught young men newfangled ideas about the sun and stars. This comedic, semi-fictional Socrates also trained youths in the latest slick techniques for making the weaker argument appear the stronger. The *Clouds* was performed at the City Dionysia in 423, almost twenty-five years before the trial. Although many jurors may have been too young to have seen the performance at the dramatic festival, some may have read the play later, and virtually all of them would have been familiar with Socrates from his tendency to hang around public places in the city. Indeed, Socrates made reference to the pernicious influence of his accusers who had been spreading lies about him for a long time, and he emphasized "a certain writer of comedies" among their number (*Apology* 18d, 19c).

During the last third of the fifth century, Athens had witnessed the arrival of a professional class of highly skilled foreign experts. These teachers came to mainland Greece from Italy and Asia Minor. In the 440s, well before the Peloponnesian War broke out, Pericles personally supported foreign teachers who visited Athens. Commonly known as "sophists," these professionals visited the major cities of the Greek-speaking world, where they taught for a fee. Being a sophist was virtually synonymous with travel in the ancient Mediterranean. Traveling philosophers would settle for a few years in a city, lecture, take on new students, and in time go on to another cultural center.

In one sense a sophist was a "sage," and some of the traveling teachers simply lectured on natural history, science, and mathematics. Some of them were also known by the Greek terms *physiologoi* or *physikoi,* men who studied natural phenomena. New astronomical theories proposing that the sun was really not a god but a fiery rock in the heavens had been introduced into Athens by the Ionian philosopher Anaxagoras in the 440s and 430s. Anaxagoras was one of several teachers who originally came from the cosmopolitan Ionian Greek cities in the eastern Mediterranean. In the cities of Ephesos and Miletus, Greeks may well have been exposed to more advanced scientific knowledge from eastern centers of learning— Memphis in Egypt, Babylon and Persepolis in Persia. These Ionian natural philosophers traveled around the Mediterranean, teaching as they went; Athens was one of many ports of call they would have frequented.

Pericles was said to have befriended and supported Anaxagoras when he visited Athens during the late 440s and 430s. But this support came at a price for Pericles, whether his traditional-minded political rivals felt genuinely threatened by the new ideas or simply attacked him where they believed he was weak. They charged Anaxagoras and others like him with impiety. The details are scanty, but it seems that in the mid-430s the Athenian Assembly passed a decree put forward by a citizen named Diopeithes. This decree may have provided the legal foundation for the *eisangelia* impeachment procedure for individuals who did not observe the city's laws and customs concerning the gods: *tous ta theia mē nomizontas* (Plutarch *Pericles* 32). Pericles' foreign friend Anaxagoras was perhaps not the only target of Diopeithes' decree; later sources indicate that another traveling philosopher named Protagoras was allegedly tried in the 420s and had his books burned in public, and another tradition holds that Pericles' common-law wife Aspasia, who actively supported new ideas, was also indicted for *asebeia*. Nothing bad seems to have happened to Aspasia; Anaxagoras may have been found guilty but Pericles helped him leave Athens safely, and Plato reports that Protagoras died with his reputation untouched. Still, these are the first examples in the historical record of individuals being charged with impiety and put on trial.

We cannot be sure what Socrates did or did not believe about natural phenomena. Xenophon's *Memorabilia* depicts Socrates suggesting that the investigation of the ultimate origins of cosmic phenomena was not a good use of a man's time, especially when there were other more pressing moral questions that needed to be explored (Xenophon *Memorabilia* 4.7.5). Following both Plato and Xenophon, scholars today surmise that most of Socrates' teaching was aimed at ethical issues, especially those sorts of ethical questions that would have had immediate and practical application for the citizens of late fifth-century Athens. In Plato's *Apology* Socrates spoke to the jury and reminded them that he was not connected with any of the natural philosophers, despite what the character that had his name in Aristophanes' popular play might have led them to believe about him.

But the term "sophist" itself was not without controversy; over time it came to mean "wise guy." Such sophists were itinerant professionals with little interest in teaching ethics, scientific knowledge, or a method for apprehending the truth. Rather, these experts excelled in the arts of speech making and rhetoric: they constructed arguments that would unfailingly persuade an audience to follow the will of the speaker. Some sophists taught ways to make a weak argument appear stronger; others advocated the position "might is right." There were sophists who became infamous for teaching impressionable and brash young men in Athens, many of whom came from the ranks of the Athenian aristocracy. Some of the leading public figures in the law courts and assemblies of Athens had been trained by these traveling teachers in their youth, or were at least influenced by their methods. Lysias, the metic who became a famous speechwriter, had connections to philosophical schools and sophists in southern Italy. Critias, the harsh leader of the Thirty, wrote plays and other poems that reveal a genuine interest in late fifth-century intellectual movements connected with the new rhetoric; he is often counted as one of the sophists in Athens.

Aristophanes' *Clouds* conflated the two kinds of sophists that Athenians were familiar with in the 420s, and Socrates had a hard time later dissociating himself from the parody. The comedy depicted a character named Socrates teaching young men both natural science and rhetoric. This

Socrates instructed students to argue in such as way as to make the weaker argument appear the stronger. The comic Socrates ran a school of philosophy with the silly name "the Thinkaterium" (the Phrontisterion), and he accepted as his student Pheidippides, the youthful son of a nearly bankrupt Athenian citizen named Strepsiades. Strepsiades had lost much of his money in the war, suffering from its economic blockades and high prices, and had recently gone further into debt: he complained that his worthless, lazy son Pheidippides spent far too much time at the racetrack betting on horses and losing. Strepsiades hoped that at the Thinkaterium Pheidippides would learn a new method of argument that would enable them to evade the claims of creditors and debt collectors. Instead, the young Pheidippides proved to be an impetuous student who concluded that Socrates was actually teaching him to disrespect his father and all paternal authority figures. After attending Socrates' lessons, Pheidippides beat up his father and then further exercised his new intellectual freedom by burning down Socrates' Thinkaterium. The eccentric philosopher was still inside the school, and as the play ended the audience could hear his screams offstage.

Even when distorted through the lens of Dionysian satire, the *Clouds'* dark humor cannot entirely obscure what scholars assume was the typical Athenian's opinion of Socrates. Some Athenians apparently did believe that Socrates had a school—or that he was the sort of person who would likely attract students. In fact there had been and still were several such informal "schools" in Athens. While some learned men taught natural philosophy, others claimed to teach virtue, or *aretē*. These teachers asserted they could—for a fee—train young men to become persuasive public speakers. The skills required to conduct oneself according to recognized standards of virtue and to persuade peers in law courts and the Assembly were highly valued in the ancient *polis;* consequently, these itinerant teachers maintained that they could teach men to be good citizens. Both groups of men, those who taught science and those who taught *aretē*, were commonly called "sophists" in the fifth century.

Although Socrates investigated the nature of *aretē* with his friends and acquaintances, he was keen to distance himself from sophists who taught rhetoric. He asserted in the *Apology* that he was not a clever speaker, and did not take students or accept fees. He simply spent all his spare time in the public spaces of the city and talked one-on-one with anyone who had the time and interest. He called himself a gadfly who had attached himself to the city and was constantly disturbing it (*Apology* 30e). He did not seek the attention or praise of the citizen body in the Assembly, and he did not seek to persuade his peers to follow one particular policy over another. The Socrates shown in the dialogues of Plato did not usually discuss current events, but rather investigated the more abstract ethical principles that underlie all actions, whether in the public sphere or in private life.

Indeed, the Platonic Socrates was known for his disavowal of public life. Several times in the *Apology* Socrates stated that he had never had any interest in pursuing politics. Assuming that he was at or near 70 at the time of his trial in 399, Socrates was a mature man in his 40s at the start of the Peloponnesian War—the prime age for an articulate and ambitious Athenian to take on leadership roles in the Assembly. He was near 40 at the time of the great plague and the death of Pericles, and in his late 40s in 423, when Aristophanes lampooned him in the *Clouds*. Looking back even further Socrates was born around 470, shortly after the Persian Wars—born to parents native to an Athens that had twice been evacuated and sacked by the Persians. Tradition has it that Socrates was trained in the craft of stonecutting; with Athens undergoing its most intense phases of rebuilding and reconstruction in the 450s and 440s, he had many years to hone his skills. As a younger man Socrates witnessed the rise of Athens under the leadership of Cimon and Pericles, and the prime of his life overlapped with the entirety of the twenty-seven-year war with Sparta. He experienced the brutal years of the second coup of 404 as an elder.

In a coincidence of historical timing, the span of Socrates' life corresponded with the rebuilding of the city, rise and fall of the Athenian empire, and the entire course of the Peloponnesian War. His complete absence from Athenian public life would have been remarkable. And yet, according to Plato, Socrates maintained that he deliberately chose to avoid public life. In the *Apology* Socrates attributed this decision to the presence of his *daimonion,* a personal, divine entity that he described as akin to a small voice that communicated to him privately (*Apology* 31d). The *daimonion* did not tell him explicitly what to do in a given situation. Rather, it somehow inhibited him from a planned course of action and questioned him about his intentions—or better, the *daimonion* led Socrates himself to examine his own intentions. It was the voice of this *daimonion* that consistently guided him away from pursuing a life of public activity in Athenian politics. Instead of taking on a leadership role in the Assembly and urging his fellow citizens to take one course of action over another, Socrates chose to engage citizens in conversation individually. In Plato's dialogues Socrates was not pictured questioning his peers about recent votes in the Assembly, the current course of the war, or the position of democrats and oligarchs. Rather, Plato depicted Socrates exploring more abstract ethical issues such as justice, piety, love, and what constitutes a good life in the *polis*.

While Socrates may have chosen not to assume a leading role in Athenian politics—he did not make himself Pericles' heir, or model himself after Cleon or Nicias or any of the other leaders of the Assembly and the military—it would be a mistake to think of him purely as a private citizen who consistently shunned all involvement in the life of the city. The fact is that Socrates was personally involved in the war, the *polis,* and the empire from the late 420s steadily through to the fall of Athens and the tyranny of the Thirty. In many ways Socrates was an ideal democratic citizen. He served in the infantry; he took his turn on the Council, and in leading the Assembly while serving as one of the *prytaneis*—at a crucial time, as discussed below. This is not to say that Socrates unfailingly supported empire and war, only that he was more involved in Athens than he initially admitted in the defense speech preserved in Plato's *Apology.*

Three Platonic dialogues give accounts of Socrates' service in the infantry, where he served as a hoplite (*Apology* 28e, *Symposium* 219c–221c, and *Laches* 181b). The backbone of the Athenian army during the Peloponnesian War was the heavily armed hoplite soldier. Adult citizens who could afford to supply their own helmet, spear, shield, and greaves registered for service by deme and tribe; regular training was compulsory. In Plato's dialogues Socrates mentioned that he had served in three separate campaigns during the first decade of the Peloponnesian War: at Potidaea, Amphipolis, and Delion. The Potidaea action in the northern Aegean anticipated the war (430–432); there Athenians besieged a city that had revolted from the empire. The Amphipolis campaign was waged eight years later in the same region. The Athenian retreat and loss at Delion in 424 happened closer to home, in a sanctuary of Apollo in nearby Boeotia. In all battles Socrates acquired a reputation for steadfast courage and endurance. He rescued companions when they were wounded, and even the heavy winter snows in Potidaea did not bother him (*Symposium* 220b).

As a responsive and responsible citizen, Socrates later served on the Council. Ideally, every man in the democratic system would be selected by lot within his tribe to serve on the *boulē* at least once, and no more than twice. Socrates served in this position when he was in his 60s, during 406/5. Each of the ten Cleisthenic tribes contributed fifty men to serve on the Council for the entire year, and each tribal committee of fifty was assigned a prytany (one-tenth of the year) during which they presided as executive officers over all *polis* business. Socrates' prytany happened to fall in the autumn that year—at the very time when the generals were on trial in the Assembly following the naval victory at Arginusae (*Apology* 32b; Xenophon *Memorabilia* 1.1.18). In fact, Socrates himself was presiding over the entire Athenian *dēmos* in the Assembly on the very day that Pericles (son of Pericles) and the other generals were tried and found guilty. While the Athenians debated whether to try the generals as a group instead of individually as required by law, Socrates felt it was his duty to observe the established laws. In his role as *epistatēs* (chief of the *prytaneis*), he opposed the men who made the motion, and he urged the *dēmos* not to vote in support of it. Feelings were running so high, he reported in the *Apology*, that orators threatened to have him arrested right there at the Pnyx. He did not flinch, and although he feared imprisonment and death in that moment, he chose justice and the rule of law over the passions of the people. The Assembly voted to try the generals as a group despite Socrates' objections. That was, Socrates says in Plato's *Apology*, his only experience with holding public office, but it was a fateful day.

But that was not the end of his experience with injustice and groups of powerful men. Just a few years later, he and four others were summoned by Thirty to the Tholos to take care of some state business. The Tholos, which had served as the headquarters for the *prytaneis* when Athens was still a democracy, had been taken over by the Thirty when they disbanded the Council and the *prytaneis*. At the Tholos the Thirty ordered Socrates and the four others to go to the home of Leon of Salamis, and fetch him so that he could be executed. Leon had done nothing wrong, nor had he had a trial; he was simply a wealthy and influential man who stood in the way of the Thirty's power. He was one of hundreds whom the Thirty illegally arrested, and then either detained or killed. As Socrates put it in the *Apology*, the Thirty wanted to implicate as many citizens as they could in their illegal actions, so they drafted ordinary citizens like Socrates to carry out their illicit commands. On this occasion Socrates refused to follow the Thirty's orders. Socrates' actions and words made clear that he would not take part, and he walked out of the Tholos (*Apology* 32c). The four others obeyed, and they departed for Salamis without Socrates. Socrates speculated in the *Apology* that this act of defiance would have soon cost him his life if the Thirty had not been removed from power.

This situation in which Socrates and the four nameless men found themselves that night was precisely the type of thing the Amnesty of 403 was aimed at. Those who remained in the city did not necessarily support the reign of the Thirty, or any other oligarchy. Countless Athenians who did not leave the city got caught up in the Thirty's authoritarian regime, and not every citizen had the backbone and the commitment to justice exhibited by Socrates. The restoration of the democracy in 403 made allowances for these men, and unless it could be proven that they had personally killed someone, they were not put on trial alongside the remaining members of the Thirty who survived the civil war.

For many who were involved in Socrates' trial, perhaps the most damning, though indirect, evidence concerned his friends and associates over the years. Although Socrates was not a wealthy man himself, or even the type of person who sought social status, many aristocrats counted him as their friend and teacher. He dined with these men in their homes, and talked with them in the Agora. Everyone in Athens knew who had been associated with Socrates over the years, and the list was long. Most notably, he counted among his friends men who had played a part in both coups, especially Critias and Charmides, both of whom were relatives of Plato. Critias had a long history of being involved in powerful oligarchic factions. He had been named by Diocleides in the Herms affair in 415 and imprisoned; the testimony of Andocides brought his release. Critias eagerly followed the visiting sophists in Athens, and wrote tragedies; he was a close friend of Alcibiades and may have suggested Alcibiades' recall in 408. After a period of exile in Thessaly he returned to Athens. Critias' open admiration for Sparta may have helped him gain an appointment as one of the Thirty initially empowered by the Spartans. Charmides was Critias' nephew; he had also been named in the profanation of the Mysteries in 415, and was later closely associated with the Thirty. Both men had associated with Socrates, both were mentioned by Plato, and indeed Plato named two of his Socratic dialogues *Charmides* and *Critias.* Both men were also killed in a battle in the Piraeus during the civil war of 403.

Some of Socrates' other friends had connections to oligarchic factions and the *hetaireiai* that were so influential in Athenian politics. Phaedrus, one of the men present at the drinking party at Agathon's in 416 depicted in Plato's *Symposium,* went into exile after being implicated in the profanation of the Mysteries. A certain Adeimantus, a name known from Plato's *Republic,* was also involved in profaning the Mysteries, and Eryximachus, another character in the *Symposium,* was named as a person involved in the mutilation of the Herms. But the most infamous of all of Socrates' friends was Alcibiades. He had been an intimate friend of Socrates since he was a young man and fought alongside the older man at Plataea. Plato named a Socratic dialogue after him, too, and he was also mentioned among those present in the *Symposium* as well as the *Protagoras*. Socrates never openly criticized Alcibiades in Plato's dialogues, even after all of Alcibiades' treasonous betrayals and all the harm he did to Athens. In the *Symposium* Alcibiades confessed to having been in love with Socrates at one time. Although on one occasion they shared the same couch and slept under the same cloak, Socrates showed no interest in Alcibiades' charms. A few months after the dramatic date for the party at Agathon's, Alcibiades left for Sicily; affairs in Athens then rapidly unraveled, with Alcibiades at the very center of the turmoil. Socrates may have considered Alcibiades his most brilliant student, but in the end this did little good for the city of Athens.

Each of the three trials in 399 in some way encapsulated the tensions and conflicts of the past. Andocides' trial bore witness to the democrats' uneasiness with aristocrats and their informal *hetaireiai;* Nicomachus's trial recalled the struggles to reestablish the laws and the *patrios politeia.* Socrates' defense speech dredged up everything for the Athenians, from revolting subject allies in the empire (Potidaea) to the most egregious atrocities overseen by Critias. Socrates personally participated in the wartime desecration of Apollo's sanctuary at Delion, and his friends profaned Demeter and mutilated the Herms. Socrates himself admired foreign teachers like Anaxagoras who understood the forces of nature in a radical new way, and at the same he time obeyed a private *daimonion* that did not resemble any god of the pantheon recognized by all Athenians. Prosecutors at all three trials evoked the civic norms of *eusebeia* when they accused these three men of *asebeia*. If some jurors particularly despised Socrates because of his past connections to Alcibiades and Critias, they could mask their hatred by decrying Socrates' impiety.

The fact that Socrates never left the city to join the democrats in Boeotia or the Piraeus during the Thirty's reign did not help matters, either. If any Athenians sought evidence for his anti-democratic stance they could look here. The terms of the reconciliation agreement did not work in Socrates' favor when he defended himself in court. The final blow came in the penalty phase of his trial. Socrates was given one more chance to speak after the jury found him guilty—he could plead before the jurors and ask that he be given a more lenient penalty than the one requested by the prosecutor. But that is not what he did. Instead of requesting a mitigation of the death penalty that Meletus had initially called for, he asked the assembled Athenians to grant him the honor that he truly deserved. He asked that he be given free meals by the *polis* at the Prytaneion, as they did for Olympic victors, respected generals, and the descendants of the tyrant slayers Harmodius and Aristogeiton. Socrates spent his lifetime urging Athenians to inquire into what constituted the greatest good, and he claimed that he was a great benefactor for the city, as great as any of the others who received honors for their efforts to advance the public good. In a city where civic piety and animal sacrifice brought political interests and the affairs of the gods into public dining rooms, there might be an ironic logic to Socrates' request.

The request inspired outrage among many jurors and they voted for execution. In fact, it was reported that more voted to enforce the death penalty than had voted to find him guilty in the first place. After their decision Socrates was imprisoned while he awaited the return of the ship from Delos. When it finally did arrive he bravely drank the poisonous hemlock. With his last words, as recorded in the *Phaedo*'s death scene, Socrates instructed his friend Crito to make a sacrifice to the god Asclepius (118a). This god was a relative newcomer in Athens, having arrived in the city from Epidaurus in 420 during a lull in the war following the Peace of Nicias. As the son of Apollo, Asclepius was a healing god. Wishing to honor this god was the last recorded act of an old man found guilty of civic impiety.

'ASEBEIA' AS POLITICAL AND RELIGIOUS ACTION

The year 399 turned out to be something quite extraordinary in Athens. It was a time for collective introspection among citizens who looked back over the past thirty years and examined the whole push for empire that the *dēmos* had supported. In their law courts Athenians become painfully aware of all the poor decisions they had made and the civic conflicts they had become embroiled in—whether the affairs of the Herms and the Mysteries, the first coup in 411/0, the total disregard for justice and established legal procedures in the trial of the Arginusae generals (406), or the final, disastrous reign of the Thirty in 404. All three trials in 399 recalled these past events and the role of civic rites in Athenian public life, but the presence of Socrates, more than Nicomachus or even Andocides, may have evoked the most intense feelings among the Athenians.

By 399 Athenians could see what the push for empire had brought them. They had lost a war and thus lost their navy, their empire, and their authority in the Aegean; broken their own laws; ignored ancestral religious custom; and witnessed the unjust torture and the deaths of thousands of innocent citizens and foreign residents. Socrates perhaps came to represent all this failure to the Athenians on the jury—all this and more. For his fellow citizens, Socrates brought to mind the dangers of imperial democracy. The method of self-scrutiny and inquiry that guided his conversations led some jurors to reconsider the condition of their *polis*. They became fully aware of the dreadful things political leaders could accomplish when persuasive skills and rhetoric overwhelmed the common sense of the voting public in a dynamic democracy. *Nomos*—the precedent of law and religious custom—made little difference to powerful men driven by raw ambition. Perhaps some jurors found it difficult to face this truth; they found it easier to point the finger at Socrates than to admit their own role in the decisions made by the *dēmos*. "Impiety" was the word detractors used to describe Socrates' public behavior and, when it came from the mouths of Athenians, "impious" was a word that could simultaneously describe political and religious actions. At this trial in 399, the majority of citizens serving on the jury agreed with those who argued that Socrates was guilty. Socrates was executed, while the citizens and the *patrios politeia* of Athens survived.

Epilogue
The City after Socrates

AFTER THE YEAR 399 the Athenians experienced no more drama for a while, as Athenian democracy returned to its full function. The fourth century was a time of relative stability for the democratic institutions that had been put in place by Ephialtes and Pericles following the Persian Wars and then revived in 403. The Athenian *dēmos* during the fourth century could take full advantage of the sanctuaries built during the period of empire under Pericles: Athena's monumental Acropolis and Demeter's Eleusinian sanctuary. In the 330s Lycurgus added to Athens' splendor by constructing a permanent stone theater in the urban sanctuary of Dionysus. That theater still stands today on the south slope of the Acropolis.

In the 380s Athens attempted to re-create a naval empire, but the situation in Hellas had changed. Thebes and Argos grew powerful, and the strength of Macedon was on the rise. As the Macedonian kings Philip and Alexander gradually consolidated a new Hellenic empire, Greeks experienced the end of the autonomous and sovereign *polis* as they knew it. But as long as the Athenians did live in their democratic *polis, ta patria* and ancestral *nomoi* were upheld by the *dēmos;* at the same time, these customs and laws supported the *polis* and ensured the well-being of the citizens. The Athenian state was built on a foundation of reciprocal relationships between democracy, law, and ancestral religious customs. *Patrioi nomoi* kept the reciprocal system in balance, and respect for the ancestral laws and customs ensured that the *polis* would remain in good working order. Athenians kept to their civic calendar of annual state-sponsored festivals. The Athenian year started off in July with the Panathenaea and festivals for Zeus and Athena. Autumn was the season of Demeter, with the women's Thesmophoria and the celebration of the more egalitarian Eleusinian Mysteries, while autumn through spring was reserved for Dionysus—the Oschophoria and Anthesteria wine festivals in the late fall and spring, and the dramatic festivals (the Lenaea and the Rural and the City Dionysia) in winter and spring. At each of these festivals, Athenians worshipped their ancestral gods and experienced themselves as a complex political community that included male citizens, foreigners, women, and slaves. Politics and religion were interdependent in the classical *polis*. In this respect Athenian democracy is quite alien from its modern form.

Plato's teacher Socrates was executed by the state in 399. Several decades later, Plato's student Aristotle stated that the human being is a political animal—a *politikon zōon*—a creature of the *polis* (Aristotle *Politics* 1.2). The Greek *polis* was an autonomous entity composed of *politeis* (citizens) and other residents of both sexes and of varying status—female, slave, free, foreign. While the *polis* was autonomous, the people who lived in it were not, or at least not completely so. The citizens and residents of Athens were all social beings who needed community to live fully. As Aristotle put it, they needed the *polis*. But human beings were also creatures—the *zōon* of Aristotle's "political animal"—and as such they also needed the natural world and its abundant resources to live full lives.

Political life and religious life were fully integrated in fifth-century Athens. Traditional practices, *nomoi,* set up a complex set of interfaces that facilitated communication in three separate but related areas: between the individual and his or her ancestors, between the individual and the ongoing social and political world of the *polis,* and between the individual and the natural environment that every human being inhabited. Athenians did not worship the forces of nature or the agricultural produce that the land provided. They worshipped by means of that natural world. The fertility of the countryside generated the meat, olives, grains, grapes, and other products dedicated to the gods and consumed by humans at civic festivals. The yearly agricultural rhythms placed a predictable structure on the collective experience of those who lived in Attica and Athens. Festivals for Athena, Demeter, and Dionysus were occasions when the *polis* experienced itself as an integrated political and religious organization, and when the citizens and residents found their proper place in that organization.

On the communal level *thysia* nourished the citizens, and through their actions the citizens reinforced what they knew as their ancestors' customs. Even as customs slowly shifted over time, the nature of piety in this culture continued to validate social and political relationships through the consumption of native produce. The gods were present when all the parts in the complex set of interfaces functioned as they should.

Athenians did not have the financial resources after 399 to build the sort of grand public buildings that they had constructed in the past. In the mid-fifth century Cimon had access to funds from the spoils of a war he waged in the eastern Aegean, and Pericles' building program had relied on the tribute of subject-allies in the Athenian empire. Those sources of wealth were gone forever, once Sparta defeated Athens and ordered the Athenians to tear down their defensive walls and relinquish their naval empire. But one notable building project was carried out soon after the restoration of the democracy in 403: the construction of the Pompeion in the Kerameikos district.

Just beyond the Agora to the northwest were two of Athens' most important gates in the city walls: the Sacred Gates and the Dipylon Gates. Today you can visit the small park in the Kerameikos and see the Themistoclean walls constructed in the first half of the fifth century. The walls take a somewhat irregular course in that stretch, and in the odd-shaped space between the two gates the Athenians built the Pompeion. The building stood just inside the walls; outside was the Kerameikos cemetery, where fallen soldiers and the ancestors of Athenians were memorialized with tombs and elegantly sculpted grave *stēlai*. Outside the walls two roads ran through the cemetery and into the countryside: one road led north to the Academy, the suburb where Plato would set up his school later in the fourth century, and the other, called the Sacred Way, was the road traveled by Demeter's initiates on their way to Eleusis every fall.

When Athenians voted to construct a public building called a Pompeion around the year 399, they were once again committing themselves to their *patrios politeia* and ancestral civic rites. This area in the Kerameikos had always been used on the days of major festivals—the Panathenaea, the Eleusinian Mysteries, the Anthesteria, and the City Dionysia. This place at the gates was where the city met the countryside; it was the physical and symbolic point of contact between the citizens and their natural environment. Here civic magistrates marshaled those marching in the *pompai* (processions). Participants young and old gathered together, expressed their piety (*eusebeia*) in the presence of the ancestors buried in the Kerameikos, and lined up at the Pompeion. The area around the Pompeion was also the meeting place where city dwellers mingled with herders, who arrived from rural pastures leading the cows, sheep, and goats that would join in the procession and be sacrificed at the city's altars. A long portico fronted the building, and inside a large courtyard was surrounded by dining rooms where citizens could recline later in the day and feast on the sacrificial meat distributed in the Kerameikos.

The Pompeion's façade was obviously asymmetrical, a design a little unusual for an Athenian public building constructed at this time: from the perspective of someone facing the building, the main doorway was offset toward the right. Archaeologists note that by placing the door so far off-center, ancient architects were guiding the steps of Athenians directly onto the Panathenaic Way and toward the Agora. Anyone leaving the Pompeion and walking along the Panathenaic Way would have seen Athena's sanctuary on the Acropolis rising above them not far in the distance. This building was where the Athenian *dēmos* erected a statue of Socrates a few years after they had found him guilty of *asebeia* and voted to execute him. Every procession that started out at the edge of the city would have passed by the statue, and every citizen who participated in one of Athens' many festivals or dined on publicly purchased meat in the Pompeion's dining rooms would have seen this image of the famous philosopher. In the end Socrates became memorialized in the city of Athens as a figure who watched over the Athenians' civic rites.

GLOSSARY OF TERMS

ACROPOLIS   literally, "height of the city": the rocky outcrop and sanctuary of Athena in the center of Athens

AGORA   the central marketplace in Athens that also served as the center of Athenian government

AMBROSIA   literally, "immortal stuff": the food of the gods (compare *brotos*)

ANAGRAPHEIS   those who "write up" the laws: the committee of citizens who researched and published the laws after the first restoration of the democracy in 410

APARCHĒ (*APARCHAI*, PLURAL)   first fruits; dedications of agricultural produce made to the gods first before humans enjoy them

APOLOGIA   a defense speech delivered in a court of law

ARCHĒ   rule or authority; later in the fifth century the word was used to denote the Athenian empire

ARCHON   one of ten civic officials who held office for a year after being selected by a two-step process that included both lot and election

ARCHŌN BASILEUS   the so-called king archon, the civic official responsible for matters of cult and worship

ARCHOUSAI (FEMININE PLURAL)   the women selected by other women to be in charge at the Thesmophoria

ARETĒ   virtue

ASEBEIA   impiety

ATHANATOI   literally, "deathless ones": the immortal gods

AXONES   the most ancient laws of Athens on view in the Agora, probably published on wooden pillars and mounted on a vertical axis so that they could be turned as they were read

BARBAROI   barbarians; a term usually used to describe peoples from Asia Minor, western Asia, and Persia

BOULĒ   the Council of 500 in Pericles' time (earlier it was a council of 400)

BOULEUTERION   the building in the Agora where the Council met

BROTOS (BROTOI, PLURAL)   mortal man

CHORĒGOS (CHORĒGOI, PLURAL)   a citizen who produced drama at his own expense at a state-sponsored dramatic festival

CHOUS (CHOES, PLURAL)   wine jug

DADOUCHOS   the person who carried the torch at the Eleusinian Mysteries, usually a member of the one of the Eleusinian priestly families

DAIMONION   a small divine presence that Socrates said was in him (and that sometimes warned him not to do certain things)

DEME   a rural village in Attica, and after Cleisthenes one of 139 political units that formed the building blocks of Athenian democracy

DĒMOKRATIA   the power of the people

DĒMOS   the people

EIRESIŌNĒ   decorated olive bough dedicated to Apollo at the Pyanopsia festival every autumn

EISANGELIA   a particular Athenian legal procedure used to impeach and prosecute alleged wrongdoers

EKKLĒSIA   the Assembly of all Athenian citizens, which met on the hillside called the Pnyx

EKKYKLĒMA   a wheeled platform used in tragic productions for displaying the bodies of characters who died

EPHEBE   a young man in late adolescence just before he assumes full citizen rights

EPISTATĒS   chairman of the *prytaneis,* or presidents; a new *epistatēs* was selected by lottery every day

EPITAPHIOS   traditional funeral oration given at the graveside at a state funeral

EPOPTAI   those initiates who reach the highest level of initiation at the Eleusinian Mysteries

EUSEBEIA piety

HELLAS what the inhabitants of ancient Greece called their land

HERMATA piles of stones (cairns) that marked territory or stood beside roads

HETAIREIA (*HETAIREIAI*, PLURAL) small private associations of aristocratic men

HETAIROS (*HETAIROI*, PLURAL) companion

HIPPEIS "knights"; citizens who were wealthy enough to own horses and who served in the cavalry

HIEROS GAMOS sacred marriage

HISTORIA "researches"; a word first used by Herodotus to describe the kind of work he was writing

HUBRIS intolerable pride, especially a mortal man's pride in the face of the gods

ICHŌR the immortal stuff that runs through the veins of the immortal gods, as blood runs through the veins of living, mortal creatures

IDIŌTĒS a private citizen who lives without concern for the larger political community

IKRIA temporary wooden benches erected every year for spectators to watch plays performed at festivals of Dionysus

KANĒPHOROS the young woman who carries the basket with the knife in a sacrificial procession

KISTAI special containers that held sacred object used in the Eleusinian Mysteries

KLEOS undying fame

KLEPSYDRA a water clock used to time speeches in an Athenian courtroom.

KŌMOS ritual revelry celebrated at a Dionysian festival.

KORĒ (*KORAI*, PLURAL) maiden

KRATER a serving bowl in which wine was mixed with water

KRATOS power

KYKEŌN a special drink consumed by initiates at the Eleusinian Mysteries

LEITOURGIA "liturgy"; public service performed by the wealthy for the benefit of the larger *polis* community

MAGEIROS the civic official who wielded the knife at a sacrifice and butchered the animal victim

MANIA Dionysian madness

MEGARA deep pits in the ground where women deposited piglet votive offerings when worshipping Demeter at the Thesmophoria

METIC   a noncitizen resident alien living in Athens

MIASMA   ritual pollution

MYĒSIS   initiation

MYSTAGŌGOS   a guide who leads an initiate into the Telesterion at the Eleusinian Mysteries

MYSTĒRIA   Mysteries, the secret initiation rites performed for Demeter or Dionysus

MYSTĒS   (*MYSTAI*, PLURAL) an initiate into the Mysteries

MYSTIKOS   "mystic"; an adjective used to describe things related to the Mysteries

NEMESIS   divine retribution

TA NOMIZOMENA   the customary things; the term often referred to the customs of the ancestors

NOMOS (*NOMOI*, PLURAL)   law or custom, both legal and religious

NOMOTHETAI   those who "place the laws": the committee of citizens who researched and published the laws after the restoration of the democracy in 404

OIKOS   an individual household

OMPHALOS   the navel of the world, a term used to designate a particular rock at Delphi

ORCHĒSTRA   the round, flat area where the chorus danced at a dramatic performance

ORGIA   rites, especially mystic rites of Demeter or Dionysus

ŌSCHOI   clusters of grapes

ŌSCHOPHOROI   young men who carry the grape clusters to Dionysus at the Oschophoria

OSTRAKON (*OSTRAKA*, PLURAL)   pottery shard used to inscribe the names of candidates for ostracism, a ten-year forced political exile

PANHELLENIC   relating to all the Greek *poleis*

PANNYCHIS   a religious festival that goes on all night

TA PATRIA   literally, "the things of the fathers": ancestral customs

PATRIOI NOMOI   ancestral laws

PATRIOS POLITEIA   the ancestral constitution

PELANOS   a grain offering made at the Eleusinian Mysteries

PEPLOS   a type of woolen dress worn by Athenian women, and presented to Athena at the Panathenaea

PHOROS   literally, "bringing in": the annual tax or tribute paid to Athens by subject-allies in the empire

PHRATRY   literally, a "brotherhood": an ancient family organization that had certain religious duties in the fifth century

PHYLAI   tribes

PHYSIKOI, PHYSIOLOGOI   natural philosophers

PITHOI   large clay vessels used to store wine

PLĒMOCHOAI   special terra-cotta vessels used at the end of the Eleusinian Mysteries

POLIS (POLEIS, PLURAL)   the autonomous city-state in ancient Hellas

POLITEIS   citizens in a *polis*

POMPĒ (POMPAI, PLURAL)   religious/civic procession

PROPHĒTAI (PLURAL)   seers who interpret religious signs

PROSKYNĒSIS   the custom of falling down on one's knees before a human king

PRYTANEION   a public dining room in Athens where honored men ate at public expense

PRYTANEIS   presidents; the men who lead the Council and the Assembly during their prytany

PRYTANY   an administrative unit of time (one-tenth of a year) during which one of ten tribal committees managed the business of the *polis*

SITĒSIS   the honor of being maintained and fed in the Prytaneion at public expense

SPERMA   seeds

SPLANCHNA   the innards and internal organs of a sacrificial victim

SPONDĒ   a libation or offering of wine spilled into the ground or over an altar; in the plural, *spondai,* a negotiated truce sealed with the pouring of libations

SPONDOPHOROI   the traveling officials who announced the sacred truce in the fall before the Eleusinian Mysteries were celebrated

STĒLAI   stone tablets used to inscribe laws, and also used to mark graves

STRATĒGOS (STRATĒGOI, PLURAL)   general in the army; ten *stratēgoi* were elected annually in Athens

SYMPOSIUM   an evening drinking party

SYNOECISM   the unification of all the distinct villages in Attica, completed by the sixth century

TEMENOS (TEMENOI, PLURAL)   the boundary that defined a sanctuary, often marked with a wall or boundary stones

THANATOS   death (compare *athanatoi*)

THĒTES (PLURAL)   the lowest class of landless and poor citizens in Athens

THOLOS   public building constructed by Cimon in the fifth century where the *prytaneis* lived, ate, and worked during their prytany

THYSIA   civic animal sacrifice, and the public feast that followed

TIMĒ   honor

TRITTYS (*TRITTYES*, PLURAL)   a one-third section of a Cleisthenic tribe; each tribe had three *trittyes*, one from each of the three distinct geographical regions of Attica

TYRANNOS   king, or an extra-constitutional ruler; the term later came to mean "tyrant"

XENIA   the most ancient customs of hospitality between a guest and a host

SUGGESTED FURTHER READINGS
BY CHAPTER

References to inscriptions are given according to item numbers in Fornara's translated sourcebook: *Archaic Times to the End of the Peloponnesian War* (1983).

CHAPTER ONE

PRIMARY

The literary sources for studying Athens (and Greece in general) before the fifth century are notoriously scanty. The Greek historians Herodotus and Thucydides, too, were interested in this era, and they provide accounts for some of the more important events. The *Constitution of the Athenians,* or *Athenaion Politeia,* attributed to Aristotle (possibly written by one of his students) also preserves some of the ancient traditions that were gleaned from sources available during the fourth century BCE, but since lost.

SECONDARY

Archaeological evidence brings many insights to this period. Camp 2001 gives an excellent overview. Connolly 1998 presents lively illustrated reconstructions of the ancient city that convey contemporary archaeologists' conclusions in accessible visual form. Travlos 1980 and 1988 catalogue the principal sites in both Athens and Attica and give bibliography for each. Polignac 1995 situates Athens amid its neighbors in the larger landscape of Greece. Osborne 2000 is a straightforward handbook on ancient Greece with chapters on basic topics; Osborne 1985 is a more detailed scholarly study about early Attica and the political relationship of the countryside to the city. Fornara and Samons 1991 covers the evidence for Athens and the traditions of scholarship in considerable detail. Connor 1987 offers provocative reading for some of the earliest stories from Athens. Hanson 2000 gives a full treatment of ancient hoplite warfare. Raaflaub, Ober, and Wallace 2007 presents current interpretations of modern scholars who continue to discuss the origins of democracy in Athens.

CHAPTER TWO

PRIMARY

The primary evidence for studying religion in Athens is not concentrated in any one particular text. Two of the earliest important literary discussions of animal sacrifice are related to the story of Prometheus and the original mythic sacrifice at Mekone: Hesiod *Works and Days* 47–105 and *Theogony* 535–60.

SECONDARY

This chapter owes the most to the innovative synthetic work of Walter Burkert (esp. Burkert 1983 and 1985), and the detailed studies of Robert Parker (1983, 1996, 2005). Bremmer 1994 brings Burkert 1985 a bit more up to date. Boedeker 2007 offers a good introduction to religion in Athens, as do Mikalson 1983 and 2005, Zaidman and Pantel 1992, and Price 1999. Connor 1988 and Evans 2004 succinctly bring together *polis* and cult, and Sourvinou-Inwood 2000 presents provocative arguments on *polis* religion in general. Humphreys 2004 is provocative and worthwhile, and gives a good review of modern ways of understanding Greek religion. On the Panathenaea see Neils 1992 and 1996; Camp 2001 discusses Athenian monuments and their part in festivals. Van Straten's 1995 volume documents sacrifice through images on vase painting, and Rosivach 1994 examines evidence for the entire system of sacrifice. On the civic calendars and festivals, see Simon 1983, Parke 1977, and Mikalson 1975. Garland 1990 discusses priests and priesthoods in depth, and Flower 2008 documents well the role of priests and prophets, especially in fourth-century Greece. Gager 1992 and Graf 1997 are good places to start for those interested in magic in the ancient world. On cultural and religious interactions between East and West, see Burkert 1992 and 2004, and West 1997. Garnsey 1999 discusses patterns surrounding food, social status, and nutrition.

CHAPTER THREE

PRIMARY

Herodotus, books 5–8, documents the Ionian Revolt and the Persian invasions of 490 and 480. Thucydides, books 1 and 2, narrates the period between the Persian Wars and the Peloponnesian War and the first two years of fighting. Plutarch *Pericles* preserves some important anecdotes on this period. A fourth-century Attic inscription recording the Oath of Plataea is found in Fornara 57. The sources for the Oath of Plataea are late, preserved by this inscription and the fourth-century orator Lycurgus. Some modern historians doubt its authenticity and believe it may be a fourth-century Athenian invention.

SECONDARY

This narrative of the Persian Wars, the rise of the Athenian empire, and the run-up to the Peloponnesian War is intended only to highlight episodes that have notable connections to religious practices. For more comprehensive accounts see Kagan 2003. Bury and Meiggs 1975 is still the standard handbook; Samons 2007, with Lendon's contribution, is more engaging and thoughtful. Osborne 2000, with Kallet's essay, also offers a straightforward and accessible narrative of the war and its causes. For a thoughtful modern study of Thucydides, see Connor 1984. Kagan 1991, a readable and informative biography of Pericles, includes background on Athenian history and culture. This chapter's account of the role of the Pythia relies most on Maurizio 1995. Fornara and Samons 1991 remains the most critical treatment of the sources and the scholarship. Patterson's groundbreaking 1981 study on the Periclean citizenship laws is still worth reading, and Blok 2005 takes her arguments about women and citizenship even further. Henry 1995 is the most current study of the traditions surrounding Pericles' companion, Aspasia. Hansen 1991 clearly outlines the mechanisms of democracy under Pericles. Ober 1996, 1998, and 2005 contain interesting essays on Athens and politics, while Rhodes 2003a offers an sharp contrast to Ober's perspective. See Samons 2000 for discussion of Athenian loans and financing of the war, especially during the earlier phases. Kallet-Marx 1989 examines the evidence for how the Athenians funded the rebuilding of the Acropolis. Lapatin 2007 has a good discussion of Periclean architecture. Hurwit 2004 is an excellent contemporary study of the whole Acropolis. On the Panathenaea and changes made to it, see Neils 1992 and also Neils 1996 with the contributions of Neils, Robertson, and Shapiro. Connelly 1996 offers an alternative theory about the Ionic frieze on the Parthenon, arguing that it depicts a traditional mythological story and not the actual Panathenaea itself. On the Athenian tradition of the public funeral, see Parker 2005, pp. 469–70, and especially Parker

1996, pp. 132–28. Loraux's groundbreaking 1986 study of the funeral oration has been highly influential.

CHAPTER FOUR

PRIMARY

The *Homeric Hymn to Demeter* gives the principal version of the Demeter myth. The most accessible and up-to-date edition is Foley 1994; Richardson 1974 is an indispensable scholarly edition of the text with full notes and commentary. For the comic depiction of women in Athenian public life, see Aristophanes *The Assemblywomen* and *Thesmophoriazusae*. For women and the typical household, see Xenophon *Oeconomicus*. The betrothal formula comes from the fourth-century comic author Menander: *Perikeiromene* 1013 and *Dyskolos* 842. For the First Fruits Decree, see Fornara 140; other inscriptions related to Eleusis and the empire are discussed in detail (but not fully translated) in Cavanaugh 1996.

SECONDARY

Familiarity with the archaeological evidence is essential for studying Demeter's cults: see Mylonas 1961 on Eleusis, and Miles 1998 for the city Eleusinion in Athens. On women and Greek religion in general, see Connelly 2007, Goff 2004, and Dillon 2002. On the Thesmophoria: Brumfield 1981 and Parker 2005. On the Eleusinian Mysteries: Brumfield 1981, Burkert 1985 and 1987, Cavanaugh 1996, Clinton 1992 and 1993, Cole 2004, Cosmopoulos 2003, Evans 2002 and 2006, and Parker 1996 and 2005. On the agricultural revolution and the shift from hunting and gathering to farming in the Neolithic period, see Diamond 1999.

CHAPTER FIVE

PRIMARY

Thucydides, books 3–8, narrates the war from 429 to 411, and then suddenly stops. Xenophon *Hellenica* picks up where Thucydides breaks off. Plutarch *Nicias* and *Alcibiades* fill in vital information. Andocides *On the Mysteries* is the most important primary source for the affairs of the Herms and the Mysteries. Aristotle's *Athenian Constitution* gives an account of what happened to Athenian political institutions during the two oligarchies and the restored democratic regimes.

The account of the Peloponnesian War given in this chapter highlights episodes in which traditional religious practices and attitudes played a key role. For more comprehensive accounts of the war and the revolutions see Kagan 2003, and especially Kagan 1987 on the end of the war. Kallet 2000 is a good overview, while Kallet 2001 is a more specialized study of Athenian decisions surrounding the Sicilian expedition. Samons 2000 with its study of finance and the empire is eye-opening. Ostwald's groundbreaking 1986 study remains highly influential. Munn 2000 is a comprehensive and detailed account of the interplay between politics, piety, and personal agendas during and right after the war. On the particular role of demagogues in Athens at this time, see Connor 1971; on Alcibiades in particular, Ellis 1989. On the affair of the Mysteries and the Herms: Furley 1996 and Parker 1996. Ober's essays in his 1998 and 2005 volumes also address issues from this period, with a focus on political theory. Antonaccio's 1995 monograph on tomb cult and ancestors lends insight into why the Arginusae episode became so emotional.

CHAPTER SIX

PRIMARY

Heraclitus fragment 12; cf. Plato *Cratylus* 402a. Plato *Symposium* for the party at Agathon's following his first victory at the Lenaea. Aristophanes *Acharnians, Bacchae,* and *Frogs.* Demosthenes *On the Crown.*

SECONDARY

Henderson 2007 has a good overview of drama. Dodds 1951 is dated in some ways, but still remains the place to begin studying Dionysus in depth. Pickard-Cambridge 1988 is essential for analyzing the evidence for the dramatic festivals, including some of the most important visual evidence from vases. Simon 1983 and Parke 1977 discuss the festivals in detail, though the discussions in Parker 1996 and 2005 are more nuanced and current. Zeitlin 1990 presents a compelling argument for the relationship between Athens and the mythical Thebes. See Hamilton 1992 for the best discussion of the Anthesteria. On the City Dionysia as expressions of the *polis,* see Connor 1989, Winkler and Zeitlin 1990, and Goldhill 1987/1990; Rhodes 2003b takes issue with these scholars as overly political. Gregory 1991 offers a compelling reading for the place of Euripides in the democratic *polis* of Athens. Henderson 1991 examines the evidence for women at the dramatic festivals—how to interpret this evidence still remains quite controversial. On Dionysian *orgia,* see Burkert 1987, Carpenter and Faraone 1993, Cosmopoulos 2003, Graf and Johnston 2007, and especially the new 2006 edition of the *Derveni Papyrus.* My whole approach to ritual inversion evident in this chapter owes the most to Turner 1977.

CHAPTER SEVEN

PRIMARY

For the trial of Andocides, see Andocides *On the Mysteries* and Lysias 6 *Against Andocides;* for Nichomachus's trial, see Lysias 30 *Against Nicomachus.* Plato *Apology, Crito, Euthyphro, Phaedo* (for thematic and technical reasons, scholars believe *Euthyphro* was written later than the other three dialogues). Aristophanes *Clouds.* Xenophon *Apology* and *Memorabilia.* Diogenes Laertius wrote a ten-book compendium on the ancient philosophers; he was probably working in late antiquity—third century CE.

SECONDARY

Ostwald 1986 is a masterpiece of scholarship and argument. Munn 2000 covers some of the same ground as Ostwald. See Ober 2005, chapter 3, for an interesting essay on the Amnesty of 403, and Loraux 2002 for a book-length study of Athenian political conflict, voting, and the 403 amnesty. Sickinger 1999 is excellent on the technology of the democracy and its archives. For Plato and Socrates, the best place to start is Brickhouse and Smith 1989 and 1994. Nussbaum 1986 remains essential for considering Socrates, his philosophy, and his relationship to Plato. Vlastos 1994 (a revision of a paper originally published in 1983) also offers valuable insights into the historical Socrates and how he may have differed from the Socrates written about by subsequent generations of Greek writers, but Vlastos does not give due consideration to cultic norms. McPherran 1996 is a detailed, though somewhat limited, study of religion and Socrates; Parker 1996, chapter 10, is stronger on this score. Partridge 2002–03 has important new insights on Socrates' *daimonion.* Hansen 1995 has a very provocative interpretation of Socrates' trial, though I don't agree with it. Connor 1991 influenced me the most as I began work on this chapter.

Antonaccio, Carla. 1995. *An Archaeology of Ancestors: Tomb Cult and Hero Cult in Early Greece*. Lanham, Md.: Rowman and Littlefield.

Blok, Josine. 2005. "Becoming Citizens: Some Notes on the Semantics of Citizen in Archaic Greece and Classical Athens." *Klio* 87 (1): 7–40.

Boedeker, Deborah. 2007. "Athenian Religion in the Age of Pericles." In Samons 2007, pp. 46–69.

Boedeker, Deborah, and Kurt A. Raaflaub, eds. 1998. *Democracy, Empire and the Arts in Fifth-Century Athens*. Cambridge, Mass.: Harvard University Press.

Bremmer, Jan. 1994. *Greek Religion*. Oxford: Oxford University Press.

Brickhouse, Thomas, and Nicholas Smith. 1989. *Socrates on Trial*. Princeton: Princeton University Press.

———. 1994. *Plato's Socrates*. New York: Oxford University Press.

Brumfield, Allaire. 1981. *The Attic Festivals of Demeter and Their Relation to the Agricultural Year*. Salem, N.H.: Ayer.

Burkert, Walter. 1983. *Homo Necans: The Anthropology of Ancient Greek Sacrificial Ritual and Myth*. Translated by Peter Bing from the German edition of 1972. Berkeley: University of California Press.

———. 1985. *Greek Religion*. Translated by John Raffan from the German edition of 1977. Cambridge, Mass.: Harvard University Press.

———. 1987. *Ancient Mystery Cults*. Cambridge, Mass.: Harvard University Press.

————. 1992. *The Orientalizing Revolution: Near Eastern Influence on Greek Culture in the Early Archaic Age*. Cambridge, Mass.: Harvard University Press.

————. 2004. *Babylon, Memphis, Persepolis: Eastern Contexts of Greek Culture*. Cambridge, Mass.: Harvard University Press.

Bury, J., and Russell Meiggs. 1975. *A History of Greece to the Death of Alexander the Great*. 4th ed. New York: St. Martin's.

Camp, John. 2001. *The Archaeology of Athens*. New Haven: Yale University Press.

Carpenter, Thomas, and Christopher Faraone. 1993. *Masks of Dionysos*. Ithaca: Cornell University Press.

Cavanaugh, Maureen. 1996. *Eleusis and Athens: Documents in Finance, Religion, and Politics in the Fifth Century B.C.* Atlanta: Scholars Press.

Clinton, Kevin. 1992. *Myth and Cult: The Iconography of the Eleusinian Mysteries*. Goteborg: P. Astrom.

————. 1993. "The Sanctuary of Demeter and Kore at Eleusis." In Marinatos and Hagg 1993, pp. 110–24.

Cole, Susan. 2004. *Landscapes, Gender, and Ritual Space: The Ancient Greek Experience*. Berkeley: University of California Press.

Connelly, Joan Breton. 1996. "Parthenon and Parthenoi: A Mythological Interpretation of the Parthenon Frieze." *American Journal of Archaeology* 100 (1): 53–80.

————. 2007. *Portrait of a Priestess: Women and Ritual in Ancient Greece*. Princeton: Princeton University Press.

Connolly, Peter. 1998. *The Ancient City*. Oxford: Oxford University Press.

Connor, W. R. 1971. *The New Politicians of Fifth-Century Athens*. Princeton: Princeton University Press.

————. 1984. *Thucydides*. Princeton: Princeton University Press.

————. 1987. "Tribes, Festivals and Processions." *Journal of Hellenic Studies* 107: 40–50.

————. 1988. "*Hiera* and *Hosia*: Sacred and Secular and the Classical Athenian Concept of the State." *Ancient Society* 19: 161–88.

————. 1989. "City Dionysia and Athenian Democracy." *Classica et Mediaevalia* 40: 7–32

————. 1991. "The Other 399: Religion and the Trial of Socrates." In *Georgiaca: Greek Studies in Honour of George Cawkwell*, pp. 49–56. *BICS* Supplement 58. London.

Cosmopoulos, Michael. 2003. *Greek Mysteries: The Archaeology and Ritual of Ancient Greek Secret Cults*. London: Routledge.

Derveni Papyrus. 2006. Edited with introduction and commentary by Theokritos Kouremenos, George M. Parássoglou, and Kyriakos Tsantsanoglou. Florence: L. S. Olschki.

Diamond, Jared. 1999. *Guns, Germs, and Steel: The Fates of Human Societies.* New York: W. W. Norton.

Dillon, Matthew. 2002. *Girls and Women in Classical Greek Religion.* London: Routledge.

Dodds, E. R. 1951. *The Greeks and the Irrational.* Berkeley: University of California Press.

Ellis, Walter. 1989. *Alcibiades.* London: Routledge.

Evans, Nancy. 2002. "Sanctuaries, Sacrifices and the Eleusinian Mysteries." *Numen* 49: 227–54.

———. 2004. "Feasts, Citizens, and Cultic Democracy in Classical Athens." *Ancient Society* 34: 1–25.

———. 2006. "Diotima and Demeter as Mystagogues in Plato's *Symposium.*" *Hypatia* 21: 1–27.

Flower, Michael. 2008. *The Seer in Ancient Greece.* Berkeley: University of California Press.

Foley, Helene, ed. 1994. *The Homeric Hymn to Demeter: Translation, Commentary and Interpretive Essays.* Princeton: Princeton University Press.

Fornara, Charles, ed. and trans. 1983. *Archaic Times to the End of the Peloponnesian War.* Translated Documents of Greece and Rome, vol. 1. 2nd ed. Cambridge: Cambridge University Press.

Fornara, Charles, and Loren J. Samons. 1991. *Athens from Cleisthenes to Pericles.* Berkeley: University of California Press.

Furley, William D. 1996. *Andocides and the Herms: A Study of Crisis in Fifth-Century Athenian Religion.* BICS Supplement 65. London: Institute of Classical Studies.

Gager, John. 1992. *Curse Tablets and Binding Spells from the Ancient World.* New York: Oxford University Press.

Garland, Robert. 1990. "Priests and Power in Classical Athens." In *Pagan Priests: Religion and Power in the Ancient World,* edited by Mary Beard and John North, pp. 73–91. London: Duckworth.

Garnsey, Peter. 1999. *Food and Society in Classical Antiquity.* Cambridge: Cambridge University Press.

Goff, Barbara. 2004. *Citizen Bacchae: Women's Ritual Practice in Ancient Greece.* Berkeley: University of California Press.

Goldhill, Simon. 1987/1990. "The Great Dionysia and Civic Ideology." *Journal of Hellenic Studies* 107: 58–76. Reprinted in Winkler and Zeitlin 1990, pp. 97–129.

Graf, Fritz. 1997. *Magic in the Ancient World.* Translated by Franklin Philip from the French edition of 1994. Cambridge, Mass.: Harvard University Press.

Graf, Fritz, and Sarah Iles Johnston. 2007. *Ritual Texts for the Afterlife: Orpheus and Bacchic Gold Tablets.* New York: Routledge.

Gregory, Justina. 1991. *Euripides and the Instruction of the Athenians.* Ann Arbor: University of Michigan Press.

Hamilton, Richard. 1992. *Choes and Anthesteria: Athenian Iconography and Ritual.* Ann Arbor: University of Michigan Press.

Hansen, Mogens Herman. 1991. *The Athenian Democracy in the Age of Demosthenes.* Revised and updated; translated by J. A. Crook from the Danish edition of 1985. Oxford: Blackwell.

———. 1995. *The Trial of Socrates—From the Athenian Point of View.* Historisk-filosofiske Meddelelser 71. Copenhagen: Royal Danish Academy of Sciences and Letters.

Hanson, Victor Davis. 2000. *The Western Way of War: Infantry Battle in Classical Greece.* 2nd ed. Berkeley: University of California Press.

Henderson, Jeffrey. 1991. "Women and the Athenian Dramatic Festivals." *Transactions of the American Philological Association* 121: 133–47.

———. 2007. "Drama and Democracy." In Samons 2007, pp. 179–95.

Henry, Madeleine. 1995. *Prisoner of History.* Oxford: Oxford University Press.

Humphreys, S. C. 2004. *The Strangeness of Gods: Historical Perspectives on the Interpretation of Athenian Religion.* Oxford: Oxford University Press.

Hurwit, Jeffrey M. 2004. *The Acropolis in the Age of Pericles.* Cambridge: Cambridge University Press.

Kagan, Donald. 1987. *The Fall of the Athenian Empire.* Ithaca: Cornell University Press.

———. 1991. *Pericles of Athens and the Birth of Democracy.* New York: Free Press.

———. 2003. *The Peloponnesian War.* New York: Viking.

Kallet, Lisa. 2000. "The Fifth Century: Political and Military Narrative." In Osborne 2000, pp. 170–96.

———. 2001. *Money and the Corrosion of Power in Thucydides: The Sicilian Expedition and Its Aftermath.* Berkeley: University of California Press.

Kallet-Marx, Lisa. 1989. "Did Tribute Fund the Parthenon?" *California Studies in Classical Antiquity* 20: 252–66.

Lapatin, Kenneth. 2007. "Art and Architecture." In Samons 2007, pp. 125–52.

Lendon, J. E. 2007. "Athens and Sparta and the Coming of the Peloponnesian War." In Samons 2007, pp. 258–81.

Loraux, Nicole. 1986. *The Invention of Athens: The Funeral Oration in the Classical City.* Translated by Alan Sheridan from the French edition of 1981. Cambridge, Mass.: Harvard University Press.

———. 2002. *The Divided City: On Memory and Forgetting in Ancient Athens.* Translated by Corinne Pache with Jeff Fort from the French edition of 1997. New York: Zone Books.

Marinatos, Nanno, and Robin Hagg, eds. 1993. *Greek Sanctuaries: New Approaches.* London: Routledge.

Maurizio, Lisa. 1995. "Anthropology and Spirit Possession: A Reconsideration of the Pythia's Role at Delphi." *Journal of Hellenic Studies* 115: 69–86.

McPherran, Mark. 1996. *The Religion of Socrates.* University Park: Pennsylvania State University Press.

Mikalson, Jon D. 1975. *The Sacred and Civil Calendar of the Athenian Year.* Princeton: Princeton University Press.

———. 1983. *Athenian Popular Religion.* Chapel Hill: University of North Carolina Press.

———. 2005. *Ancient Greek Religion.* Malden, Mass.: Blackwell.

Miles, Margaret. 1998. *The City Eleusinion.* Princeton: American School of Classical Studies.

Munn, Mark. 2000. *The School of History: Athens in the Age of Socrates.* Berkeley: University of California Press.

Mylonas, George. 1961. *Eleusis and the Eleusinian Mysteries.* Princeton: Princeton University Press.

Neils, Jenifer, ed. 1992. *Goddess and Polis: The Panathenaic Festival in Ancient Athens.* Hanover, N.H.: Hood Museum of Art, Dartmouth College; Princeton: Princeton University Press.

———, ed. 1996. *Worshipping Athena: Panathenaia and Parthenon.* Madison: University of Wisconsin Press.

Nussbaum, Martha. 1986. *The Fragility of Goodness: Luck and Ethics in Greek Tragedy and Philosophy.* Cambridge: Cambridge University Press.

Ober, Josiah. 1996. *The Athenian Revolution: Essays on Ancient Greek Democracy and Political Theory.* Princeton: Princeton University Press.

———. 1998. *Political Dissent in Democratic Athens: Intellectual Critics of Popular Rule.* Princeton: Princeton University Press.

———. 2005. *Athenian Legacies: Essays on the Politics of Going on Together.* Princeton: Princeton University Press.

Osborne, Robin. 1985. *Demos: The Discovery of Classical Attika.* Cambridge: Cambridge University Press.

———, ed. 2000. *Classical Greece.* Oxford: Oxford University Press.

Ostwald, Martin. 1986. *From Popular Sovereignty to the Sovereignty of Law: Law, Society and Politics in Fifth-Century Athens.* Berkeley: University of California Press.

Parke, H. W. 1977. *Festivals of the Athenians.* London: Thames and Hudson.

Parker, Robert. 1983. *Miasma: Pollution and Purification in Early Greek Religion.* Oxford: Clarendon Press.

———. 1996. *Athenian Religion: A History.* Oxford: Oxford University Press.

———. 2005. *Polytheism and Society at Athens.* Oxford: Oxford University Press.

Partridge, John. 2002–03. "Socrates' Daimonion in Plato's *Phaedrus:* The Literary and Philosophical Significance of the Divine Sign." *Skepsis* 13–14: 75–92.

Patterson, Cynthia. 1981. *Pericles' Citizenship Law of 451–450 BC.* Salem, N.H.: Ayer.

Pickard-Cambridge, Sir Arthur. 1988. *Dramatic Festivals of Athens.* 2nd ed. revised by John Gould and D. M. Lewis. Oxford: Oxford University Press.

Polignac, François de. 1995. *Cults, Territory and the Origins of the Greek City-State.* Translated by Janet Lloyd from the French edition of 1984. Chicago: University of Chicago Press.

Price, Simon. 1999. *Religions of the Ancient Greeks.* Cambridge: Cambridge University Press.

Raaflaub, Kurt, Josiah Ober, and Robert W. Wallace. 2007. *Origins of Democracy in Ancient Greece.* Berkeley: University of California Press.

Rhodes, P. J. 1992. "The Athenian Revolution." In *The Cambridge Ancient History,* edited by D. M. Lewis et al., vol. 5, *The Fifth Century B.C.,* pp. 62–95. 2nd ed. Cambridge: Cambridge University Press.

———. 2003a. *Ancient Democracy and Modern Ideology.* London: Duckworth.

———. 2003b. "Nothing to Do with Democracy: Athenian Drama and the *Polis.*" *Journal of Hellenic Studies* 123: 104–19.

Richardson, N. J. 1974. *Homeric Hymn to Demeter.* Oxford: Clarendon Press.

Robertson, Noel. 1996. "Athena's Shrines and Festivals." In Neils 1996, pp. 27–77.

Rosivach, Vincent. 1994. *The System of Public Sacrifice in Fourth-Century Athens.* Atlanta: Scholars Press.

Samons, Loren J. 2000. *Empire of the Owl: Athenian Imperial Finance.* Historia Einzelschriften 142. Stuttgart: Franz Steiner.

———, ed. 2007. *The Cambridge Companion to the Age of Pericles.* New York: Cambridge University Press.

Shapiro, H. A. 1996. "Democracy and Imperialism: The Panathenaia in the Age of Pericles." In Neils 1996, pp. 215–25.

Sickinger, James. 1999. *Public Records and Archives in Classical Athens.* Chapel Hill: University of North Carolina Press.

Simon, Erika. 1983. *Festivals of Attica: An Archaeological Commentary.* Madison: University of Wisconsin Press.

Sourvinou-Inwood, C. 2000. "What Is Polis Religion?" In *Oxford Readings in Greek Religion,* edited by Richard Buxton, pp. 13–37. Oxford: Oxford University Press.

Stone, I. F. 1988. *The Trial of Socrates.* Boston: Little, Brown.

Travlos, John. 1980. *Pictorial Dictionary of Ancient Athens.* New York: Hacker Art Books.

———. 1988. *Bildlexikon zur Topographie des antiken Attika.* Tübingen: Wasmuth.

Turner, Victor. 1977. *The Ritual Process: Structure and Anti-Structure.* Ithaca: Cornell University Press.

Van Straten, Folkert. 1995. *Hiera Kala: Images of Animal Sacrifice in Archaic and Classical Greece.* Leiden: Brill.

Vlastos, Gregory. 1994. "The Historical Socrates and Athenian Democracy." As revised in *Socratic Studies,* edited by Miles Burnyeat, pp. 87–108. Cambridge: Cambridge University Press.

West, Martin. 1997. *The East Face of Helicon: West Asiatic Elements in Greek Poetry and Myth.* New York: Oxford University Press.

Winkler, John J. 1985/1990. "The Ephebes' Song: *Tragôidia* and *Polis.*" *Representations,* no. 11: 26–62. Reprinted in Winkler and Zeitlin 1990, pp. 20–62.

Winkler, John J., and Froma I. Zeitlin. 1990. *Nothing to Do with Dionysos? Athenian Drama in Its Social Context.* Princeton: Princeton University Press.

Zaidman, Louise Bruit, and Pauline Schmitt Pantel. 1992. *Religion in the Ancient Greek City.* Translated by Paul Cartledge from the French edition of 1991. Cambridge: Cambridge University Press.

Zeitlin, Froma. 1990. "Thebes: Theater of Self and Society in Athenian Drama." In Winkler and Zeitlin 1990, pp. 130–67.

INDEX

Acropolis, 1, 13, 16, 17 fig. 1, 25–26, 30 fig. 2, 102, 154, 160, 171, 211, 241, 244; during Archaic period, 25–26, 32–33, 50–51; destroyed by Persia, 72–75; festivals on, 44–45, 50–58, 89–91, 108, 169, 229; inscriptions on, 155, 162; rebuilt, 87–88, 90–92; slopes of, 54, 74, 110–11, 127, 171, 193–94, 201–2, 211, 219, 241; treasury on (or near), 85, 87–89, 157, 202

Aegina, xviii map 2, xx map 3, 84

Aegospotomi, xviii map 2; 166, 169

Aeschylus, 9, 81, 120, 191, 196–98, 204

Agora, 1, 91, 109, 161, 218, 243–44; during Archaic period, 24–26; Assembly and Council in, 151, 160, 171, 211, 223; Demeter near, 109–11, 118, 128; Dionysus in, 171, 175, 177, 189; Eponymous Heroes, 222; festivals, processions and dining in, 58–60, 89, 175, 218; herms in, 146; laws on display, 60, 220–24; Painted Stoa, 80, 122; Socrates in, 237; twelve gods in, 25, 89

Alcibiades: as Alcmaeonid, 140; cursed by priest of Demeter, 155, 159–60, 162, 212; death, 169; as friend of Socrates, 190–91, 217, 237–38; as Olympic victor, 142, 144; pardon of, 160; and Pericles, 63, 131, 140; and Persia, 159–60, 162, 169; profaning the Mysteries, 149–54, 161–63, 212; return to Athens, 162–63; and Sicilian Expedition, 144–46, 150, 154–55, 238; and Sparta, 141, 155–58, 160, 169

Alcmaeon, 33

Alcmaeonidae, 13, 32–34, 63, 71, 81, 99, 140

Alexander the Great, 6, 9, 59, 241

alphabet, 65, 184

altar, 13, 20, 33, 36 fig. 3, 38, 102, 106, 124, 128–29, 146, 147 fig. 10, 218, 244; of Apollo, 72, 142; of Athena, 26, 45, 50, 54–58, 62, 88, 90–91, 108, 124, 219; of Brasidas, 138; of Demeter, 110, 113, 123; of Dionysus, 184, 193–94, 205; as scene of sacrifice, 36, 48–49, 55–59; of the twelve gods, 25, 89; of Zeus, 44–45

amnesty, 4, 168, 170, 211–15, 219, 236

Amphipolis, xviii map 2; 137–39, 235

anaktoron, 119–20, 124, 126

Anaxagoras, 92–93, 204, 230–32, 238

Andocides, 149, 151–52, 154, 161, 209, 215–21, 224–27, 230, 237–39

animal sacrifice. See *thysia*

Text: 11.25/13.5 Adobe Garamond
Display: Adobe Garamond
Compositor: Westchester Book Group
Cartographer: Bill Nelson
Printer & binder: Maple-Vail Book Manufacturing Group